out of the mist and steam

ALAN DUFF

out of the mist and steam

a memoir

TANDEM PRESS

Dedicated to my father, Gowan, for always holding reason above the storms of emotion, and for providing enlightenment.

First published in New Zealand in 1999 by
TANDEM PRESS
2 Rugby Road
Birkenhead
Auckland 10
New Zealand

© 1999 Alan Duff
ISBN 1 877178 58 6

Cover design by Phil O'Reilly Design Limited
Text design by Jacinda Torrance
Edited by Linda Cassells
Printed and bound by Brebner Print, Auckland

acknowledgements

With much gratitude to the combined advice of editor Linda Cassells and publishers Bob Ross and Helen Benton.

The photograph of the rugby team is reproduced with kind permission of Christchurch Boys High School.

introduction

I t's August 1999. Four hundred guests have gathered in Manukau Road, Auckland, at a private car museum. We are here to celebrate the Alan Duff Charitable Foundation's Books in Homes programme, which has put one million brand new books into the homes of disadvantaged young New Zealanders in just four years. This nationwide programme has now reached over 63,000 low-income homes, the majority of those Maori, with the aim of spreading the good word that 'Reading is Cool!' as it says in the trust's brochures in the 284 schools where the programme currently operates.

A group of young Maori children from Northland entertain us with an extraordinary performance of haka and dance and poi action songs, showing the guests that Maori can be excellent and inspiring too. And then the place reverberates with our new theme song 'Read About It', a brilliantly catchy tune encompassing all the energy and positivity of the programme.

Christine Fernyhough, the executive trustee, has made a huge contribution, along with a host of other people: the other trustees, the dedicated staff, the business sponsors, the families who privately sponsor their own schools, and the teaching staff at every school involved in the programme. I pay special tribute to Bruce Plested, managing director of Mainfreight, for what he has done personally and what his company has done for Books in Homes. Together we achieved a vision I had. Now the formalities are over, we can party.

Off the stage the first person I go to is my wife, and we hug and she says that I must be proud of myself, and I, having a previous problem with accepting myself, can this time answer a very definite yes. This is a dream come true. I think of Beth Heke in my first novel *Once Were Warriors* wandering around her bookless house in stark realisation that her entire social group, her Maori race as she knows it, is also bookless. And going nowhere. We have done something about Beth's realisation, and left the rhetoric and empty promises to others. I think of my own past which did not promise anything like what the trust has achieved, except in my occasional wildest dreams. Oh yes, I am proud of myself all right.

Next I go to my twenty-one-year-old daughter, Katea, a third-year student at university studying literature, herself now a published author. I take that child seed of mine in my arms and hug her long and meaningfully. And I think to myself what a long way this is from her early beginnings. What a long way this life has come in the last twenty years....

Back then, I'm waiting for her and her mother to arrive and I see her appear, this child of mine, with her dark eyebrows and trusting face with eyes so quickly picking me out amongst the numbers and me puzzled that she is standing on her own, for she is not yet one year old. Then she comes towards me, making those ageless first steps on unsteady feet that take her into another world of swifter movement and greater adventure and growing confidence.

I put my arms out and urge Katea towards me. I have tears in my eyes, prompted not least by the circumstances of this momentous day for child and parent. She picks up speed as she gets close to me and makes it just in time as I scoop her up and express a father's delight. Her mother Paula stands smiling proudly and gladly in the doorway and then she comes over and the visit starts. We have half an hour.

The room is full, maybe a hundred people, strained, stressed wives and girlfriends, confused or all-too-knowing children. They in their variety of colourful and differently styled civilian clothes, some of them drab, most world-weary. And us in the standard uniform of prison inmates, of jeans, striped shirt, coarse wool navy jacket, clumpy black shoes, and underpants that never stop telling the wearer how badly fitting they are beneath your jeans. For they're kind of half long-johns, shaped and reshaped by the variety of bodies that have worn them. Of all the things you are aware of, the most tangible is these underpants that can't be seen, and what they signify of the new life you are trying to adjust to. You have no choice. You have a sentence beside your name. A finite period with room within to punish you if you misbehave by deducting remission days. These underpants symbolise the dignity you lost at those front gates when the van brought you in and the gates closed on the outside world and this became the universe where you had not only to find your place, but do so by being immediately and permanently reduced by the ignominy of these ill-fitting undies.

You quickly saw that only a few of you were trying to make something of this awful experience, turn it into an advantage, make something of yourself, your personal qualities – or lack of them – and yet constantly thinking you were as doomed as everyone else, a loser, a misfit, a failure, just another of society's outcasts.

But it was too early then, just a few weeks. I had hoped that things would change and was fighting to keep myself together against this onslaught of humanity in the raw, of society's rejects as my residential company. Paula's trick had worked, for I only cared for my daughter making it all the way to my table. When I picked Katea up I began a little ritual between us that day as I sang the song, 'Don't Cry for Me Argentina.' Visit after visit I'd sing that to her and she'd go quiet every time for the whole duration of it being sung softly in her ear. The same child I would later, on gaining my freedom, take outside at night, just as my father had done with me, to say goodnight to the stars, the child I would also have custody of from the age of eleven and watch blossom.

That was 1979. London, England. Now it is 1999, Auckland, New Zealand. And so much has happened in those years, especially the last nine, since the publication of *Once Were Warriors*. My child has herself taken her first literary steps with her children's book *Just One Seed*. And now our organisation was endeavouring to help disadvantaged children take their first reading steps, their first steps into a lifelong love affair with the written word.

Three days earlier in the week we had celebrated our one millionth book at Tairangi Primary School in Wellington. The Minister of Maori Affairs, Tau Henare, was there. So was John Delamere,

Associate Minister of Immigration. And the Prime Minister, Jenny Shipley, was our guest of honour for this great occasion. The following day our executive trustee Christine Fernyhough received her honour of Officer of the New Zealand Order of Merit conferred by the Governor General, for her work in Books in Homes.

This same night I was staying at the home of Bruce Plested, who had not only contributed hugely to sponsoring our programme, but in the three years since I have known him has been one of the most significant influences on my thinking ever. Bruce and his dear wife Nancy were at the party of course. All night, though, I kept thinking of how far I had come from that time twenty years ago. I'm not saying that I had become another man, just the potential man. A man I can now live with and rather like. But the dreams had always been there. They just looked highly unlikely, if impossible, to believe back then.

1st Oct. 1980

Dear Ngaere

Thanks for your letter. Well at the moment I'm waiting on a parole decision which if favourable could see me home by Xmas – this year!....I'm not doing this sentence any easier than when I started. But I don't quite agree with you when you say that it's a waste of a young life. It might well be had I not been in need of such a period in my always dramatic... life. I've been plucked out of a river of my own making and I'm glad I was. I'd have been surely drowned otherwise. I think it's best to wait and see what I've made of this imprisonment. I'm confident more than a few people are in for a surprise but I make no predictions from my present prone state. Just look out for me though for I have something to say....

Those poems of mine embarrass me. I don't know what Dad sees in them. They were just bursts of voice from a fledgling artist who didn't know who the hell he was. He's not that certain who he is now but his voice has learned a refinement which is beginning to appeal even to him.

There is one poem however which I quite liked although I don't know if Dad got it published. He was going to try the Listener *as far as I know. It's called 'Father. Father?' It has a nice rolling rhythm which I have since worked on. I enjoy writing prose rather than poetry. I get the best of both worlds then.*

Roger Paulin the Cambridge University tutor came to visit me a while back. Have you met him? He's quite nice and a typical Duff – highly intelligent and at times unsettling. He has real Duff eyebrows dark and pondering as if he is forever contemplating great and wise things. I do wish I had known Oliver from an adult view. I'm in no doubt at all that I missed out on something with his passing at the time of my very troubled coming. I was in Borstal at the time and I still remember his letter to me. 'It doesn't last forever.'

Well?… No of course it doesn't but it feels like it at times! I got a nice letter from Alison yesterday. At last she is writing to me as an adult to another instead of an aunt to her teenage nephew. I might appear (my actions) childish to certain narrow-visioned people but I'm a man beneath it all. Despite my being here I have always behaved – in the past 6 or 7 years anyway – with loyalty and integrity to my friends and though I broke the law I would not dream of stealing from an individual and have never done so. These are different times and I have grown up in an anyway tumultuous childhood as you well know. But my head is high.

Love to you and be assured this Duff will make his mark.
Alan

Ngaere is my late step-grandmother, Grandad's second wife. I wrote this on an ancient prison typewriter that had a broken comma key. No apologies for the poor grammar. I'm said not to be great in that area anyway. I'm confident enough to think that some of my writing may well force a few changes in the rules! I think I have made my mark. And it's been an interesting journey and one which I would mostly do all over again and hardly change a thing. Or I wouldn't be writing this would I? But no way will I put a child of mine through a life remotely like it. We must give our children the key to the future, and that starts with love. And reading, of course.

one

O urs was just another of the houses sprouting up all over the country under the government's state-housing programme in the late 1940s. The Second World War had ended in 1945 and the government was determined to ensure their returned soldiers and families had a roof over their heads. My father was one of those returned soldiers. It was a time when people were grateful to the government and considered this grand plan a wonderful thing, which it surely was in the context of New Zealand in a state of post-war which had drained our economic resources.

My father had painted our house black. Creosote black. This black house alone amongst others of gleaming white or cream or a wan colour. The smell of creosote was a part of our lives. Dad thought it was a practical sort of paint application, 'practical' being one of his favourite words. But living in a black house surrounded by weather-board creams and pale greens and light browns wasn't much different in that we all knew they were exactly the same inside, these single-storey dwellings.

The entry to the back door of 29 Matai Street was on the side of the house, down a dirt footpath, unless you knew someone who had access to concrete supply, on a pot-holed street that would remain unsealed for a few years. In the rain, if it was heavy, and in Rotorua it often was, the houses sat there, islands in lakes, and for days mud was everywhere. And parents shouted at their children for traipsing mud into the house when the children couldn't help it. Though our father never shouted at us, ever.

The front door was off centre to the front of the house, but hardly anyone went in and out of the front door since the back door was closest to the kitchen. You went in through the wash-house (laundry wasn't a word anyone used then except for the commercial laundries operated by the stereotype Chinese), opened a door and there was the kitchen, quite a small room, though not that a child would have noticed or cared. It had windows a child couldn't look out of, a bench with a sink, a basic stove, and that was it.

Out of the kitchen was the passage, or the hallway, always dark because there were no windows and the doors off it were usually closed. On the immediate right was the toilet, next to it the bathroom with a bath, a vanity cupboard, a basin with cupboards underneath, and a high opaque window giving it some light. Across the passage opposite the toilet (my father called it the lavatory and won our mother to this usage when he told her it was only the lower classes who called it a toilet) was a bedroom, with one of its walls on the other side of the kitchen. Windows ran about half its width.

Directly ahead where the passage turned right was the main bedroom, Mum and Dad's shared with whoever the baby was at the time. Left was the sitting-room, the largest room in this one thousand square feet of house, with an L-shaped corner of windows, and an open fireplace.

The passage went the other way up to the front door at the end, and to the last bedroom, which we called the top bedroom, off towards the left. This was also a reasonable size, or so we thought and never knew any better, not for some years. Several of us shared it, first in single beds with two top and tailing, then we had our own bunks.

There was an older half-sister, Josie, from my mother's first marriage, and two brothers, before me, Kevin born in 1947, Nick 1948, and then me in 1950. Sister Donnelle came in 1952, Neil in 1954, and Roger in 1956. The three older brothers shared the top bedroom; Donnelle slept in Josie's room, though I remember she slept in our room too if she felt like it.

Most of life took place outside. Our footpath was a typical one of the neighbourhood, with holes dug out for our games of marbles. But that was in the school years. The glass marbles were our currency;

everything of swap value was converted to a certain number of marbles. Boys had favourite firing 'tors', which were ball-bearing 'steelies' or clear glass marbles of deadly striking power. The opaque glass ones with little pockmarks were for some reason the most prized. We kids ascribed many magical, mystical powers not just to these coveted superior strikers, but to the lucky kids who owned them.

But in the house it was mainly the kitchen where we spent the time, and secondly the sitting-room. You furnished your own home. Dad preferred the varnished floorboards at any rate, though we did have coarse wool carpet in the sitting-room at one stage, just that I don't remember when or that it was of any importance. Dad had installed lots of shelf space for his books in the sitting-room. Books had always been part of our sitting-room, even before Dad purchased our sofas. One of his wardrobes stored a set of encyclopedias on the Second World War. For many of the returned servicemen, this was the event around which the rest of their subsequent lives revolved. But not for our father, though he did talk almost thematically about it, used it as his most common reference point. It was without question the most major event in his life. Even given the marriage he had.

Dad was a bit of an incongruity, perhaps a curiosity, living in this state-housing area. He was a scientist at the Forestry Research Institute, an educated man with a university degree living in a suburb that was virtually all working class. That, and the fact that he was a white man married to a Maori, were the obvious differences. He was a most well-read and therefore well-informed man who was reasonable almost to the point of irritation at times. He had a mind that loved knowledge for its own sake. And yet he married, inexplicably, someone to whom knowledge was a pragmatic affair and simple at that. This man was an intellectual above all and born of two fine parental minds, and yet for some mysterious reason he took up with a hedonist, an egotist, and sadly a violent bad drunk to boot. But she was also a powerful personality, funny and indomitable, gregarious and positive.

My father, Gowan Duff, was European. He was born in Central Otago in 1910, went to Beaumont Primary School and when his family moved to Christchurch he went to Papanui School and Christchurch Boys High, and then to the University of Canterbury. His father was Oliver Duff, renowned as a newspaper, magazine and journal editor and a highly respected public commentator. His mother Jesse (neé Barclay) was a self-taught classical pianist, an art lover, and had a novel published in 1945. Dad's brother Roger was the youngest appointed director of Canterbury Museum and one of the country's youngest ever to receive a doctorate of science for his contribution to anthropology. Dad had a sister who had taught fine art at university and was a sculptor and artist. He had a brother who taught and ended up lecturing in education at different universities, both in Australia and New Zealand. Later Dad became known as Pat, a name he was given because he never really liked Gowan as a name, and at his work there had been another Duff, so Pat he became. My first-born grandson has the name Gowan, but seems to be proud of it.

My mother was Maori, born Hinau Josephine Raimona, but all her adult life was known as Kuia, which means 'old woman' in Maori and is a term usually given someone who is revered. Mum had been educated only to Standard Two level, through no fault of her own as there was not enough money to give all of her family an education. My maternal grandfather, Raimona Mikaere Heretaunga was born in 1870. He reversed his name after being refused credit at a grocery store because one of his brothers was a bad debtor, so Heretaunga Raimona he became. He lived in the village of Te Wairoa until the eruption in 1886 of Mount Tarawera, which killed hundreds and smothered forever the famous Pink and White Terraces. He then moved to Matata in the eastern Bay of Plenty, where he is buried beneath a carved pole representing the ancestors of the great chief Rangitihi, his grave right beside a meeting-house. Also buried in the same urupa is my Uncle Hini, whose son Michael is now the family spokesman since he is the eldest son of the eldest son. My grandfather spent years living in Rotorua, was thrice-married and according to legend fathered up to thirty-five children. In his job as a translator for the settlements around the lakes in the Rotorua area he provided services to communities that had no money and so they paid him with women of his choice. He was a teetotaller and kept a diary in a Bible in a beautifully crafted hand, which I have but glanced at many years ago.

He married Arapine, whose maiden name was Kereama, but she had been married previously to Natanahira Wiwarena to whom she had three children. I think she was born at either Te Haroto, a tiny Maori settlement in between Napier and Taupo, or at Nuhaka on the east coast. Yet she had land-owning connections in the tribal area of Tuwharetoa, and in Whaka. Arapine lived with our family at Matai Street for some months before I was at school. I remember her sitting up in the front room, which looked out over the alleyway connecting our cul-de-sac to Clinkard Avenue. She would call out to passers-by in Maori. She was suffering mild dementia and I understand my mother had her put into a mental hospital, Tokanui, which had a Maori psychiatrist director, Henry Bennett. I recall visiting her there with my Uncle Jim and Aunty Mary and my mother, and giving her a small bar of chocolate. My grandmother died when I was five and my only other memory of her is being at the thermal baths of Whaka, giving out walnuts to all and sundry and talking in Maori to them.

My maternal grandfather died in 1940, ten years before I was born. The photograph I have of him is a group one taken at Whaka's Model Pa in about 1920, an assemblage of chiefs and high-ranking males, most of them wearing traditional feather cloaks, including my grand-father. I understand it was posed for a re-enactment of the signing of the 1840 Treaty of Waitangi, rather an irony considering no Te Arawa chief signed the Treaty.

Few of us know much of our Maori background, except that there is family land at Taupo's now exclusive Acacia Bay, and my mother's family receives regular lease and timber royalty cheques from various land holdings throughout the Rotorua and Lake Rotoiti area. I re-member the land money as the reason for Mum and her sisters running around in taxis and getting drunk.

Mum's two older brothers, Hini and Tupu, were educated at Te Aute College, at that time a prestigious Maori boarding school in Hawkes Bay, the area I've now settled in; and an older half-sister, Mary (or Mereana, the Maori version), went to another Maori boarding school, Queen Victoria, in Auckland. Hini Raimona was dux of Te Aute College. A brother, Nat (for Natanahira) had been killed in the Second World War and a sister, Jean, a rather strikingly attractive young woman, had died of some disease during the war years.

My mother and father were vastly different. My mother scoffed at my father's intellectual interests. She laughed in his face at where his mind took him. My father would ponder the origin of the universe, for example, something that interested him his entire life, but it was of no account to my mother whatsoever.

'Stars?' she'd say at my father posing yet another question of the heavens. 'Only star I care about is the good luck one that's going to shine on my next card game.' She didn't give a damn about mankind's beginnings let alone the origin of the universe. Her universe was personal and peopled only by those around her and those who affected her, no more. She read little, and no evidence of my father's reading convinced her that there was anything, any advantage, to be gained from it. She simply existed without ever reflecting.

She saw life in terms of what physical, sensual pleasures could be taken from it. She measured much of it in terms of insult, of what degree of offence she would take at any given slight. Whilst her husband contemplated Plato and Einstein, and read Faulkner and Shakespeare, she thought about tactics and her opponents' strengths and weaknesses for the next poker game. Or she smouldered over some intended act of revenge she was going to take physically against someone. On my marriage certificate stating parents' occupations, I put 'Father: research scientist. Mother: card player'. There was no more ill-suited couple than Pat and Kiua Duff.

It was an unlikely marriage union and to most who got to know the couple, an inexplicable one, though I understand it was a typical early marriage of bliss, with the usual relationship difficulties anyone can expect. An incident between my mother and her mother-in-law Jesse, when they met once at Jesse's house in Auckland, sums up my parents' two irreconcilable worlds. The discussion turned to art and classical music and Jesse asked my mother what she thought of Beethoven. 'Oh, I like his paintings,' said my mother innocently and to her mother-in-law's immediate outrage. Jesse chided her daughter-in-law for her ignorance, which was a big mistake, for my mother started in on the sherry and fumed. In her home Jesse had a piece of sculpture by my father's sister, Alison, a somewhat abstract piece. My mother, by this time well inebriated, picked up the work of art, smashed it to pieces on the hearth and stormed out of her mother-in-law's house. Several days later, after getting on the booze with friends, she turned up in Rotorua, having caught a taxi from Auckland, a distance of 160 miles. She demanded my father pay for the fare to make up for her embarrassment at his mother's house.

I have to say that my memories of my parents' marriage come as a blast, like an explosion. And of course those memories can't be right, for my parents stayed together until I was ten and there were definitely some good times for both the couple and their children. Except that's not what my memory drags up. My memories of those very first years are of course gone, or sketchy at best. Going out with Mum to hang up the washing on our wooden clothes-line, her humming tunes or singing a song to herself; playing in the dirt on the permitted edges of Dad's vegetable garden; being in the fowl-house with Dad or Mum or an older brother or sister, finding eggs our hens had laid; staring in fascination at the newly hatched chickens, wanting to grab these fluffy yellow balls and crush them to death with love; watching wood being chopped by Dad, seeing how he made kindling; seeing the same axe remove the head of a hen for our oven, the blood spurting as the headless creature runs crazily around the back part of our quarter-acre section.

At night, in the evenings, I remember Dad taking us out to look at the stars, hearing his voice explaining, us too young to understand, but not too young to know it was a most pleasant bonding time with our father. And yet he wasn't the demonstrative type, more the affectionate sort; his was the rational man's way of showing love for his children, restrained somewhat by the logic that was the engine of his mind. We would not have had any other Dad, who would sit us around the fire in winter and read to us, or tell us stories from his war experiences, his time as a prisoner of war or from his own childhood of growing up in a farming district in a small South Island community, surrounded by the large, extended Duff clan, many of whom were characters.

In my memory my father is quite a fine-looking man, fair-skinned, with strong features but diffident blue eyes, brown hair, an air of intelligent dignity, of average height, and surprisingly muscular, especially his chest which was well-defined well into his seventies. My mother is Maori of feature, full lips, round face, attractive, superb teeth, black hair, strong challenging brown eyes almost taunting you, and unlike most Maori eyes that usually averted your gaze, hers never left you. She had a full figure, once it had been good, and her laughter, funny thing, stays in my mind.

My brothers are good-looking, especially Kevin the oldest, and we all know from an early age that the Duffs are very intelligent. Josie is pretty, Neil is dark and handsome, and when Roger came along he too is handsome. Donnelle doesn't look like us, she's darker and has Fijian features, though we didn't notice, not for years until we linked the whispers with the comparison between ourselves. She is our sister.

Dad reads a lot and reads to us and tells us stories. He takes us everywhere on his bike on a seat he's had built with footrests and you hold onto the inside of the handlebars and the wind is cool in your face and the speed feels so exciting. He explains things to us, whoever's turn it is on the bike; he'll go all the way into town, a couple of miles, down to the lake, to Sulphur Point; he'll swim in the lake with us, ride us out into the deep on his back. Maybe we'll all walk to Sulphur Point, Mum included, and make a day and a picnic of it, with an ice-cream on the way back to stop the moaning about being tired. I think I used to throw glances at my mother, hoping she wouldn't get angry at anything and spoil the day. I can't remember that she ever did, not the Sulphur Point swimming days. Maybe she wasn't there most of the time. Perhaps my memories of her are too subjective and unfair, though I have had every incident I recall confirmed by family or family friends. I know she did not feel comfortable with her role as mother, and I have come to know it extends to the role of wife. In my older adulthood I understand – at least I hope I do – that she is just her own person. Maybe it's a quality that has stood me in good stead.

We're Maori and Pakeha. We're both, we know that early. It's part of our parents' often clashing conversation. They disagree on so many things. But then we notice other parents in our friends' houses disagree too. So it's not the end of the world, not when it's all yours out there, waiting to be discovered, and there aren't too many rules about where you can go. Just avoid where the storm-water pipes are being laid all over the neighbourhood, in case there's a flash flood. Don't go near that house because they've got a mean dog. Nor that one because the woman or the man or both are nasty. In one house they make comment on your being 'half-castes'. As if it's a disease. But apart from them, it's a friendly few streets to be growing up in.

I grew up with contradiction, I was born of two races, two opposite sides of the intellectual and cultural fence, of two oppositely behaved parents, of white and brown, passivity versus volatility and violence. I was born on 26 October, 1950, at Rotorua Hospital. I started school at Glenholme Primary, a half a mile down Rimu Street, which cut our street in two. I was there for five years and in my last was dux of the school whilst being one of the worst-behaved. But then coming dux whilst being a bad boy felt perfectly normal to me. By then it did. And so did everything else that happened, after the formative years had done their forming.

two

I feel the presence of my father within me little different to a part of my body. I have his ashes on a wardrobe shelf not two metres from me. I have his father Oliver's framed photographic portrait on my desk, and alongside it sits a clay bust of my father's mother, Jesse.

It was late 1992, October. I was living in Havelock North, Hawkes Bay, and my father was in hospital in Rotorua and really unwell. My second novel, *One Night Out Stealing*, had been published in September. Bob Jones – Sir Robert, as is his official title – launched it and I was proud of the novel. Some critics had called me a 'one book wonder' after the publication of *Once Were Warriors*, which by this time had been out just short of two years. But I didn't care for what the literary establishment or the academics thought. It was my father's opinion I wanted before anyone's.

Dad knew language, and he knew literature as good as any expert there is. He loved language. He loved words. He loved the written word most of all. My father's major influence on me was in language. He taught us all correct grammar. We knew from an early age the difference between 'bought' and 'brought' and the usage of 'me' and 'I'. He dwells in my mind as a man of intellect who never ceased being curious and interested in the world. He was always challenging conventional thinking, but was a stickler for rules of grammar and correct spelling. He also believed in truth unto itself, thus never allowing anything but truth to be his judgement. I knew he would have been blunt and honest enough to tell me if he didn't like *One Night Out Stealing*, and the reasons why.

I remember the Christmas after *Once Were Warriors* was published. It was the same day that my ex-de facto wife gave me and my wife custody of my daughter Katea, then aged eleven, this little girl I'd not been responsible enough for after her mother and I had gone our separate ways several years prior. I went for lunch with my father to the International Hotel at Whakarewarewa in Rotorua, a place with a huge history for me. We ran into a Maori elder, the highly respected local kaumatua and former director of the Maori Arts and Crafts Institute, the late Kuru Waaka and his family. He and Dad knew each other well from the war years and occasional social contact at parties or war remembrance events such as the Dawn Parade. Kuru and his family expressed their pride in me as a 'Whaka boy' for being published and Kuru asked Dad how he felt.

'I'm happy to bask in my son's glory,' said my father with typical diffident pride. I was feeling pretty proud myself, not so much at the compliments, but at my father being so proud of me. It was not something I was used to, from my school days of achieving first in classes and being school dux. Dad just didn't believe in being too generous with compliments and praise lest it give the recipient a swollen head. I think he was wrong there, very wrong.

On that day in October I sat talking to my father in his hospital bed, and then suddenly I made the conscious decision that he wasn't going to leave this life without my showing how much I loved him. So I put my head on his chest and my arms over him and I bawled and told him I loved him. For the first time in my life. It was a moment of purity, I knew that. But I could also feel his arms rigidly tight beneath me, not coming out to return my embrace. When I pulled away I asked, 'Did that embarrass you?'

He shook his head. Words took just a moment to come. 'No,' he said. 'Definitely not.'

Then he looked at me, which wasn't Dad, as he had shy eyes that only held you for brief spurts. He said, 'But I could never have done that with my father.'

About three years before this I'd had a most disturbingly realistic dream in which my father lay on the kitchen floor of his house and I cradled him in my arms, weeping as I cried out the words, 'Oh Dad, please, not your brain! Not your beloved brain!' 'Beloved' as a term for a brain, whilst seemingly inapt, felt perfectly the right word, for my father had a love affair with the intellect. I was so troubled by my dream that I made it an excuse to drive the three hours to Rotorua to see him, and I told him of it. We chuckled and as usual he allowed for the possibility that he could be afflicted with dementia or even a brain tumour one day, but he didn't mention cancer as a possibility. Not of the brain. He did recall that his mother had died in a state of total dementia, being unable even to recognise him.

The next time I visited Dad from Hawkes Bay a few weeks later, I found him in a deteriorating state; he could speak only in a pain-racked croak and the nursing staff informed me that the diagnosis was cancer of the brain. I went in to my father and under the circumstances I don't know why I had such a need to ask this, but ask I did of my struggling father, 'I don't suppose you had time to read *One Night Out Stealing*?'

His head came up with a surprising sudden energy. 'Ye—ess,' he croaked. And flopped back down.

'What did you think of it?'

Again he came up from the pillow, with a physical vigour of the man I had always known. And he looked at me with milky, red-rimmed eyes and that mask of death descending, and he croaked out one word: 'Powerful.'

It was all I could do not to burst into tears. Of gratitude. Of total admiration for a man who can find the strength from within his ebbing body to leave me with his own 'powerful' last memory of a wonderful, good man. This was his legacy to me, and it turned out to be his last conscious utterance to me. I knew that my literature in its second attempt had reached his standard, and that he had had to muster all his physical strength to tell me in the way he had: 'Powerful.' His boy, the one who had always been in most need of encouragement and affirmation, Alan the insecure one, getting all and more than he could have asked for in his father's last utterance to him.

A week or so later, I think it was a Thursday afternoon, I came home from an out-of-town speaking engagement. My wife was looking serious, and I knew my father was dead. When she told me the news, I stood there weeping and crying out that I should have been there for him in his last moments, just as he had always been there for me, through all my troubled years, my times of being a lost wretched confused soul who didn't know who or what he was, time and again being overwhelmed by a sense of smothering insecurity. So many times Dad and I discussed this. I never told a soul nor, I am sure, did he. I felt I was his closest son, though he was appalled by favouritism. So he would never admit to such a thing himself, not even on his deathbed. But we had an understanding that we were especially close.

This moment, hearing of my father's death, is one of only a handful of absolutely pure moments of love, of grief, that I have ever felt. And writing this down is my best way of paying tribute to the man who helped shape me and whose intellectual joy and moral integrity gave me so much. He gave me a profound belief in fairness and in looking always at both sides of an argument. He gave me the true power of not envying people and therefore being free of what envy and jealousy do to a person. It took many years of immature adulthood before I would reclaim those influences, but claim them I did in the end. All my adult books are dedicated to him. With love, of course.

My father's thinking mind was inherited from his father Oliver Duff and from his artistic, creative and somewhat flighty mother Jesse. His father became famous as the founding editor of the *New Zealand Listener* and, after his retirement, was the much-loved columnist 'Sundowner' in the same publication. He was one of the most respected literary voices in the country in a career spanning many decades.

Dad's mother was the daughter of a Dunedin publican. Her creative urges had her playing classical piano, self-taught; she painted, she sculpted and she had a novel, *Otago Interval*, published in the mid-1940s which won a literary award. In her seventies Jesse Whitworth (she remarried) went to Europe, travelling second- and third-class on boats and trains, to see Europe and to visit her favourite composer's grave in Austria (it might have been Mozart or Beethoven). She brought home to New Zealand a handful of dirt in a treasured little box, now long lost, from that last resting-place of whichever illustrious musical genius it was.

During the sixties my grandmother travelled overseas with the young novelist Janet Frame. I met this writer whilst preparing these memoirs, and I admire her work most of all New Zealand writers. We sat in her living-room and together quoted one of our mutually favourite poets, Gerard Manley Hopkins. She spoke highly and fondly of Jesse, recalling that on one ship voyage my grandmother travelled lightly, with only two frocks, a change of underwear, one warm top garment and that was it. I have an exchange of letters between my great-grandmother and her son Oliver on his pending marriage to Jesse, of whom she disapproves strongly, evidently because of her different religion. Oliver's letter in reply despairs of his mother's narrow-mindedness. I wonder what my grandfather thought of the woman his oldest son married.

My father gained his Bachelor of Science degree from the University of Canterbury in 1933, the same year his father resigned as editor of *The Christchurch Press*, over a dispute with the owners who did not like their editor's lead article in support of striking tram workers. Oliver Duff was a man of strong principles and no amount of financial argument would sway him from resigning over this issue, not least the fact that the Depression was in full swing throughout this country and the western world, and anyone who had a job with a high salary, as he did, must have been considered mad to resign in the middle of such worldwide economic strife.

After gaining his degree Dad moved to Rotorua, as that was the centre of the forestry industry, close to where the world's largest man-made forest, Kaingaroa Forest, had been planted by prison labour earlier in the century. The fledgling Forestry Research Institute was housed in airforce barracks out by the village of Whakarewarewa. Whaka, as it was usually called, was the country's number one tourist destination and a major influence on me in an emotional, perhaps cultural, way.

Before the war Dad did jobs like taking weekly supplies up by horseback to the keeper of the fire watch-house on top of Rainbow Mountain overlooking Kaingaroa Forest. He culled deer for a couple of seasons, deer hunting being one of the loves of his life, as was simply being out in the forests and walking along lonely roads with his thoughts in his beloved nature's surroundings.

Dad signed up for the Second World War in the first echelon. He was a wholly committed anti-Hitler, pro-democracy advocate. He was one of the few who had read extensively about the politics and events leading up to the outbreak of the war. On his departure his father gave him a revolver from his South African Boer War days; a gesture my father said he saw as a symbolic act of fatherly love in place of an embrace.

He was captured in Greece, without even the dignity of being armed, as the commanding officer had ordered everyone to discard their weapons to help facilitate faster retreat from the advancing Germans, which was a sore point with my father. He spent over three years in a prison camp in Austria. We heard tales about the prisoners of war being squeezed like sardines into train carriages; of one small man who got himself out of a tiny window whilst the train was stopped somewhere and his mates watching him being pursued by German shepherd dogs and of course armed Germans. Dad remembers vividly how easily this tiny man handled the first dog that tried to attack him. He threw it effortlessly into the air. I suspect he told me this story in particular because he knew I was afraid of dogs. Not least the Kiels' pig dogs up the road.

As prisoners he said they were treated well, although the same could not be said of the Russians. We heard tales of Russians being put outside the barracks in the snow on punishment, some of them not surviving the cold, and the prisoners inside hearing their singing. I played a recording of Russian music at Dad's funeral and had in fact played him the same piece at home some months before he became unwell. He was so moved he was weeping, and it was only the second time I had ever seen him in tears, the first being at my oldest brother Kevin's funeral.

One incident my father told about the war never ceases to astound me. A group of about forty prisoners were allowed to go to a local pub, on the strict understanding from their tolerant guards (who no doubt wanted a beer themselves) not to let the side down by getting drunk or showing any signs of alcoholic indulgence on their return. Just before camp they all went into marching mode and returned to being prisoners of war in a half-sozzled state. I think Dad told us that story to show us that our perceptions can often be stereotypes and wrong assumptions.

The war ended for Dad in late 1944 because he contracted bad diphtheria as a prisoner of war and went blind for several weeks. He was part of a prisoner swap and returned as an invalid soldier to Rotorua, where he intended taking up his forestry science career. His job was actually less glamorous than that, but was complicated and required complex mathematics.

I understand he met my mother at a dance in Rotorua at a favourite dancehall called Tama, down at the lakeside Maori settlement of Ohinemutu, itself steaming with thermal activity. Or perhaps it was at a party and they met through Mum's brother, Tupu Raimona, who had also been prisoner of war, though not in the same camp.

By the time I came along, in October 1950, my parents' third child but my mother's fifth (she had two children to her first husband, one of whom, Maxine, had been adopted by my Mum's sister Mary, and the other, Josie, was brought up with us) they had moved into a new state house in Matai Street about a mile or so from Rotorua township. They had previously lived at Te Hemo flats, an early century building converted to flats and now a renowned restaurant overlooking Whaka. Te Hemo is named after the gorge that runs out of Whaka, through which the infamous Maori warrior renegade, Te Kooti, was pursued by loyalist Te Arawa hired soldiers. The Te Arawa tribe chose to side with the British colonisers in return for keeping their tribal land, or at least much of it.

My father was the only university educated man in the neighbourhood. He was also the very last to own a car. Most of his neighbours beat him to car ownership, but only because it was one of their priorities in life. He was perfectly happy with his bicycle and I think perfectly happy not having any goals in life other than private self-enlightenment. And he was a most generous man who never stinted on us his children nor on anyone who needed help.

He was fair on virtually every subject, no matter how close it might be to his heart. The only mild exception was his left of centre political thinking. But he had more moments than most when he could see the flaws in even his own political arguments. I think therein lay his secret and his failure at the same time. He could see both sides of an argument, but could rarely take an adamant stance.

He was consistent and rational. Once my two older brothers hid behind the sofa playing with matches and set it on fire. My mother doused the flames and was about to hit the children when my father intervened. 'Ask them why they did it first,' he insisted. And they answered, 'Because we wanted to see what happened.' That was good enough for Dad, and he instructed my mother that she was not to punish them.

For a man who suffered an affliction of shyness that had measurable effects on his career and stunted his social life and any chance of finding another marriage partner, my father was the most unselfconscious person in Rotorua when it came to riding proudly to and from work, into town, and all around on his bicycle. He had a routine, as he had with everything he did, of folding his trouser cuffs carefully at a certain angle and pushing his bicycle clip over to avoid catching the cuffs in the chain. He always checked his tyres to make sure they were firm, an excuse for a physical man like him to grab the pump attached to the bike frame and give the tyres a few shots of air. Then, left foot on the pedal, over his right leg would go, and he'd be off, Pat Duff on his bike.

At one stage in my younger days I was embarrassed at the sight of my father on his bike because the girls laughed at him, and my new male friends refused to believe that this man, the silly old fool on the bike, with the bike clips on his trousers, *and* wearing a cravat, was not only my father but a *scientist* as well! He was simply the most incongruous identity for miles.

He had discerning taste in clothing. His selection of cravats stands out in particular, as do his well-looked-after sets of shoes. But taste eluded him when it came to house décor and furnishings. He was a wholly pragmatic man in this regard, our kitchen tables were a succession of formica-topped lumps with stainless steel edging, usually a hideous yellow. There was barely an item of furniture in the house that didn't have a practical purpose. Function, not aesthetics, was my father's primary concern. Yet he had an artistic bent himself, and his drawings as a child are to my eye suggestive of a real talent. But no art adorned our walls and no fine furniture acquisitions occurred to him. Our furnishings were austere, and if it hadn't been for our extensive bookshelves the house would have looked pretty grim. I think it all reflected a most unpretentious man who didn't care a damn what other people thought of him.

Dad had planted a large vegetable area in our quarter-acre state property. He kept a good front lawn and a footpath with well tended edges. He was tidy and rather fastidious, in keeping with his job which involved measuring logs. He had developed tables of measurements and systems in his time, which I am told by his Forestry Research Institute contemporaries were world class. He had a team of others under him, and was an exceedingly conscientious government employee. He allocated minor tasks according to the salary scale of the person, reasoning that it cost the government less if a lower-salaried person did the task. He would have made a good businessman. His salary was high in comparison to most of his working-class neighbours, though obviously there were self-employed contractors who made a lot more money than he did.

So we lived better than most, certainly food-wise and where clothing and footwear was concerned. But luxury was not in our house. Dad, being a fitness man as well as being very aware of good health, raised us on daily supplements to our diets: tablets of cod-liver oil, vitamin C tablets, a spoonful of wheat germ. Breakfast was porridge but we spoiled it according to Dad as we had as much sugar as we could filch and chunks of butter that melted and made the taste just perfect.

At night meat and vegetables were our standard fare. Dad got good quality cuts of meat such as porterhouse steak, and pork chops, and legs for roasts, though of course we also had cheaper meat such as sausages and mince. But Dad insisted the butcher give him lean mince and that most of the fat be trimmed off his lamb chops. I presume Mum carried out Dad's food shopping wishes without much complaint, as I certainly remember her cooking us delicious meals suited to Dad's smiling taste, though her own food preference was the Maori boil-up.

Dad had a thing about Mum's boil-ups. For he well knew the dangers of fatty food and never failed to point out to Mum that this kind of food was very bad for her and therefore he didn't like his children partaking too much of it. Except we loved boil-ups and we were glad that Dad didn't like to stay around if we were eating boiled pork backbones with watercress and potatoes. He also hated people making slurping or sucking noises when they ate, which was what every Maori we knew did. I have inherited my father's intolerance of eating sounds, but definitely not of the boil-up, which remains my favourite today, apart from Bluff oysters.

We weren't allowed sweets, or at least not to purchase them with our pocket money, as Dad had a middle-class concern with his children's dental health. He discouraged our well-meaning Maori relations from giving us sweets when they visited, which offended them, for to Maori the giving of any form of food is honouring the recipient or showing your love, and at the very least being kind. They weren't to know sugar is bad for you. As an adult I don't have a sweet tooth and wouldn't consume directly more than a few teaspoons of sugar in any year. And yes, my teeth are good. Three fillings.

Some of my clearest images are of my Maori relations' expressions of outrage, unable to comprehend my father's edict not to give his children sweets. In private Dad told us that the Maori people did not take a long-term view of life and that this would always be to their detriment. He spent, I'll never forget the sum, £8 on getting one of my teeth straightened when I was about nine. Back in 1959 this was a week's wage for a worker and yet my father was prepared to spend it on a mere tooth of his child's. How glad I am that he did.

Every fortnight when Dad's salary was paid he bought us apple squares. We were also allowed dark chocolate as this gave us energy, which he believed we easily burned off. He had us eating dates and dried fruits when we knew no other kid who ate such stuff. There were sheep brains and livers, blue vein cheese and tinned sardines, wholemeal bread, and lots of fruit. He could never reconcile this diet with his wife's one of fried and boiled fatty foods, and lots of it. She did get plumper over the years, whilst Dad's build remained lean and muscular.

They argued frequently about this cultural difference in food, Dad insisting that his argument was won on the simple premise that it was demonstrably better for one's health. Mum insisted her argument was won because her food tasted sweeter and juicier. She proved her point, with a wicked smile in her eye, by always having second and sometimes third helpings. Food was but one of many subjects on which their views were polarised.

It was our household where differences manifested themselves as racial and hopelessly irreconcilable. It was our household, and those of our mother's relatives and friends, where all was anything but well. It seemed our house and our family were chosen as extreme examples of the polarised differences between the two races, Maori and Pakeha, the differences of intellect, culture, everyday living routine, and attitude. It was like tectonic plates rubbing up against one another – at any time an earthquake could happen, and did happen.

three

I can smell her. Long before she starts walking up from the kitchen. Stinking of beer. And anger has a smell its own. I can smell something else about her, to do with her inner being – if she has one – the person she is. I'm up in the top room with my brothers, I have two sisters in another room, nearest to where the fuss is coming from. We can smell her before she leaves the kitchen. The moment we hear the door open to the passageway, her voice tells us she's headed this way. Before that we could hear her yelling. Thumps of her assaulting Dad. And he's restrained her as usual when we want him to punch shit out of her, give her some of her own back for once. But he won't. He won't. Even at eight, seven, six, maybe younger, you know something bad is happening to you beyond just the immediacy of the event, the incident itself. Your life juices are leaking out, your soul container has been ruptured, you're spilling out and can't stem the flow.

We're in the top room and we know she'll come. Sooner or later, she'll make her dramatic appearance. That foul apparition in her children's bedroom doorway, beer-fuming breath finding her young ones' nostrils and standing our hair and every poised nerve on end.

'Kids…?' she always starts off pretending she's a mother. 'I'm sorry to wake you up. But I want you to know something,' she lies. If she was sorry, she wouldn't be waking us up. And anyway we know, we already know this story, this same tale of woe. Heard it a hundred times. It's your father's fault. Never hers. His. And each time she tries to convince us that she, this beer-stenching, swaying apparition in our bedroom doorway, backlit by the passageway light, is innocent, and that he, the sober, rational, non-violent man imploring her to leave us alone, is the guilty party. How stupid does she think her children are?

'It's not me,' she says in that plaintive voice.

She's mother of four of us in the top room, and of two in the room closest the kitchen in this state house, with one more yet to be born. A thousand square foot state box, painted creosote black. There is no other state house like it. It's as if Dad wants us to stand out even more than what Mum's notorious deeds have done already, yet we know Dad's not like that. Our father has a mind, he has reason. And that's what he's yelling at her. 'Be reasonable, for God's sake!' Again. And again. Why the hell does he bother imploring her like this? Be hard on her! Finish this nonsense once and for all. For your sake, for all your children's sakes. This can't go on. And on. And on and on, incident after incident. It can't. Your kids are drowning, Pat Duff. Your wife, the kids' mother, is holding their heads under the water.

Down the passage she comes. Up in the expectant bedroom we are making our adjustments, readying for it yet never really able to. Turn right, Mum, not left you drunken fool. Past the telephone – hold it. Who's she going to ring this time?

'Mary, that you?' Mary is Mum's sister. She knows. We can hear her without having to hear the voice, asking Mum what the hell she wants at this hour when she was asleep and so should her sister be.

'Sis, can you come around?' No, sis can't come around. 'Mary? Mary...? Mereana, don't you hang up on me!' But Mary has. So now Mary's a bitch and she'll keep, she'll keep. We can hear that muttered dire promise. Mum will get her back. It's the best-kept promise of her life.

Now the breathing again. Breath is not always soft, breath is voice, breath is a signal, all words pour and trickle and scream and whisper and joy out on breath. Here she comes. I'm so anxious. It's the anticipating of it, a mistake I've made in this mental, emotional process. I should have taught myself to switch off.

'Kevin ...?'one of us will say.

'Shuddup. And let me handle it.'

'Kevin ...?'

'And you shuddup too. Everyone shuddup. And don't cry. Don't scream. I'll talk to her.'

'Kids…?'

'Mum.'

'Oh, my oldest son. I love you. You know that, eh? I love you. I love you all….' As she waits for the right response. Then forces it. 'Answer me.'

'I know that, Mum.'

'It's him, your father, who makes me like this. But you kids think it's me. Tell them, Kevin.'

'They already know, Mum. We're asleep, Mum. Go to bed now, Mum. Please.'

'That's what your aunty just said. Well, I'm not going to bed, not until I've had my say.'

Not until she's had her say. This is instant gratification. Our father has taught us this term. He says too many Maori are like this: they feel angry, they must express it instantly, hit someone, yell at someone, threaten them. Hungry: have a feed. Thirsty: have a beer and have another one and another, cos it tastes sweet and if it's sweet, why stop?

Not until she's had her say. About her, who else? Not her effect on her kids. But how *she* is affected by her husband, by what he says and how he says it and even if he's silent it's how he's looked at her. And if he's not looked at her, it's why he isn't looking. She'll find something to put her entire case on. Then she'll go for him.

Kevin gets up. We know that figure moving the few steps across our room so well. He's our protector. That's her hugging him. Her sobbing. Thinks it's got meaning, when we know it's called being crying drunk.

'I love you the most, son. I know your father says I shouldn't have a favourite. But who cares what he says? That's our way. Maoris have their pets and why shouldn't we? Who the hell does he think he is telling us – me, a mother – I can't have my favourite child? He's got his favourite book hasn't he? His favourite place to hunt? Why can't I have my favourite child?'

Our father will appear behind her any moment. Know that face too: weary. Kuia-weary.

'Leave them be, Kuia.'

'Who invited you to speak! I'm here talking to my children. To my oldest, favourite son.'

'Don't be telling him that, Kuia.'

'Tell him what I fuckin' like.'

Even at ten, eleven at night. It's important to tell one of your six children he's your pet and the others aren't. Important for her.

'Just come away from their room and let them sleep in peace.'

'They were awake.'

'Because you woke them.'

'Tell your father, Kevin. I said, tell him. Tell-your-father-Kev-in. Go on, tell him.' Tell him, tell him, go on, tell him, shrills in our ears when we should be asleep dreaming. '*Tellim!*'

It used to go on for an hour, maybe two; she'd come in and out of our room several times, sometimes she'd attack Dad in our room, or we'd hear the thumping of her hitting and he restraining her down the hallway. Once she even got Dad's rifle from the wardrobe in our room and pointed it at him.

She demands we get out of bed and come down to the kitchen. Dad protests of course. He protests, but we're out of bed. Troop off down the passageway, past the phone, wish I could phone someone, get them to whisk this woman away. Wish she'd just stop, there at the turning, and turn instead back to me and hug me and tell me she loves me. Wish she would.

Sisters are waiting in the kitchen. Younger sister has this amused look, as if even at four or five she knows how to handle this. Or maybe I'm deliberately hazing the picture over, maybe she's really distressed. Maybe I don't want to let the other's pain in. Yet I do see Donnelle's little covering smile, a twitching mouth, yet big bold eyes. Our big sister, Josie, the oldest in the family, is the sibling in charge. She's afraid of no-one, not even our mother. She has a born decency which she uses as her best weapon, her defensive bulwark to protect her sensibilities. She's not going to let this woman affect her future existence, she's locked the best part of herself away, safe from this woman. Dad, he sees Josie's best side, is her staunchest ally. They love each other. That's part of Josie's secret: she has joined her strength to our father's moral strength. But me, I can't find a way to lock any part of myself away from Mum. Even in my dreams she's the witch. Chasing me, wanting to murder me.

In the kitchen there's this long, drawn-out melodrama. The only player on the stage doesn't care for her audience. This is her play and she'll act it for as long as she likes and how she likes. Cupboards open and plates come flying out. Dad rushes to restrain her, Kevin herds us into the corner, by the hot-water closet, the heat has warmed the door, it gets through our pyjamas, but doesn't stop us shivering, those who are. This is but the start of how this night, any night, will go. We know the ending but we've never found a way to harden ourselves to it. Every time it happens it comes as an explosion, as if she knows it is at risk of losing its dramatic impact, so she has a variety, a repertoire of different fireworks.

Your mother's going mad now. Launching herself at Dad in a fury. He has to use all his strength to hold her down. For a scientist, an intellectual, he's a contradiction, for he's very strong, has a well-cut muscular body, is an avid hunter, a physical fitness stalwart. She's on the floor. We can see her underwear. The dark patch where we each emerged. She's on her back and shrieking and struggling and flailing. I can feel my face so flushed with shame I fear it might explode. I'm glowing. I want to die. She's on her back and we can see where we came from and it's a horrible sight, you shouldn't see that side of your mother, not in these circumstances. Dad's saying, 'For Chrissake, have you no shame?'

Shame? No. She has no shame. You have to have a heart for your children, you have to actually love them before you can feel shame at being like this....Shit, this marriage was never going to work.

Our mother thought the world needed no explaining, it was what it was and you simply reacted to how it affected you. I think of the neighbours and how many times they have heard this and yet I wish, I cry inside, that she would take note of this, what it does to us her children, the weight it puts on our heads out on the streets. The defensive anger it puts into our eyes. It is like a deformed seed planted in us – and we know it. Each of us knows it.

So it's another day after school and you've taken your time coming home, first playing up in the forest. You'd better get home, she might be mad at you not coming straight home, not because she cares but because she has to impose her authority and anyway she might feel like an excuse to vent her anger. You step out of that dappled oak and elm and fern surround, place of your growing secrets, site of your pain to trickle out onto the dirt in your hiding-place, your comforting place. You become aware of that familiar excitement in the street. All the heads are looking down the hill at your house. The necks are straining, the hands are twitching at the eyes' disbelief, the rigid leg stances register social disapproval at its greatest. Fuck it, Mum's at it again. Oh, fuck, it's not fair.

Hear her voice, her screaming reverberating up the street, feel and see the neighbours' eyes on you, hear their muttered, 'Poor kids,' because it's the plural of you. Kevin you hope will be somewhere close, so will the others. Your mother is in the centre of it, she's the cause, even though she's telling the whole street, neighbourhood, the whole town that she's not to blame, it was someone else started it but she sure as hell is gonna finish it. Through her teeth. Her beautiful, pearly whites, through that spitting aperture, that shrieking cave from which the warrioress emerges from time to regular time.

'Come on, you bitches and bastards!' she yells at them all. 'I'll take the lot of you on!'

This is someone's mother, don't forget. This is tomorrow's news-paper court page. You can sit in your classroom at school, dreading the mid-morning break and then the longer lunch break to follow, because everyone will know. Their parents will have pointed it out to them the night before. Look, there she is, tch-tch-tch, at it again. Poor kids. Or who gives a shit about the kids. This mother is not like any other mother in the entire school.

That's her brawling in the sprawl with herself, and there are others and they're all in the same enraged, engaged, drunken condition. They're having a scrap.

'Jus' a scrap, whassa fuckin' problem, officer?'

If you were their lawyer in court next week, you'd say on behalf of your client to the magistrate, 'Your honour, my client had been owed a debt for some time from, she admits, an illegal game of cards for money. Upon seeing the debtor sit at a table and gamble heavily all day whilst not offering to pay her debt, my client, if you can understand the situation your honour, became considerably inflamed. With a liberal intake of alcohol involved – though I add, your honour, it was only beer and not strong spirits – things got a little out of hand.' Blah-blah-blah.

If someone owes you a long-standing card debt, you attack. It is not only perfectly reasonable, you'd be a weakling if you didn't. That this attack should take place in front of your own children is completely irrelevant. Personal pride takes singular priority. Money can't buy it, only revenge can. The Maori word for that is utu. Utu means to gain terrible revenge. Utu carries with it a compelling, all-consuming obligation to honour, to make good the slight, the wound, the pain, by causing worse pain in return.

The fight's broken up by tired old cops who know every participant. The old sergeant talks to them like the children they are.

'Peta, I thought you'd learned your lesson the last time. As for you, Missy Davis, this is the second time in a month I've been called out to an incident you're involved in.' The sergeant shakes his head and sighs and flexes his muscles rigid in readiness and asks, 'Are you going to come along quietly, Mrs Duff?' Mrs Duff? She doesn't deserve the title, nor the name.

And she says almost as quietly, 'Are you going to listen to my reasons first?'

And he says, 'Kuia, Kuia, we've gone through this a dozen times.'

And she says, 'I thought it was more than that, actually. So you must have learned by now. Listen, that bitch Connie…'

'I'm sorry, Kuia. You're under arrest. Anything you say can be used as evidence against you.'

Sure. But try arresting her physically. She's strong. And she can't stand being manhandled, even though it's her way of handling every situation herself. Something about anyone laying a hand on her enrages her. But he's an old hand and though she puts up a huge struggle, he's a lot stronger and he has her in an armlock and is begging her not to make him use any more force, or he could break her arm.

And though the Maori men involved are getting excited again and want to hoe into the sergeant and the constable and those busybody Pakeha neighbours standing around staring (worry about the court consequences later), they manage, just, to restrain themselves.

Dad has rushed to the scene with a friend in his car because Dad doesn't have a car. He's in time to see his wife being driven away. Or he's got there just before she is, and always asks quietly of the arresting officers what the charge is and is there any way that she might just be taken down to the station and let off with a warning, as they'll understand without him having to prostrate himself.

I don't know how many times the cops let Mum off with a warning not to breach the public peace. But sometimes she gave them no choice and they'd cart her off down to the station for a couple or three hours, and there was always great relief at home immediately afterwards, knowing we'd be free of her for a period. The shame didn't kick in, not in its fullness, till next day. Or at night, when you lay there thinking about it, reliving it, playing it back in your mind. God, why are Maori so instantly ignited into violence? Why do they get so blind, staggeringly, vomiting, abusively drunk? What angers them so? And what did we do to deserve a mother like this?

She comes home usually quietened, almost subdued. She hates the police process, the court process. She's even said sorry to us on occasion, but that only makes you, the kid, burst into uncontrollable tears and has you want to hug her and say you forgive her, you'd forgive her anything when she's like this, contrite and vulnerable. And she's had her times of weeping back in my arms and slobbering sorry all over me. And hell, I liked that, I did. Why the fuck did you never *stay* sorry?

Hey, but the morning after it's porridge for breakfast with sugar and butter on. Mum might have got up and made it herself, but usually Josie or Kevin does. Dad is quiet in the kitchen, he's up before us, done his press-ups on his fingertips in his room, his running on the spot, shaved, put on the shirt he's pressed himself, sometimes but not often a tie, unlike most of his work colleagues, a jacket and neatly creased trousers. Fixed his breakfast, toast (wholemeal in times when most of the population have no idea wholemeal bread exists), he's had his wheat germ and we'll have our daily roof-of-the-mouth-sticking ration. He'll have two poached eggs and make his boiled ground coffee in a tiny blackened pot on the electric stove. He'll make his lunch, sandwiches with sardines. He's a most ordered, tidy man of routine and eating discipline. He'll have our cod-liver oil capsules laid out on the bench. We've been awake earlier than usual, always are the day after a major incident. A minor incident like 'only' a face-clawing attack on Dad is a sleep-in, so inured have we become.

I cannot recall ever having a single discussion with any of my brothers or sisters over our mother's behaviour, nor any talk of her being named in the local newspaper on charges of breaching the public peace. The rule in our house was: Don't cry. When she broke out we had to train ourselves to hold back our responses, to keep our reactions, let alone our despair, in check. Kevin made sure we kept to this dictum. You learn to cry like this: 'Mmmmmmmmmm.' With a dry face.

I knew by the age of five that I was scared of my mother and that once she had a drink or two, or if she was sulking or upset about something, she was not a person to whom I could take my troubles and even little ailments to. In fact we all learned to keep well out of her way, even earshot in case her bellowing voice summoned us. Anything could happen at any time. A pleasant Saturday afternoon visit could turn into a nightmare of drunken mothers trying to tear each other's scalps off, and fingernails slicing one another's faces to shreds. They punched like men, screamed like banshees, and bled like animals on the slaughter line. And my mother most of the time was in the thick of it, if not the cause.

It wasn't all misery and violence and booze. Mum had sober periods. She was house-proud and was a very good cook. We enjoyed her marvellous Sunday lunchtime roasts, a chicken or a leg of lamb, a creation of her own. Hearing her humming as she prepared the lunch, seeing the contentment on my father's face as he brought in freshly dug potatoes from his garden, the look that said he was once again forgiving her, and if only the marriage could stay like this.

She even had times of turning quite clucky. I had baths with her when I was little when I sat behind her and soaped her back. I have a few pleasant memories of her lovingly tending to my grazed knee or needling a prickle out from my foot. I remember her dabbing my child's play wounds with purplish Mercurochrome. I remember once her look of delight and relief for me when she lanced a huge boil on my knee first with a hot cloth-wrap and then a gentle squeeze; my own delight and disbelief at seeing an eruption of pus that leapt across the room, the continued ooze of it being squeezed by her always painted nails of (scratching) fingers. The feeling that my mother had helped make me pure again.

She had a good sense of humour, and a reasonable singing voice. In a good mood her smile could light up the room. We sat around our living-room in winter and contentedly read books. Our parents chatted and Mum would warm her rump up against the fire with her dress hiked up and Dad would tease her and we'd all get into the act and the bad memories would wash away.

Though our only hope was she wouldn't have even one drink, as she found it impossible to stop at one or two. It had to be all or nothing. Just like her children's lives: we had it all and we had nothing.

four

I am of two peoples, white and brown, two cultures, two races, two natures, two types of intellectual outlook. At school I am a half-caste Maori, but never a half-caste European. The official forms have boxes that break the amount of Maori blood you have into sixteenths. Every child with a quarter or more Maori blood is considered Maori, but no child with a sixteenth Maori blood is considered European. Not quite.

Ours was a typical mostly working-class New Zealand neighbourhood. There were Maori households and Pakeha households, and quite a few mixed marriages. I don't think there was much of an anti-Maori attitude, though of course some must have existed. Our neighbourhood was made up of chiefly English, Irish, Scots, and Welsh stock from several generations back, and the people had tolerance and a willingness to mix socially.

There were one or two foreigners, like Mr Otto, the German, over our back fence. We kids used to say he was a spy for the Germans, even though the war had been over for many years by that time. But Dad told us Mr Otto was in fact a very nice man and ashamed of what his erstwhile country had done.

A lot of people living in our area had higher aspirations, if not for themselves then for their children. There was almost full employment then. I seem to recall the unemployment figures numbering just a few thousand. With no television and not too many cars, children made their own fun and those adults who frequented pubs had to put up with the astonishing closing hour of 6 p.m. So people had parties and the men brought home beer in half-gallon glass jars called flagons, or they brewed their own, as did my father in the wash-house copper – we had a washing-machine unlike most who still boiled their washing in the copper. I know that everyone went to bed quite a bit earlier than they do now, perhaps by nine o'clock. Life socially was a very limited affair and so was the outlook to go with it, though some of that had a classical, timeless simplicity to it.

Two houses up from us lived the Kiels, a growing Maori family of eventually thirteen children, and close friends to each age-corresponding member of our family of seven. Two of the brothers, Kohi and Gary, I was close to. Kohi Kiel junior had all our envy by being a runner on Saturdays to the bookmaker for his father's bet on each race, earning Kohi a shilling a run. The Kiels always had visiting relatives and friends, their house a hive of social activity and mean pig dogs one of which, Rolly, had a taste for my buttocks. Kohi and Gary and I had grown up from babyhood together.

For many years throughout most of our adulthood we saw virtually nothing of each other, but that all changed the day they came to my father's funeral. It struck me how emotionally close they were to our family, how well they knew our upbringing, how they were amongst the few first-hand witnesses who would have understood our mother's effect on us with her often outrageous and quite beyond-the-pale behaviour. They'd seen us in our abject misery and fleeing terror of any one of our mother's violent rages. They had witnessed the big brawls on our front lawn, and the ugly drunken scenes at our house. They had stood on the street watching my mother make a public fool of herself and her children, watched her being driven away in a police car, struggling violently. They heard but never took part in the teasing at school of my mother's publicly known court appearances for her anti-social, violent behaviour. None of our father's efforts to stop this never-changing cycle of drunken behaviour made the slightest impression. My mother, her friends and extended family, kept right on partying. And many of their children became the victims of this mindless, hedonistic, and too often violent behaviour. Yet the Kiel kids judged us not. We were just the Duffs, mates of theirs. And they were same to us.

The Kiel boys hunted with my father, with my brothers and myself. I loved going hunting, the sleepless excitement and then the agony of being woken at 4.30 a.m. by Dad after only a few hours' sleep. The night before we'd done most of the preparation, sorting out our packs with rain-wear, spare socks, extra singlet, bars of dark chocolate, tins of sardines and corned beef, a few ounces of butter wrapped in grease-proof paper, salt and pepper shakers, all the paraphernalia of a man who planned, a man who thought things out. We'd breakfast on poached eggs, porridge for me and whoever of my brothers was coming, then make sure the rifles were all ready, having been oiled and pulled through the night before, and checked the ammunition supply was packed where it should be. Then our transport would arrive, usually Dad's close mate Des Marks, the grocer, who was often accompanied both by his wife Betty and son Noel. Des was a rugged man, typically modest and self-effacing, to the point of never mentioning any exceptional deed or act that lesser men could not wait to tell the world. He ran a very successful grocery business, which he later turned into a shopping centre, was strong as an ox, yet modest to an extreme. At my father's funeral service Des's son Noel gave a most emotional tribute to my father.

When Des arrived early in his van to go hunting, he'd have his pig-hunting dog in the back and off we'd go in the dark heading out to the Kaingaroa State Forest before the dawn broke. Dad was a stickler for paying his share of the petrol and any other expense incurred. I remember he and Des, both being honourable fellows, arguing over Des refusing Dad's money and Dad getting annoyed and insisting Des take it and Des telling him to go to hell.

Driving slowly along in Des's van, windows open, the sliding door open, everyone keen to hear the sound of the dog on to a pig, watching the vast scrubby plains before they turned to pine forest. Such excitement. Or, if Dad felt like walking, the crunch of boots on the pumicey ground along the forestry roads, over frosted, iced-over puddles if it was winter, the dog out there somewhere in the forests seeking out our quarry, the men in quiet conversation, stopping to roll a smoke, take in the scenery, ask if we were okay, offer something to eat, but always with a look that meant, 'be strong out here, this is the place for men.'

I went hunting countless times for many years and it was one of my favourite activities with Dad. Somewhere along the line I figured it wasn't me, that my interests lay elsewhere, unlike my brother Nick who was passionate and remains so to this day. The Kiel boys would spend countless occasions talking for hours with Dad in our kitchen about hunting and all sorts of other subjects, and Dad would keep them enthralled with his vast knowledge and his kind manner.

Oh they knew us all right, did the Kiels; that huge family who were money poor and love rich. With a formidable mother, Dudda, who kept her family together tighter than a jar of her preserved fruit, and a father, Kohi senior, a giant Maori of great dignity – even when drunk – who made up for what he lacked in money by taking his children hunting and fishing and going on shellfish-gathering trips to the sea and of course showering them with love. But tough love, in keeping with the big powerful man he was.

The Kiel family literally overflowed their house. Yet we heard mostly laughter coming from there. They never got ugly when they had a few drinks. Now whenever I'm in Rotorua I hardly see anyone else. It is still laughter and wit from the Kiels, now shifted to another part of Rotorua, where the family, through their grandmother on the Mitchell side, has had a long history of hosting homestay tourists from all over the world. There is a signature book that bears some famous scrawls, including George Bernard Shaw and British royalty. I call it aristocratic royalty visiting commoner royalty.

Next door was an older Pakeha couple, the Slaters, who must have heard every fight and angry utterance issued from our household just across a short stretch of pedestrian thoroughfare which we called the alleyway. Mr Slater had a wooden leg and we called him 'peg-leg' behind his back. Sometimes the cheeky kids would shout the name out within Mr Slater's hearing and he'd come clopping out angrily demanding to know the boy's name. They shared a state twin unit, which meant only a wall separated them from their neighbours, whom I don't remember. Yet they rarely said a word if we stopped to chat, and often would invite one of us for a cup of tea, or to help them pick peas and get a bowl for our house.

Right across the cul-de-sac street was the Pore family, Maori, and starkly different to my mother and her crowd. They had great dignity. Mrs Pore did not like our mother – and for very good reason – and quietly discouraged her children from forming too close friendships with us their neighbours, though we were friends regardless. Her husband was a carpenter, a fine man, quiet and dignified, whom my father respected. I think they resented Maori being seen as the violent, volatile drunks they witnessed at our house, though I later found out from them that Mr Pore had grown up witnessing the same drunken carry-on.

Up at the corner where Rimu Street cut our Matai Street in two was the Robinson family; Mr Robinson seemed odd to us. He had a moustache that was a bit like Hitler's and rumour had it that he was indeed Hitler living secretly amongst us and the ex-servicemen who had fought against his German people. The truth was he was a New Zealander, an engineer, who liked his own privacy and so built a high wooden fence around his house. Rimu Street was our domain too. There were perhaps a hundred families in all and we were one and the same with our Rimu Street neighbours. For some reason at the top end lived the town mayor. So the street was a colourful mix of families of various occupations. The Humphreys' father was a speedway car racer and the owner of a large logging truck which he kept in pristine condition. There was the MacMillan family, one of whose sons put a wasp down my back which stung me repeatedly. Yet what I remember more than the pain was the exquisite sight of Mrs MacMillan thrashing her naughty son for doing this to me. There was the railway worker and his family, he a drunk with an unsociable attitude and he'd stand in the middle of Rimu Street yelling at kids, and at the adults who were chiding him.

Down the other side of Rimu Street were the Walkers. One of the sons, Bobby, was a tough customer who boxed. There was the Hansens, who had attractive daughters that the boys went after. The Bucktons, whose father was an electrician with his own business, and their boy Bob, one of my good mates. The Spry family were tough, but good people and hard footballers. One of the Spry boys played senior representative rugby for the Bay of Plenty province for many years. Our neighbourhood produced great rugby players and athletes, and very good netballers, my sister Donnelle amongst them. Even the minority sports of soccer and cricket produced a few good players from our area, including my oldest brother Kevin who was outstanding at both. And so on it went, this rather diverse mix of people whose off-spring were destined mostly for better things.

Through the alleyway was Clinkard Avenue, where we Matai and Rimu Streets kids had a lot of friends too. My best friend Owen Bryson was one. The boy I ran away with at the age of twelve to Wellington was another. Beside them was the local bookmaker. Betting was illegal of course, but those in the know used to place their Saturday all-day bets with the Clinkard Avenue bookies. There were several families of Irish stock with wild reputations who drank and brawled and roared around drunk in their hotted up cars, just as there were tough Maori families whose fathers and extended adult family would challenge all and sundry to a fight.

Of course in the same neighbourhood we had bizarre, perverted, emotionally afflicted individuals who also helped add colour and darkness to my childhood perceptions, the inevitable crazy person, the recluses, the eccentrics. I recall a house painter who sexually abused all of his three daughters, two of them simpletons. He'd invite us kids up to his house and give us biscuits and talk dirty. The law convicted and gaoled him for a period and when he was released was allowed to return to the house and take up abusing his wretched daughters again.

Another neighbour had an endless succession of nice cars, which we used to admire in utter incomprehension that we could ever get to own such a gleaming work of metallic art on wheels. Not with Dad's indifferent attitude to owning a car. We used this neighbour's pathway as a shortcut to get to the playing field area of public land where we all played rugby or Kingasini or just mucked around. A sprinted shortcut was thought to be the prudent way of brief trespass, out to a world that was purely physical and so much fun.

But ours was also an area with a singular difference. Right in our ever-encroaching state-housing midst, atop a small hill surrounded by its own copse of exotic trees of oaks and elms, there was a two-storey mansion, replete with multi-gabled roofs and bay windows and curtains that hung like rare tapestries. The Bertram family lived there, and to us they represented class. High class. Their lives, their social inheritance, the Jaguar Mr Bertram drove, made them quite different. Two of their children went to the same primary school as us, and I recall a certain aloofness, if I didn't mistake it for shyness. I don't think they felt comfortable with working-class people, nor do I blame them. You relate to your own.

So many of the settings and characters of my novels are from my childhood. It was not difficult when writing *Once Were Warriors* to recall myself in spying witness on that Bertram family, the Tramberts in the novel, and like the character Grace Heke I have at times throughout my life considered suicide. A little part inside me knows the feeling of that grey blanket coming down and turning to the blackest black that engulfs reason. You just have to be stronger, if that's the way your mind and emotions get inclined at times.

In later years we were invited to join the Bertrams by their kindly Gran who lived with them for tea and home-made biscuits or even cake of the most exotic design and exquisite taste. They had fine china and manners and grace to go with it. I remember picking up on the strained smiles and the forced good manners and it hurt. But I don't know what either side could have done about it, for we were just letting our awkwardness show. I think the Duff children may have got more invites because our father was educated and had a good job. The references to my mother were a different tone altogether, but couched in polite terms, as if they were trying to exonerate us, 'that woman's' children, from her distasteful behaviour.

But to me the Bertrams meant more than high class. They personified good breeding, civilised behaviour, peace and love and family unity – the opposite to that of my own home, my mother and her volatile sisters, and the rough company they kept. But not my father, whom one of Mum's brothers, Uncle Jonny, once described as 'a lone rose in a blackberry bush.' That big two-storey rambling Bertram mansion with its many eaves and rooftops surrounded by an English-like forest of oaks stood supreme. I would spend hours concealed in the trees, listening to the piano playing somewhere inside.

There was an old macrocarpa tree at the back of our property that was one of our favourite playing areas. I loved climbing to the top to look down over the world and get a good view of Rotorua, along with neighbours and some of their more private goings-on. Dad had built a platform tree-hut and nailed a few handholds to the trunk. It was a good place to go when Mum was in a foul mood or the adults were fighting during the day. It was where I could be in private and let my imagination roam. One day in the higher Standards I got the idea that I'd do my bit for the election and the political party Dad voted for, and I went to the top of our macrocarpa tree and shouted for a good hour to the neighbourhood that they should vote for National, only to come down and be told by my eldest brother that Dad always voted Labour!

Each of us children had our own patch of garden, with Nick being the most efficient of us. I remember envying his immaculately tended area sprouting radishes and carrots and the green leafy promise of potatoes, far better than my spring onions and lettuce. We also had a nectarine tree right outside the kitchen window, a prolific producer; and a fowl-house with laying hens. We knew the delight of seeing chickens hatched from eggs incubated in the warmth of our oven, or just running, newly born, around the fowl-house, little movements of yellow fluffiness and energy.

I remember my first day at school, somewhere after my fifth birthday on 26 October 1955. It was raining and my father delayed going to work so he could take me there on his bike. I was wearing a yellow plastic raincoat and a floppy plastic matching hat. I don't remember my mother being part of my first day, but she may have been. I recall sitting on a very coarse mat in class that made my legs itch, and feeling scared and excited.

I was a few months behind Kohi Kiel and we were in the same class right through to intermediate. Gary Kiel was a year behind us, though after school we all played together with our other neighbourhood friends. So it wasn't a lonely or a miserable experience. It was home that was hell.

I did well at school. In those days they had grade markings, from first place to thirty-first, depending on how many were in your class. My two older brothers, Kevin and Nick, also did well, and being first in class was a standard event in our household. By Standard Two I had established myself as a top student, though I was always pushed by

Louise Armstrong, who I understand became a doctor, and Anthony Brown, whose fate I know nothing of. I don't remember showing an exceptional talent at writing, but I was a good speller and had a vivid imagination, and I wasn't afraid to venture out into the wide world of real adventure and experience. Hardly anywhere was out of bounds for me.

I was first in every subject except art. Art I just never got, even though Dad had been exceptional at drawing and my brother Nick won a national school prize first equal with, astonishingly, our father's sister's daughter, our first cousin Mary who lived in Auckland and had a different surname, so no link was known. The artistic streak came from Dad's mother Jesse.

In Standard Four we had an art exam, a home project. I worked hard on my masterpiece but when I checked with my classmate Kohi as to how he was going, I found his older sister, Wanda, pencil in hand with Kohi's work before her, and the supposed artist on the other side of the work. We took our works of art to school for judging. The teacher would let us know the results the following day. When she read out the top three places the next day, it turned out I came second, which was fine by me as I didn't consider myself all that good. But certainly a lot better than my mate Kohi. Then I heard the unbelievable. 'Kohi Kiel, congratulations. I have judged your work first.' Kohi first – *in art*! I think he laughed at me every day for about a month, and his sister gave me ferocious looks, warning that I had better not be asking *her* any questions.

In Standard Four I also asked to be exempted from any form of Christian worship or study, as I did not believe in God. I had my father's written support, and without him my case would have been lost from the start. But the outraged headmaster told me he'd 'fix' me for this, after first trying to break my will with his adult own. I remember his face being thunderstruck at the thought that a mere nine-year-old should have the right to make up his mind on whether he believed in God or not. Well, I didn't believe in God, and it was with an equally passionate vehemence. My teacher packed a lengthy sad and all the other teaching staff would give me funny stares when they walked past. So, every morning whilst the other kids were in assembly, I was put on weeding duty in the school gardens and held over at that task until everyone had filed out of the assembly hall and were off to their classes. Only then was I given permission to go to my class. Naturally kids looked at me sideways for being so outrageously different to them, though none dared laugh because of my violent temper. I don't recall lasting much more than two weeks of being different. My class teacher informed me when I surrendered my puerile principle, almost spitting out her words, 'We have God on our side.'

Although my two brothers were at the same school, we didn't necessarily have much to do with each other. We were rapidly developing a 'system' in our family of the next oldest one up not talking to you unless absolutely necessary. So Kevin would talk to me but not Nick. I would not talk to Donnelle, but to Neil the next one down. This happened at our meal table, around the house, out in the streets, up playing in Bertram's forest, and at school. So I only saw Nick from a distance for most of my early years, and I did my share of ignoring the existence of the one down from me, sister Donnelle. Our sibling fights were full-on fisticuffs and when Mum's violent pattern of behaviour started to become something we had to accept, we got harder with each other, scorning, deriding whoever broke up into tears or, even worse, screaming.

At school I established myself as the fastest sprinter in my age group and I never lost that to anyone all through my school years except when I competed at provincial level, where I was usually in the placings. I was a pretty good rugby player too, in the school first fifteens at primary and intermediate, but my tackling could have been better. I played centre and wing, although I locked for my intermediate school first fifteen for a couple of games and rather enjoyed fantasising that I was a future Colin Meads in the making.

I also discovered fighting because I was quite good at it. I went to wrestling with my best mate of several years, Owen Bryson, from about Standard Two, under the coaching of a Rimu Street resident, Lofty Houghton. Lofty was good to us, he and his kind-hearted wife were always having their 'wrestling boys' around to their house for cups of tea, cakes and biscuits, and long chats. They seemed to take a particular interest in me and I remember the embarrassment of Mrs

Houghton struggling to say kind things about my mother even though we all knew what she was like.

Lofty coached us on how to take pain and then how to do something about who was inflicting it, in a considered way. He taught us the holds, and how to fall. I loved it. I felt this immediate understanding of the flow of one human body matched against another. I could sense which way an opponent was going to move and my sprinter's muscles gave me superior speed. When I was up against someone stronger, which was invariably Owen Bryson, I used a bridge position that few could break. I could prevent my opponent from winning the match as they would be unable to force my shoulders to the mat. I made a lot of draws – too many – this way.

I'll never forget the first time Lofty let us have a tag-team wrestling bout. I felt in my element. My fantasies had come true, of being like my professional wrestling heroes, Haystacks Calhoun and Gorgeous George, and being in the same room with Lofty Houghton, who was also on the New Zealand professional circuit.

Not that I was the toughest kid on the block – not when you lived two houses from the Kiel family, or had Bobby Walker the champion boxer just around the corner, or the crazy Fitzgerald clan through the alleyway on Clinkard Avenue, not to mention the Rimu Street toughs, the Spry brothers and my mate Bob Buckton. But I was no retiring weed by any stretch of the imagination. And if I was pushed far enough, I would defend myself against any boy my own age. It seemed the lower my self-esteem got, the more I took from getting into fights and winning them.

And yet throughout the whole neighbourhood there were many kind, good people. The wives all helped each other out, as these were not prosperous times. So it was common for someone to drop off a gift of jars of preserved nectarines or jam or pickled vegetables. The Kiels gave out buckets of mussels and pipi and cockles, and the many hunters in the neighbourhood gifted cuts of wild game to their neighbours. Neighbours would turn up with a freshly picked cauliflower, a cabbage, new potatoes, or some shellfish if someone had been out gathering them at Maketu beach forty miles away, or it might be a leg of venison, some wild pork, a smoked trout, a basket of steaming hot scones. That was the way it was in the fifties. Simple, almost naïve.

I believe growing up surrounded by this kind of salt-of-the-earth people of both races made an everlasting impression on me. I learned to respect men for what they were, not who they were or how much money they had. Their qualities of manhood were not so much with fisticuffs but in their basic decent outlook, and the character that the beloved game of rugby bestowed on each and every one of them – playing for the team first and foremost, doing your part to contribute to that team effort, having to find within your individual self the mental and physical efforts the game required each and every winter Saturday. Though naturally there were times when men sorted out their differences with their fists. But a fight was an honourable matter and doing it dirty was an unforgivable crime. You fought when your line had been crossed, or your honour offended. Men back then were of more simplicity and greater dignity. When it wasn't rugby adding character and durability to a man, it was hunting and fishing and diving too that gave them an unpretentious, honest outlook on life.

Certainly in my growing up I knew a hardy, rugged type of man who was tough and uncomplaining, a kind of self-contained man of few words but plenty of action. He shared social activities as equals and mates with Maori or Pakeha. He worked hard, played his rugby hard, and he drank pretty hard too. But I have few bad memories of our neighbourhood where booze turned men ugly. Many of these men were bushmen, tree-fellers who worked all day with heavy chainsaws and on weekends returned to hunt for pig and deer. Or they were tradesmen who did an honest day's work or they had small businesses, operating as panelbeaters, builders, painters, engineers, truck owners, or running a mechanic's garage. We grew up with the sons and daughters of these families and if we weren't close mates, we had a mutual respect.

I had adult friends all over the place with whom I used to confide or just chat with. Mostly they were women. I think I had a desperate need to find decent female company, most of all a mother figure, a female symbol that would be an ideal and not betray me. One was a cripple, Elva Fares, who lived at the end of our alleyway on Clinkard Avenue. She was a cerebral palsy victim and shook so violently she had to force her hands under her rump. She was a friend to all of us Duff kids and lived within earshot of the worst fighting noises issuing from our house. She had a will of iron and a heart of gold. There she was, in her condition, and yet she could cry her eyes out for any one of us Duffs and what she knew we were going through.

Elva had the strongest views on motherhood, which is why she would get so upset at our mother. She'd been told she could not have children, and so she married and had a son she named Des. When we knew Elva, she had a boarder, an American who drove stock cars and who pushed her everywhere round Rotorua in her wheelchair. Her conversations with me were frank and always tried to come to some positive conclusion. She'd say, 'Well all right, so your mother is how she is – but that isn't you is it? You haven't got a dress for starters. And I don't see any breasts developing!' She'd cackle as she joked.

I can still see her, in that rather dark state-house kitchen of hers, a kettle on the permanent simmer on the woodfire stove, that bent, misshapen body in a wheelchair, with her head at an angle, and one hand pushed under her rump and the other shaking as she smiled good morning or good day to me. Though sometimes I'd catch her in a pensive, even miserable mood, where she'd be seated at her kitchen window staring out at the able-bodied world and she would ask of God, 'Why would you do this to a person?' The self-pity never lasted long and usually it was something else making her morose, something she'd heard said about her beloved son and her frustration at not being able to get out of her wheelchair and go and sort out this or that bad-mouthing person. Not that son Des needed any help, for he was all sinewy muscle, and did lots of running and worked hard as an apprentice carpenter.

My mate Owen Bryson's mother was another Clinkard Avenue woman confidante. I spent a lot of time in my primary school years around at the Brysons', and knew all their family well. Mrs Bryson was always there with a sympathetic and patient ear. Mr Bryson was a feisty Scot who spoke with a heavy accent even though he'd been in New Zealand for decades. I made a terrible mistake with him when one day he caught me laughing at Owen's older sister's poor spelling. Mr Bryson abused hell out of me and told me never to laugh at one of his children again and I slunk out of that house feeling thoroughly chastened and vowing I'd never laugh at anyone like that again. It was a good lesson.

My Aunty Margaret, or 'Bunna' as she was better known, was another on my list of woman confidantes. She was so sweet and loving, and yet so tragic. She was a most understanding woman, but when she had drink in her was abusive and highly critical of us Duff kids for 'having brains'. As she grew older though she became our favourite aunty, the one who always had an understanding ear and was always ready to feed you. Probably the lifetime rivalry she had with Mum had engendered a sense of inadequacy in comparing the respective sisters' children. But we Duff kids were close, and remain close, to our half-Fijian first cousins. Two of our Sasson girl cousins were killed in the same car crash as my brother in 1972.

There were also a few women out at Whaka that I could spend long periods talking with. And a couple in my neighbourhood in Rimu Street. I never discussed Mum's behaviour with my brothers or sisters. But the whole neighbourhood talked about her and the effects on us children, and so would half the town sometimes if she ended up in the newspaper court pages. So I was grateful to all those sympathetic adult ears. It may be why I regard myself as being a good, understanding listener now: because others showed me by example. All in all not a bad place to grow up in, were it not for the situation at home.

By Standard Three our parents' marriage was in a hopeless state. Something beyond my mother's normal, inexplicable anger was driving her to worse depths of drunken depravity, of assaults, not just on Dad, but nearly any adult who dared upset her. Her violence against us children had never been terrible, just the occasional thrashing. Nearly every kid you knew also got them, so it wasn't as bad as it seems. It was the other violence that destroyed our souls, seeing our mother in such a state of undignified fury, or just plain staggeringly blind drunk. I should have been happy – I was doing well at school, enjoying my athletics and rugby and wrestling. But I was thoroughly and deeply miserable. I had moments of wanting to die.

five

We used to go to Christchurch by aeroplane once or twice a year to spend school holidays with our grandfather and step-grandmother, who seemed a little more exotic to us because she had a Maori name, Ngaere, but was European and from Rangiora. We all loved going there and of course the plane trip made it even more exciting, leaving from Rotorua Aerodrome and getting to see our town and half the country from the air. This is where some of Dad's money went, ensuring his children had direct contact with his family. It made us children stand out not just amongst our Maori relations but in the neighbourhood as well, the fact that we flew regularly to the South Island.

Grandad and Ngaere had a farmlet out at Landsdowne Valley in Halswell, a good half-hour drive out of Christchurch. They were always there to meet us, this smiling couple with an age difference of twenty-seven years between them, Grandad the older. We'd stop to buy an ice-cream in town at a shop owned by Grandad's friend, Ernest Adams. Ernest had been a supporter of Grandad's when he resigned from the *Christchurch Press*, helping set him up in a rural newspaper, the *Rangiora Sun*. The best cakes and biscuits were made in this bakery. Its proprietor had a literary side. He and Oliver would converse for quite a time whilst I, or we if one of my brothers was with me, would happily eat our ice-creams.

Out to 'Spylaw', the farmlet of about thirty acres that Grandad and Ngaere had retired to. Sun-baked hills, the sweet scent of pine needles and macrocarpa hedge and flowers, fruit trees with fattening apricots, plums, apples, a lovely little cottage partly hidden by trees and shrubs, and wafting from it Ngaere's home baking – absolute bliss. A sheepdog, Scamp, who knew us, a milking cow, Betty, who seemed to remember us, and the sun-baked Port Hills where we'd go shooting rabbits in the evenings with Grandad.

The vegetable garden had a large area of peas. My favourite memory is sitting on the back 'stoop' as Grandad called it, shelling peas into a bowl, three for the pot, one for the sheller, and Grandad chatting to us all the while. I cannot remember anything of what he said, only that it felt highly pleasant being with my Grandad.

We'd be up at the crack of dawn to walk down to the cowshed to help milk the cow. I had an uneasy feeling watching such a large weight of mobile beast being manoeuvred into its milking bay, seeing those strong hands of Grandad's manipulating forth squirts of pure white milk from udders, and hearing the sound of it against the metal milk can. Try as I might, I could never master the skill of getting those damned udders to render me milk!

The full pail had its own quality now, set in the water-tower storage-room, covered by a fine-mesh gauze to keep the flies out while the cream slowly rose to the top. The result was cream poured on our porridge and desserts, or whipped on Ngaere's hot scones. I never got used to the idea of drinking the same milk from a glass, not after I'd seen it coming out warm and smelling quite pungent. There was an abundance of home-made raspberry jam to spread over home-made oatmeal biscuits and dark home-made slices of toasted bread, and roasted coffee beans ground in the wall-mounted porcelain grinder with its blue European landscape painted against a white background. How very different to the Maori side of our existence, to our own home which had only fragments of this whole picture as it might have been; our home was like a rural painting that was broken, disfigured by something, someone.

The people who visited 'Spylaw' were civilised and kind; they were educated and conversational. They took an interest in anything we visiting Rotorua grandchildren might be doing and showered us with most unfamiliar praise. No-one swore and screamed drunken obscenities, no-one drank themselves into a mindless condition. The idea of these people brawling was unthinkable.

We had hills to walk and explore, small valleys, the odd cave or two, and every evening before dusk would go rabbit-shooting with Grandad, on the understanding we were not to show Ngaere the shot carcasses, as she loved animals and had a very sensitive nature. We were accompanied by Grandad's dog, who tended a very tiny flock of never more than thirty stock. Many of them had become pets which our grandfather wrote frequently about in his fortnightly *Listener* column under the pseudonym 'Sundowner'. We were under strict orders to stay behind Grandad if he was taking a shot at a rabbit. Grandad taking aim, squeezing the trigger, the shot ringing out over the hills, catching an echo if we were near a gully, running to retrieve the rabbit, but no chance with Scamp around.

Later, watching Grandad skin the rabbit, the warmth still in the limp body and the pelt peeling off, felt nothing less than an exciting outrage against the dead creature's existence, as if killing it wasn't enough. We had to do this to it, roll its furry hide off like a glove to reveal a glistening, perfect body. I hated the rabbit stew Ngaere turned our hunt kill into and only nibbled miserably at the vegetables in it. I had the same trouble eating the fowls I had witnessed Dad axing the heads off. And despite my years of hunting, I haven't acquired a taste for wild game either.

I was only four when I first visited 'Spylaw' so I didn't get a chance to test my shooting skills with the .22 rifle until a few years later. I have a photograph of myself at about this age holding a handful of straw, with my grandfather behind me, looking over the boy just started school. I have a memory of this aching with wanting to tell Grandad something… about our home and what was going on in it. Somehow I doubt that I would have wanted to cry so young on someone's shoulders, so perhaps it was later.

But if four or five was the age, then I don't know why I didn't just blurt out these troubles, these confusions, this sense that something awful was happening at home that wasn't anywhere else. Perhaps I instinctively sensed that telling Grandad would achieve nothing, as he lived so far away, six hundred miles. It might have upset him that he couldn't do anything, for he was always a man trying to find a solution, a logical, rational path out of any situation that was troublesome. Each time I went to 'Spylaw' for the school holidays I remember saying to myself that this would be the time I would tell him what was happening at home. I never did.

My grandfather was a good man, a kindly man, who gave you an attentive ear and sometimes a very indulgent one. I once told him he didn't look so good with his moustache and he disappeared for several minutes and came back with this solicitous grin and asked what I thought of my grandfather clean-shaven! This was a man whose photographic image was famously known wearing a moustache.

Even at a young age I understood only too well that he was highly regarded by everyone and indeed that he was famous. Perhaps I feared that telling him of the incidents at home would somehow spoil his own seemingly idyllic life, of order and civilised, moderate behaviour; of stimulating, unheated conversation, wit and laughter and classical music and bookshelves that went from floor to ceiling, where reading was a nightly activity. Just the sight of Grandad sitting in his armchair with his reading glasses on told a child that this image truly meant something good and noble and most of all important. For the face that those written words awakened was one of a man caught often in the sweet, glowing light of knowledge, just as my father could look in times when Mum seemed at peace or, better still, was absent.

To put the words that were in my head into this perfectly ordered household was doubtless what held my tongue in check. To this day I have a fear I cannot overcome, of walking into someone else's home without feeling I am disturbing their peace, their serenity, and I even feel decidedly unwelcome, as if surely they would not welcome some-one like me. I feel this even with friends, which of course has them puzzled and perhaps a little insulted that I cannot take the friendship beyond this childhood fear. I can with a few people, and know from these friendships what I am missing out on in the extended sense.

Grandad had a small office that yet seemed to house half the intellectual world. It was full of books and papers and framed photographs of family, of himself pictured with some famous international identity. And even the foyer area between sitting-room and kitchen and Grandad's office was full of paintings and a piece of sculpture depicting entwined cats, done by Alison, my father's sister. All these things seemed to be saying that the goings-on at 29 Matai Street had no place to be mentioned here.

It was another world at 'Spylaw' and I only remember wanting it never to come to an end. I came home once to my father greeting us at Rotorua Aerodrome with his face covered in scratches, and he had an air of distracted quiet. That explained the telephone conversation I'd overheard between Grandad and, I was sure, my father. For Grandad had spoken in a firm, almost shouting tone, and told my father to 'do something about it.' I think he added, 'For God's sake.'

Our Uncle Roger, the famous Canterbury Museum director and anthropologist, was a regular visitor who sometimes took us on outings or had his younger adult sons come and take us for a drive in the country. He was Dr Roger Duff, the doctorate being not just an ordinary doctorate degree, as he himself was proud to inform us, but a Doctorate of Science for accumulative contribution to science, and only rarely awarded. I remember my father had a copy of *Who's Who* which contained entries for both his brother and his father. My mother when drunk once grabbed this *Who's Who* and opened it on the page with the Duff entries, and she demanded to know where Dad's entry was. And then she laughed in a most hysterical manner because Dad's name wasn't there. I remember it because I saw for a brief moment Dad's hurt, as if Mum had touched a raw nerve. Not that he was ever jealous of anyone, including his family members. I think he just knew that he would never achieve that much prominence and yet many years later I found out he was regarded as world-class in his own, modest, unheralded occupational field. Mum would see this *Who's Who* entry as somehow excluding her from what she perceived as Dad's higher social rung. Yet paradoxically this same person proudly showed off those two Duff entries to her friends and relations.

Across a stretch of paddock from the cottage about the length of a football field was Grandad's sister, Anne, married to Will Sinclair who was also a cousin to the Duffs. They were typical older people of their time: kind-hearted, simple and decent of outlook, and happy. Although now I know more of them and of course of life, I realise it wasn't so much happiness as a joy of living. There was a certain stoicism behind those civilised façades which concealed a suffering from the normal ailments of life, depression, diseases, marriage problems, and most certainly sexual problems. But still, they were never torn asunder either as individuals or as an extended family unit.

Most nights Grandad and Ngaere would pop over to Will and Anne's to have some home-brewed beer, and Ngaere a gin. The routine of going over of an evening gave me a feeling of warmth and security, latching each gate after us. We'd pass through Betty the milking cow's territory and Grandad would never tire of his game of warning me to be ready 'to take to your scrapers' if Betty indicated a foul mood, and I never stopped believing him. I felt I belonged here and only here, and it seemed so unfair that it would end and I'd be back in the other world.

I don't know what Uncle Will did previously. I think he farmed. He was a most practical man who could put his hand to anything. But he would get very frustrated with Oliver for thinking he could do practical things, for they were always breaking down or not working even after his efforts to fix them.

All this generation had an unhurried way of speaking, thoughtful and full of common-sense without for a moment being pretentious or self-important. They were kind and patient with children, and loved explaining all sorts of things to us, from how tension is achieved with a farm fence, to the intricate workings of wool. I remember a particular flower in Uncle Will's and Aunt Anne's garden that flowered only once a year anytime from 10 p.m. to midnight, and which we were allowed to stay up and witness at least twice, as I recall. For me it was nothing short of a miracle that a plant could somehow have a memory, and that it should unfold like this in secret late at night was even more astonishing.

They used gelignite to split pine trees for firewood. I see a fly-blown ewe's behind oozing maggots. Lambs with their eyes picked out by magpies; and me the child shooing angrily at every magpie and yet being afraid they might peck my eyes out. I'd stand on the other side of the fence observing Betty the cow for long periods. Watching her breathing like hide-covered fire bellows, listen to the steady munching of her chewing the cud, marvelling at the sound of that phrase. I enjoyed my own company, though of course had periods of being utterly bored if I was at 'Spylaw' without one of my brothers. And if one was there, we fought like hell, especially if it was Nick.

I recall the sounds of this haven, of bees, birds, the quiet phut-phut-phut of the water pump down by the mailbox, the gentle panting of Scamp, a radio playing some classical piece, perhaps a Sunday hymn, adults exchanging laughter, or just discernible intellectual tones of some weighty subject being discussed, perhaps argued over. So much peace here.

I was about eight or nine when one day at an afternoon extended family gathering of Duffs and Sinclairs, I looked at these people, my blood relatives, bearers of my surname, my father's father, his sister, my father's uncle and aunt, his first cousin Helen, his brother Roger, various first and second cousins, and I suddenly felt I was not one of them and never could be. It was because of what was happening at home, which had by then escalated into violence beyond anything imaginable. I looked at these people and I saw myself a stranger; I who had been amongst them regularly for over five years, who had sat on Uncle Will's knee, on many a knee and been told a story or just kind words, and now I was not one of them. Inside I started getting in a panic, feeling flushed, as if out of the blue I was exposed, my mother-tainted condition, my unworthiness to be here amongst these good, decent people.

My cousins seemed to be suddenly distant. Some were my age or close. I'd spent many long hours doing things around the farm with them. We'd caught eels up in the creek past Jim Minson's farm, worked at picking raspberries down the road at the raspberry farm (I was hopeless), and talked for endless hours on all sorts of things that interested us intellectually. Everyone was in their usual happy state of exchange, so much of it with a certain sensitivity which was a quality of the Duffs and the Sinclairs, so it made the feeling worse that I had stopped belonging. And I could not have given the reason even if asked as to why. It just seemed to me that my destiny was going to be significantly different – and certainly of worse outcome – than theirs.

six

I moved between the European world and the Maori with ease and hardly gave it a second thought. I spent a lot of time at Whaka, where my mother's brother, Uncle Tupu, Aunty Baby and our five Raimona cousins lived, along with many other relations.

Whaka, pronounced 'woka' and short for Whakarewarewa, was Rotorua's main tourist destination, and a wonderful playground for children to grow up in. What sights were there for any child, not least one with imagination – swimming lakes, azure blue, greeny yellow, shallow and clear, and ground textures you could inscribe in a geographical book; and the Pohutu Geyser, seeing it in action, hearing the rumble from deep within the earth, and then watching the spitting of boiling water signalling the roar as it finally erupted, white silica rock splashed with sulphur yellow, small volcanic cones, hissing fissures, like an extraterrestrial surface, boiling pools of grey mud sending up bubbles like eyes of unworldly creatures. Deep pools of boiling water, searing depths that you dared to edge closer to, stare into, and feel afraid of yourself falling or being pushed into. Differing landscapes, shallow saucer lakes in constant steam veils, gaping fenced-off holes of angrily boiling water leaping several feet and invading the ground around it, enlargening the hole as if threatening to engulf all of Whaka. Oh, it was some sight for the imagination to be sure.

They say the founding European inhabitants of Rotorua were intrepid people, for they were prepared to endure the long, arduous journey over the Mamaku Ranges through near impenetrable bush, along a track cut early last century to this magical thermal area of erupting geysers and boiling pools, glistening lakes and rolling hills. This was where in the mid- and late nineteenth century travellers from overseas journeyed to see 'the eighth wonder of the world', the Pink and White Terraces about twenty-five miles south of Rotorua, and buried forever in the eruption of Mount Tarawera in June 1886. Several stories I have read about this event stick in my mind. There was the Englishman who, knowing he was going to die, wrote a farewell letter to his family in England. There was the postmaster from the nearby village of Te Wairoa who sent an urgent Morse code message to the outside world about the eruption, likening it to Pompeii. There was also the phantom canoe of old Maori warriors sighted not only by a local Maori woman who acted as a guide to the Terraces, but also by her boatload of foreign tourists. The eruption itself was foretold by a tohunga, a Maori priest, who survived the eruption. He was dug up by rescuers several days afterwards, only to die later in Rotorua hospital after they broke his heart by cutting off his hair for hygiene reasons – to do such a thing to a traditional Maori was an unspeakable outrage. After the eruption the main tribe of Rotorua, Ngati Whakaue, gifted the land at Whakarewarewa to the survivors of the village of Te Wairoa, and a sub-tribe in the Thames area in the Coromandel also welcomed visitors.

This thermal landscape had a river, Puarenga Stream, from which we earned money by retrieving coins thrown in for us by the tourists. We could make bigger money by jumping or diving off the twenty-foot high bridge for a shilling a jump, two shillings a dive. The more spectacular divers like Clive Hemopo and 'Gullagulla' Eparaima did graceful swan-dives or toe-touches or even a somersault, and could get an extra bob or two after the dive when an admiring tourist would call them back up to receive a bonus.

Our father's bike route to work took him by choice over the bridge crossing Puarenga Stream which divided the village from the rest of the Whaka area where state housing was springing up. Priority was given to housing the returned servicemen and their growing families. The airforce barracks of the Forestry Research Institute were sited about a mile from the bridge. Dad had taken us on his bike many times along this interesting route of unseen bubbling mud pools and pools of boiling water constantly issuing steam, patches of manuka bush and then the planted exotic varieties of the Institute's experimenting. Sometimes in the school holidays we might be in the river when Dad was coming home from work. He didn't approve of the penny diving. He called it a form of begging, which I suppose it was, strictly speaking. But I never felt like a beggar when I launched myself after a coin and followed it, flitting in different ways according to what type of coin it was, down to the sandy bottom; then surfacing in triumph and holding the coin aloft to the benefactor who would always smile and often exclaim in compliment, and then into the mouth the coin would go, to join the others of that day. We had to compete for every thrown coin and some of the kids were not slow in coming forward.

We had a large pool called the Round Bath to go and get warm in; like all the baths, heat was added by removing the rag stoppers from the concrete channels that ran from an elevated boiling shallow lake. We also had the Top Baths, a series of six concrete vessels, open to the sky, which were set down the bank with the river gurgling by tumbling over rocks, and on the other side a high bank thirty feet or more sprouting tenacious manuka. And then we had the Down Bath, a few hundred yards the other way, which was a huge pool, usually a grey muddy colour, thirty feet wide and a hundred the other way, surround- ed by tall manuka. There was a rock area where we gathered around that ran alongside the road. From our large pool ran a concrete storm- water pipe about eighteen inches in diameter under the road. It came out the other side, dropping into yet another bathing area called the Hirere, meaning waterfall. This was the most magical pool of them all, with ferns finding a hold on the steep banks, an enclosure of rock in a reducing half moon, the hot water cascading down from the highest point, and where it channelled out, a view of sulphur-yellow patches on green growth and grey rock and steaming fissures.

Picture it – a bunch of Whaka Maori kids, boys and girls, in our array of swimming outfits, rarely the conventional togs, shorts, shirts for the girls, teeshirts, sitting in our warm pools with mouths stuffed full of coins which we spat out into our hands and counted carefully, knowing the exact value of a penny and a shilling. Brown bodies, with mine and a couple of other half-castes the paler ones, sunk down in the thermal warmth as we sent runners to buy us food and sweets. We spent our money on sweets, ice-creams, pies, and, best of all, half a loaf of barracuda bread with a tin of cream-style sweet corn to eat with it. The poorer coin divers offered their services as runners to the local grocery store which opened our corn cans. We knew every style of lolly in the place – aeroplanes, spearmints, hard jubes, pineapple chunks, winegums, red and blacks, smokers, the list was endless. And we ate mince pie with ice-cream, a bite of pie, a lick of cold ice-cream!

We watched the tourists, and there was a huge range of them, and we saw how they interacted – their relationships, the incidents of love and niggles and occasional arguments. We heard magical tales from friendly Americans of how wonderful their country was, and realised how patriotic they were. We saw different styles of dress, heard different languages and accents, and understood the bearings of different ethnic groups. Most of these people were extremely interested in our steaming surroundings, in us, in what they perceived as the Maori race.

The Whaka locals dwelled here as inhabitants, roamed as guides, and were themselves of great colour and personality. Guide Rangi was our world-famous personality. Our women had a distinct air of self-confidence so lacking in many other Maori women. I remember the old women, kuia, shuffling out of the steam in the early mornings when we were having a bath before school or at dusk; these slow-moving figures were like apparitions stepping out of our very past. The kuia spoke almost exclusively in Maori, whereas every other adult conversed more in English and did not teach many of their offspring the Maori language, although they could speak it themselves.

The guides were beautifully articulate in explaining their fascinating landscape. Old men and women, with their sad old eyes and tattooed chin and lips, spoke eloquently in their own language, gazing at their beloved landscape, speaking of the times that had been left behind. There was guide Rangi, hostess to the visiting powerful and rich, and later guide Bubbles and guide Emily, and singers galore with superb voices, both men and women, and all the children growing up imitating them. There were women who did traditional crafts, weaving flax kits, making traditional puipui skirts for the males in the concert parties or for tourists to purchase. They made poi, which the women used with extraordinary dexterity tied to a length of slender rope, making a rhythmic slapping sound as they twirled them this way and that. Culture was strong in Whaka, especially in the form of the concert parties that used to tour all over the world with their poi dances and action songs and haka and waiata.

Music is the forte of the people of Whaka. When our Whaka uncles and relations were youngsters at what was then called the Whakarewarewa Native School, an enlightened European headmaster decided he would train these raw voices in operatic harmony. In their older years these men would still go to him to practise their harmonies. Powerful female singing voices also enter my early childhood memory. I see big women standing proud as they sing. I see the same women leading the hymns in the meeting-houses at tangi. I hear them at parties. They symbolise feminine strength and dignity. I remember, too, the old-style Maori chanting, the waiata, a kind of monotonal warbling in which I could hear the slight inflexions of lifting and falling notes, of words in a language that flowed. I hear old women and a few old men chanting these hauntingly beautiful waiata, ancient voices in the Whakarewarewa thermal steam. My father would explain the musical structure of these ancient chants to me, the inflexions, the flawless stream of words recalling deeds and tales of ancestors, and family lineage. He told us what he knew of their history with an admiration for a people he said were truly exceptional.

Dotted all over this uneven, steaming landscape were houses, some of them falling down having succumbed to the steam, the constant damp, the sulphur. They perched on hillsides, atop hill rises. Many had traditional carved gables, and some had old-style verandahs where older women sat weaving or smoking a pipe, or just watching the world of tourists and locals go by – people so different to each other and yet the same human species enjoying the same wondrous landscape of hiss and roar and bubble.

I have confused memories of a meeting-house just beside the store, but it burnt down at a date I have no idea of. The old communal dining-room, called a wharekai, was on the thermal reserve side of the bridge right near our bathing pools, but I think that either burnt down or fell into disrepair from the thermal activity attacking its structure and indeed its very under-earth foundations. I have a memory of this dining-room in the late fifties, of the happy chaos of women preparing food, of strong men cutting up pig and sheep carcasses, potatoes being peeled and washed in large concrete sinks, the adults chattering in a mix of Maori and English. A woman would be singing, maybe my Aunty Baby, and others would join her and soon the place is ringing with song as harmonies are taken up. I feel the concrete ground hot beneath my feet. My imagination fears the thermal activity will break through. I once got sent to cook a large bag of watercress in the main cooking pool, a sight from Dante's Hell of bottomless boiling water plunging down white silica sides to a deeper and deeper blue until it turned black. And I remembered the tale of the old blind woman, a local, who walked into this pool, and they had to fish out her cooked flesh with a fishing-net.

There is a magnificent meeting-house in Whaka at the far end of the road coming over the bridge, which was erected in 1940; it has intricate carvings and woven flax-work wall panels, every carved wooden figure representing an ancestor, part of the history. Then there were the tangi, the unique Maori way of grieving for the dead, with several days of tribute, oratory, songs, underlaid by a near constant formalised wailing of women, one taking over from another, a kind of melancholy yet reassuring sobbing. The elders would frequently break out in a haka, and sing ancient waiata in that half-tone chanting style from another age passed down. This meeting-house is where my brother Kevin and two first cousins were farewelled and of course where the tangi of all my Whaka relatives were held.

●

Maori were in a state of flux in my growing years, and probably in a state of confusion and cultural disorientation too. Most Maori lived in rural areas or in the smaller towns. Thus a funeral would often be in a rural area where the living standards were pretty basic. I remember homes that had newspaper as wallpaper, and a few had dirt floors. There are muddy tracks and slippery dirt paths leading to dimly-lit houses. I smell the pungent odour of boiled cabbage, with boiled meat in the same pot; fatty brisket, pork backbone (still my favourite dish) pig trotters, mutton flaps, sheep hearts, any one of these cheaper cuts and as often as not with puha, a wild weed used as a vegetable, or watercress, boiled soft, absorbed of the fat. When the air wasn't strong with boiled food, it was heavy with frying. The smell of fat is embedded in my brain.

A place we visited quite regularly was my Aunty Mary's. It was where my half-sister Maxine lived and she seemed so much more exotic than us, her real siblings. Tall, lean and good-looking, Maxine was more like a foreign cousin. Often she wasn't at home when we were there – she might be staying with other relations or with friends, as she was a teenager when I was becoming aware of her existence. She seemed to want to keep an aloofly smiling distance from us. To Maxine her 'brother' was 'Jimmyboy'. In fact he was her first cousin, but they were closer than most siblings. And she wouldn't have traded her adoptive parents for anyone.

We'd often be invited to spend a weekend at Aunty Mary's and Uncle Jim's – usually myself and one or two of my Whaka first cousins. As a place to roam, Ngapuna on the eastern outskirts of Rotorua where our uncle and aunty lived was ideal; the neighbouring farmland was our playground, with 'Boot Hill' looking down on us, and up there a Maori graveyard which overlooked Lake Rotorua. You had to go through a paddock of bulls to get there, but their scare value was more talk than likelihood. From Boot Hill we could see most of the township and the island of Mokoia in the middle of the lake which we spread of cousins knew well from our excursions there with the Ex-Prisoner of War Association, which had family picnics there a couple of times a year. Dad would invite various of our cousins along. The Raimonas at Whaka were entitled to go anyway through their father being an ex-POW, and so were several other Whaka families, including the Raponis, whose sons were my good mates.

Aunty's husband, Jim Rangi, worked at the abattoir about half a mile up the road from their house, which was a rental from the meat company. We could go up and watch the animals being slaughtered, and hear the men sing as they worked, or laugh and joke or talk rugby.

Mary and Jim's house always had plenty of free meat from Jim's work, and terotero was a favourite, this being sheep intestines which we had witnessed earlier on the Saturday half-day being run through uncle's practised hands, squeezing out the faeces as the train entwined like an endless length of glistening, bloodless penis, since each set of intestines was tied to the next. We had this fried for breakfast or boiled for tea. Or we had huge steaks, huge everything when it came to meat.

Breakfast could be steak, or any number of cooked meat items, accompanied by eggs from the free-ranging chooks and gathered by us children. Aunty Mary busied herself thoroughly tidying the house, right down to last specks of dust up on high window ledges, each photograph frame dusted and the glass cleaned if necessary, every cushion in perfect place. Uncle Jim would come home from work just before noon on these Saturdays, his apron spotted all over with blood; he'd have a quick bath, a bite to eat, and then off we'd go, to Whaka, to the Geyser Hotel.

Uncle and aunty in the cab, big cousin Jimmy – we called him 'Superman' after the comic book character, as he was exceptionally strong and a gifted athlete – all the children on the back of uncle's big work truck with its steel tray and sides nearly as high as a nine-year-old child, off on their regular Saturday trip to the Geyser Hotel public bar. Aunty, as a Maori woman, was not allowed by law inside the bar where her husband was, but she did her drinking with her regular female companions on the road islands opposite the pub, my mother amongst them. Aunty Mary would make sure we had money enough to buy lunch and a few treats before she settled down to playing cards with her buddies, even though she knew we would surely earn a few shillings from the river. That is how she was, as was her brother Tupu, who if he saw us would always offer us money, but on the strict understanding that we would never accept if someone had already given us some.

The Geyser Hotel was a real institution, and every Saturday afternoon you could hear the singing of the Whaka men in the public bar. Outside the rambling two-storey hotel the road was a wide avenue of potholes, a rutty thoroughfare. In the middle of the road were two grassed islands with cabbage trees that provided shade. There was a public toilet area and some covered seating which the old kuia of Whaka made their gossiping-spot.

These road islands would assume significance for me, and for any of the children whose mothers made these islands their drinking-spot. Thursday afternoons, that being payday for most workers, and Friday afternoons, because that was the end of the week, and Saturdays from about noon onwards, until six o'clock closing came. By then our mothers, our aunties, had turned the six-inch grassed elevations into their version of heaven: a drunken orgy, with jitterbugging and waltzing and the occasional fights – making public displays of themselves under the contemptuous, but hapless eyes of the old local women. The world of the kuia did not belong to this disintegrated drunken behaviour of modern days.

It was an odd feeling seeing Mum there on the road island, or arriving later, after she left us. It was as if I was looking at someone more removed, and yet of course it was my mother. Always well dressed, she carried herself with pride, but a ferocious pride, not the quieter dignity of the older local women. Naturally Mum greeted us, and more often than not she had money to give me and my sister, the two children in our family who loved Whaka most. But I remember it being a cursory greeting, a dutiful acknowledgement of her children. There was something of the excited child in her that couldn't wait to get to the card game, the beer drinking, the company of the other women. Of course I would observe my mother from a safe distance, noting her mood and whether she was on a winning streak or not. If she was winning she could be generous with her money. She was usually the most boisterous, extroverted cardplayer of them all. And the most regular winner. That winning smile of hers would light up half of Rotorua, and yet the taunting eyes on her defeated opponents could well be the start of a brawl later.

The Pork Bone Man used to turn up with his truck stacked with pig backbones and my Aunty Baby would give us money to get some and take them to her home and put them in the meat safe or, in later years, the fridge. Fish vendors sold fresh fish and shellfish from vans. Maori would take a package of fresh raw mussels over to the road island and eat them on the spot with whoever wished to partake.

The pub was usually full by early afternoon, as working men and office workers and management types arrived in their array of transport which could be anything from bicycles to brand new cars, to trucks and vans, and vehicles held together by No. 8 wire, rope, home-welding, or simply the occupants' thirst willing the ancient vehicle to get them to that pub. From a quiet start at eleven in the morning, with many men there on the hour, it would gradually build to a mid-afternoon roar and an hour or so later to a cacophony of men transformed by the rapid intake of beer from the week-day habit of drinking it quickly.

Sometimes a fight would spill outside and children would come running from all over to witness the big men belting each other. The women on the island, especially if well on the way to being drunk, would yell encouragement and catcalls and some would scream for blood. But fights weren't all that common, not at the Geyser, as the local culture of friendliness and singing ruled supreme, along with the iron fists of my Uncle Tupu who could knock most men out with a single punch if trouble was what someone was out to be causing. He was head barman and then bar manager, a position he was so proud of gaining, as it reassured him that a Maori could make progress the same as his white counterpart, just as long as he was prepared to apply himself. There were lots of other locals who could sort out trouble-makers, so usually it was a happy place.

But by the time the six o'clock closing bell rang out over this side of the Whaka bridge there had been quite a transformation in these sober, spotlessly clean and well-groomed Maori women on the island. Staggering, vomiting, cursing, fighting, publicly urinating, they were unrecognisable apparitions of female humanity. Being helped home by their older children, or shoved into vehicles to be driven home, or wandering in an unseeing drunken state or fast asleep like innocent children on that grass island with not a hope of stirring them. Lord knows what the overseas tourists thought of these sights. Certainly the old local women disapproved. I have images of the kuia telling them off in Maori, and yelling at them in English to behave themselves. But to no avail. Their authority had been lost, to modern times and alcohol.

The men too, emerging blinking in the sunlight after five or six hours of rapid beer intake, hardly able to walk, getting onto bicycles and promptly crashing, or making a weaving path that looked most unlikely to reach its destination. And Uncle Jim, normally a placid, happy fellow, coming out with features all twisted up and calling for his namesake son to drive us all home, or insisting that he was going to drive. Cousin Jimmy who learned to drive at only nine grabbing the truck keys and soon we were ready to depart. But first we had to help Aunty Mary into the cab. If she was too drunk my uncle would throw her onto the back tray with us and we'd have her incoherent company for the five or six miles to her house. Aunty Mary would be rambling on in English, in Maori, cursing every one of her sisters, a brother or two, enemies, and then would halt to extract a name, saying, 'Oops, sorry, dear, not you. Your sishta loves you. It's those other fuckin' bitches,' and then she'd break into Maori and presumably curse them in that language.

We would hear the cursing all the way home, as we bounced along on the back of Uncle Jim's abattoir truck, onto the last stretch of unsealed, pot-holed road, dust kicked up, cows lowing in the dying day. Home to that immaculate house, and the person who kept it that way tripping and stumbling through the front door, lost of all her dignity, trying to prepare the evening meal, a sight both amusing and alarming, especially if aunty was in a foul mood from losing at cards, particularly to my mother.

On Saturday nights we'd play in the spooky vastness of the old abattoir, with its old crumbling brick and big creaky wooden doors and paneless windows and dust-covered wooden and steel beams and spider webs and light plays that gave eerie effect through different openings. It was where the abattoir stored salted cattle hides and sacks of salt, along with discarded machinery and rusting tools, and there would be salt granules on the floor that got into the cuts in your bare feet and stung. I had many a terrifying moment in there having the wits scared out of me by my older cousin and sometimes his mates. A nightmare if I let my vivid imagination and those echoing screamings by my older cousin get to me. Couldn't wait to get out of there, and couldn't wait to go back another weekend for more.

●

Unlike Aunty Mary's and Uncle Jim's, most houses we went to made me uneasy, even terrified. Nervous and near crapping in my shorts with fear as we sit at the table of one of our relations. Afraid to make the tiniest clink of fork or knife against plate, because there's trouble brewing, from the brew that the adults have been drinking all day long. Years later when I'm learning the lyrics of a song for a band I'm involved with I get a shockwave of recognition at this line: 'Had my fill at the still got to kill.'

He's got to kill. The uncle. It isn't just this house, but any of the houses we go to, have school holidays at. Had his fill of beer and so has she, the aunty, whoever it is this time, and she's looking anxious and her body sways drunkenly at the table as he, her husband, glares at her and his chewing starts to slow down and so does ours, the children's – I want to go home! Even if to Mum going mad, at least we've got Dad, or Kevin – we can barely swallow our food, so tense is the atmosphere.

He gets up, gets something from the cupboard, or the bench, shoots glances at his wife as he returns, mutters something. She says, 'What was that, dear?' in a fawning, appeasing voice. He doesn't answer. He's past that point, of reasoning, of talking. The warrior tough man doesn't talk with his mouth; he talks with his overpowering sulking, brooding silence, towering not just over his wife but every child at that table. Then he talks with his fists. He suddenly throws a punch across the table, hitting her square in the face. Sends her toppling backwards in her chair. Her scream fills the room. And he, Mister Fists, starts eating again. Look at those jaw muscles pulsing. The woman gets up. She's pouring with blood.

'Did you have to do that in front of the fuckin' children – again! Did you?'

No, probably not. So he walks around the table, grabs her by the hair and drags her off down the passageway and confines our experiences to the audible. Thump! Thump!

●

What is dark too of these memories is the crude, often violent way people behaved, their arbitrary and immediate dispensing of violent justice. A child is slapped before trying to find out why they did something. Children receive thrashings for petty misdeeds, hidings out of all proportion to the crime. A kid gets beaten senseless for showing disrespect to an adult. One of my strongest childhood impressions is of being in fear, of being intimidated by most of the adult Maori company I was in. I remember fear at some arrivals of Mum's relations, the noise they made, the explosion of voice and laughter and seemingly rough utterance. Their conversations were crude and gutteral, their every action either menacing or teasing and primed always to explode. They intimidated me.

The Maori adults were worse when they were drunk. It was the adults' hurtful comments and deeply resentful eyes on me that I struggled with. My mother's boasting that I was the best in my class academically did me no favours either. Not too long into my school years I began being singled out for abuse or scornful comment by some drunk adult, often as not an aunty or an uncle. They'd say, 'You're a brain box, eh?' Loaded up to gun you down, whatever your reply. Being a 'brain box' meant you thought you were 'smart', which doesn't mean clever smart, but cheeky smart, and daring to have an intellectual existence.

It was the predictable unpredictability of every situation, of knowing that things could always break out, but not knowing the reason why. There was no logic that I could discern, no code of behaviour that I could understand. We'd go and visit one of our aunties, and we'd see holes in the wall from where of few of her husband's punches had missed her head; there'd be blood smears on the walls, on the floor. And whoever of the wives it was, she'd be a picture of facial wounding, her eye swollen shut, and her lips so battered she could hardly utter a sound. But beyond even that, her eyes looked out at you as if from behind a prison where you could not even visit.

I have the most vivid memory of one mid-year school holiday

staying with another aunty out of town, and her head being held under a tap over a sink and the blood being washed from her face. My uncle held her by the hair like this, after he'd beaten the hell out of her in front of us, his own children and myself and another visiting first cousin from Rotorua, right in the middle of the meal aunty had just served us. Words had been exchanged. He demanded she shut her mouth. She wouldn't. So he beat her up. We knew to sit there and to act like we were still eating, as that was the way demanded of children witnessing violence.

In various houses around Rotorua we saw the same pattern. Men, our uncles, our adult male cousins, friends of our mother, smashing up their wives and, just as often, thrashing their children, particularly their sons, since it is sons who have to live up to the physical model of being tough. I had cousins whose fathers beat them as if their son was another man and this was a grudge fight and therefore of greater fury and ferocity than normal. I have a second cousin, a childhood mate of mine, whose father would punch him full in the face, from the age of about ten, as I remember. My mate would carry his black eyes and grossly swollen lips with a burning hurt so intense we thought he'd either burst into inconsolable tears at any moment, or he'd kill his father one day. He did neither. He didn't return for his father's funeral and when I heard the whispers of complaint about him that day I laughed inwardly at his small gesture of revenge against a man who was nonetheless well respected in the community. That was and still is the problem – that violence gets to wear the cloak of acceptance.

Our mothers fought too. Countless times we stood in silent or screaming witness to a scene of several women yanking out tufts of each other's hair, raking gouges and scour-marks down one another's faces, these punching, kicking apparitions falling to the floor, or down on my father's well-tended lawn, on any bit of grass or house footpath, wherever. They flew at each other whilst kids were sitting at the same table eating. An upset, an insult, a slight, just had to be avenged immediately.

Of course there were Maori households where violence and heavy drinking didn't get a look in. The Pore family across the road were not the slightest bit violent, and their father liked a beer and a good time.

The Kiel family had the odd dust-up between adults but mostly they were a happy family. In Whaka violence wasn't too visible a problem, though in some households it was bad. Sadly, one of those was my revered Uncle Tupu's household, the family I would live with soon after my parents separated, moving between Whaka and home, as Dad had been granted legal custody of all us children by the court. Uncle Tupu was widely respected in the community. He was manager of the senior rugby team, and a huge contributor to the community well-being. He was a lead singer and organiser of the war remembrance occasions, a speaker at tangi, and one of the most highly regarded figures in Rotorua, a man of great mana. Yet in his home violence prevailed.

There is no doubt that many of the children survived their violent upbringings. My first cousins, the offspring of Mum's sisters and brothers, have almost all grown up to be intelligent, thinking people. Most of them have broken the cycle of the violence they knew as children, my half-Fijian female cousins in particular. Not for a moment has it been easy for them. But under no circumstances would they raise their children as we were raised. We all remain appalled by the legacy of violence. That must change before it destroys all that is good and hopeful for the Maori people.

seven

We came back from school one day to find Dad home early from work with a most grave expression on his face. He told us our mother had left home and was likely not coming back, or not to live. She was living with another man, he said. And we all felt his shame, this final nail in his coffin of trying to make this marriage work, if only for his children's sake.

I paid a spying visit to where Mum and her new lover lived and observed them through their sitting-room window. It didn't reveal much. Mum was gone and that was that. Well, she wasn't gone, for she'd turn up from time to time, drunk out of her skull, angry as usual, and think she had the same rights of possession, the same claim to causing an argument with my father, with the same old violent outcome. But we didn't like her one bit. Funnily enough, that took some of the fear of her out of it. We were just world-weary observers who couldn't wait for her boring, coarse carry-on to end. Several times we called the cops to have them remove her from our house. And oh, her outrage! The way she spat at her betrayers, at all of us standing on the front doorstep as she was carried, yet again, to a police car. But at least we didn't have to wake up to it, not anymore.

There's a paddock, an empty section of unused land up the other end of our Matai Street cul-de-sac. I've climbed a tree, one of a line of about thirty or forty of them, macrocarpa pines. I climb to the top and for some reason look down the line and ask myself if I can leap from one to the other the whole distance. For some have quite a leap, and at maximum height a miss could be painful. I jump onto the next tree.

Can't believe the thrill it gives me. The next. The next. I miss one and come hurtling earthward but manage to grab a branch. I can't believe my luck. I continue on. One after the other, getting bolder and bolder. Is this what confidence feels like? As if you can take on the world? As if you can fly, like in dreams? There is one large gap near the end. I launch myself without thought into the air and find a branch with my hands, my legs following with a grabbing that kids know best. I've done it, for the last few are close together. I climb to the top of that one and look back and I feel more proud than I've felt in my life. I have conquered something. If only it wasn't so fleeting.

I walk back counting the trees. Forty-two. I want to do it again and so I start at the beginning. And I do it all again and my legs are scratched and bleeding, so are my hands and face, but I'm triumphant. I head home, past the Kiel's place two houses up from us. I would have normally boasted to either Kohi or Gary but this day had no intention of doing so. This was mine, the tree-jumping act. All mine.

That night, in my bedroom, I am under the blankets in my private secret world and I am telling someone of my proud, dangerous exploit. That person is my mother. I dream that night, though, of telling her again but she is laughing at me and telling me I'm a liar.

In Standard Four I was getting more rebellious. I stood up to my teachers when I thought they were instructing us to think in a wrong or palpably stupid manner. They taught us in absolutes that could not be challenged. If they said it was so, then it was. Oddly enough I can barely remember anything specific that had me rebelling. I only remember my frustration at *knowing* a certain statement or lesson was wrong, and yet we were supposed to sit there in our classrooms accepting what we were told.

After I had taken my stand on not believing in God, I decided I'd take on the teachers directly. This was towards the end of my Standard Four year. I chose the right teacher, a man who was later convicted of sexual abuse of his school pupils, who came out to enquire about a petty playground altercation. Everybody was in a state of excitement, there was no-one being hurt, but for some reason this teacher decided he must gain immediate authority. So he demanded we be quiet instantly and whoever so much as said hello would be severely punished. So, I piped up, 'Hello!' right in his face.

I remember the power I felt as this chubby man pursued me, the school sprint champion, with me running backwards and laughing at him not being able to catch me! And that sense of freedom at getting outside the school gates and seeing this puffing man give up the chase but stand there pointing and uttering dire threats of physical hurt. But we both knew who had the upper hand and I laughed deliriously at him.

Except I didn't count on big sister Josie, who was at home when I turned up at 1.30 in the afternoon, and she wanted to know why. I told her and she hit the roof, though I did manage to calm her enough to wait till Dad got home and we could discuss it. I could count on Dad being reasonable. But he said I'd gone too far and I had better go back to school and apologise. This meant reporting to the headmaster, who was not a fan of mine because of my earlier stance on enforced Christianity. I made my apologies even though that teacher's face fairly screamed to my instincts that something was badly amiss about the man. He fairly oozed something raging inside.

The headmaster informed me that I had been chosen as dux of the school but if I misbehaved again he'd give it to the second-placed person. Funny, though I wasn't surprised at being chosen dux, I was still in disbelief, as if somehow I didn't deserve it. So I was on my best behaviour, proving that even the worst-behaved boys, or those who feel undeserving, still like to be recognised and acknowledged. Dad gave me £2 as extra recognition, that being the long-established deal in our house, that first in class at year-end got £1, and dux was worth twice the amount.

It was over the subsequent Christmas holidays when I was spending lots of time out at Whaka that I got even closer to my Whaka relations – my cousins and my new best mate, Mark Takarangi, who was tough and intelligent, had exceptional sporting ability, and could fight like crazy, yet loved having 'intellectual' conversations with me. We were inseparable and talked and talked for endless hours. He had a confident mind, hungry for the knowledge I had from my father. I had an enquiring mind in need of stimulating company. Our shared love of sports, our natural born fighting natures, made us perfect mates. Mark Takarangi, my first cousin Koro Raimona and a handful of other Whaka boys and I became very close. Mark picked up the game of chess (which has never interested me) faster than most. He could play rugby, run fast, and dive better than most for coins in our river. How I loved being with Mark, to share both mind and physical exuberance, and how I loved having the Whaka playground to express that exuberance in.

Uncle Tupu and Aunty Baby also represented family stability to me, and my uncle was such a powerful personality that just being spoken to by him felt like a blessing from God. I have this memory of uncle leading a group of Whaka Maori returned servicemen singing in a foreign language that turned out to be Italian. He was a strong family man, though naturally according to his lights, which to some might seem partly to dwell in parental darkness, for he believed in using a heavy hand if he deemed it necessary, as did virtually all of the Maori men of his time.

One of his less admirable qualities and a common one among Maori, was that of having a favourite child. In this instance it was a niece, my oldest sister's first born who was named after our maternal grandmother and whom Uncle Tupu used to dote on, lavishing more attention on her than his own children.

We used to fear, terribly, Uncle Tupu's disfavour. And he was strict. If we didn't catch the first bus after the 'flicks' in town we, his sons and I, were punished. That could range from one of his icy stares to a clip round the ear for all of us. He believed truly that he was imparting discipline. But our fear of Tupu didn't stop us riding the backs of the Whaka bus hanging onto the pram hooks on the outside. Being carried along at thirty miles per hour, how exhilarating! And how we hated the do-gooder citizens who honked a warning to the bus driver that he had illegal passengers.

The feel of the Whaka community appealed to me. Everyone knew everyone else; any adult could claim the nearest kid and get him or her to do an errand. They'd greet you by the name of your uncle, 'Ah, Tupu's nephew. How you, boy?' Or in reference to your mate, 'Mark Takarangi's mate, eh. The two intell-ectuals!' You were Kuia's boy, Mary's nephew, Kahui's cousin, Arapine's grandson, related to so-and-so.

In the mornings just before dawn we used to walk up our unsealed road with my uncle for a bath. The night before Uncle Tupu might have roasted a leg of mutton, or wild pork given by one of his numerous mates always keen to be on side with him, and that would be reheating in the fire oven, along with roasting potatoes and pumpkin, for our breakfast on our return. Roast meat for breakfast! We loved it. Or it could be sausages cooked in several inches of fat. And no table was complete without thickly sliced white bread spread thick with butter. Every meal was a feast. The time of day mattered not. Boiled fish heads for breakfast, the eyes a ritual of exaggerated salivating consumption, the body skeleton with its sweet bits of flesh to be sucked off each bone, the prime bits of cheekbone, the flesh just below the top of the head and around the gills, every last morsel sucked and picked and accompanied by buttered bread. Obesity in my half-adopted Whaka family was considered a sign that we were a well-fed and therefore well-looked-after household. My nervous energy must have burnt mine off!

I can still see my father's face when he came to visit me in the evening after work. He'd lean his bicycle against the house, undo his bicycle clips, cough to warn he had arrived, and into the kitchen he'd come; the shy man but with that pleasant smile, his sister-in-law Baby always having a kiss for him, and Tupu the standard handshake and the respect he gave my father. Though Dad almost always declined his brother-in-law's invitation to join us for tea, as he threw eyes at the table laden with all the fatty, unhealthy food he disapproved of. Though he had so much respect for Tupu I think he applied a different standard to him. Dad knew I was happier at Whaka with its family environment than at home, though he always asked if everything was all right and whether I wanted to come home. Sometimes he insisted that I accompany him to stay a night or two as he missed me. I usually did go home for a day or two but couldn't wait to get back to Whaka.

I started intermediate school, Form One, and kept the company of my Whaka pals. But the incidents of Uncle Tupu's violence began to take a toll on me, and so I was phoning Dad more and more to ask if I could come home for a few days. Not that Uncle Tupu was violent to us kids. But he seemed unhappy at something. Perhaps his bowel cancer was partly to blame.

I did well enough at school, except that I was unsettled, unhappy. Always in fights, always in trouble for arguing with teachers over what, more often than not, was nothing worth getting into trouble over. But I couldn't stop myself.

Girl awareness came in Form One and I was besotted with one girl after the other. I had an eye for the 'classy' girls, the ones who came from middle-class homes, or so most of my fancies seemed to me. I had a fumbling, confusing first sexual experience, which presumably lost me my virginity, though I only remember it as something I had to do. But I'm not even sure that strictly speaking my virginity was lost on this occasion. I bloody well hope not, if only for the girl's sake! We were in the age where sex was a sin and unmarried girls who got pregnant were more often than not sent away to an out-of-town relative to have the baby where it would be quietly adopted. Speaking openly about any sexual matter was strictly taboo. But normal pre-teenage sexual turmoil was the least of my problems. A dam inside of me was about to burst.

●

I can't believe this, I can't believe this, I can't believe this, as I watch the railway track spew silver-topped parallel lines out behind us, and blackberry bushes blur their prize crop to impressionistic brush strokes of black on dark green. A swamp. Steaming wisps of thermal in a park. I know that park: Kuirau. And isn't that Tarewa Road, where Mum goes to a card school and she had that big fight, her and two of her sisters against some other dames? Yeah, that's the street. Gives me the creeps, but not from this flashing-by vantage point. Here I'm king of the world.

The countryside, so quickly reached, racing past. Sheep and cattle grazing, is that Ngongotaha Mountain? My heart is hammering with excitement and fear. This can't be happening and yet it is. We're on our way!

He's a mirror of me in the seat beside, my mate. We daren't let our giggling escape. Our faces are suffused with the effort of trying to stop it. And oh God, here comes the guard for our tickets. Put on serious faces – no, not that serious, you fool!

'Good morning, boys.'

Good morning, sir. Sir? He's not a sir, he's not a teacher, he's a bloody rail carriage guard with a stupid hat and a self-important look. His uniform is shabby, even I can see that. Say nothing. Give him the tickets. I look out the window and elbow idiot to do the same. Guard coughs. Our hearts leap, I can say that much on his behalf, my mate's.

'Yes?' I turn and I think I am starting to blush.

'Getting off at Frankton, eh?'

'Yessir.' Call him Lord now.

'What, a holiday? Visiting a sick gran perhaps?' He's a frustrated cop.

'No, we're going to a funeral.'

'Oh, that's no good. Sorry to hear it.' He looks at each of us and frowns. One's a half Maori and the other's a fair-haired deadset Pakeha.

'A close relation is it?' He nearly has us as we both go to answer at once.

'No,' I get in first. 'It's his grandfather and I'm going with him because we're best mates at school.' Kids with imaginations make the best liars.

I know I'm only young, but I am looking at this oaf and I understand why he is in a job like this: he has nowhere else to go. He thinks he's important and yet his essential self wants approval, he just wants to be loved, forget about even respecting him. I swear I can see all this in the man, as he runs those life-confounded eyes over us and then he makes some joking remark which we both burst out in laughter at, our relief vented, our gladness that he's so stupid and we're so clever.

He says, 'You should try the pies at Frankton station, if you get a chance. Lots of meat in them and peas too.'

We sure will – sir. So we get a lesson right here that if you make a man feel important he's yours. Nice uniform. Neat hat. Must be an exciting job, sir. You must get to meet *everyone*. How many famous people have you met, mister? We heard a story that a murderer was caught on this railcar, is that true? And was it you?

And Oaf gives that aw-shucks-it-might've-been-me look, and shuffles in his tired old regulation, railway-issue, union-entitlement leather shoes, and rubs his chin and says, 'Well, there was an incident....But we're sworn to secrecy, you understand. A job like this, you know?'

Yeah, we know. We know now that we're safe, that we'll complete this journey unless by some horrible coincidence there's someone else in the up front carriage who not only knows us, but that we're up to no good. For we're runaways. At age twelve. Two Form Twos from Malfroy Road Intermediate, me and my mate from Clinkard Avenue.

Bush, soaring trees, and soon impenetrable jungle to most eyes, except mine have experienced hunting with Dad, for pig when he's with his favourite hunting mate, Des Marks. So I'm the expert telling my mate all about the pigs that'll be rooting around in there in the thick fern and bracken, and how the finder dogs sniff them out and then the bailer dog works the pig into a tight spot for the holder dogs to go in and get a mouthful of hind leg or testicles, until the hunters arrive either to shoot the creature if it's a big nasty boar too tough to manhandle, or get in behind it, flip it on its back and plunge a knife into its throat. Hunters are real men, I inform my pal. But then so are twelve-year-old runaways.

The guard keeps coming back and chatting with us. He's a well-meaning chap, but excruciatingly full of himself. I think this is an awakening of the observer in me. I see that some men are just not funny, or dynamic, witty, prepossessing. Just as I have felt that there is something about me which does not quite fit. Maybe that's why I've got an eye for it.

In an hour, it might be longer, we've travelled through the wild, untamed countryside and now it's gently undulating farmland, the mighty Waikato. Place where they produce the rugged farmer rugby players, dairy capital of New Zealand according to our local history lessons. Now lessons which will be left behind us forever, so I am convinced.

I see all these faces, mostly adult. I'm dying to talk to them, anyone. I want to know what the world's like, where do we find a job, what do you say, how much do you get, where do you find a place to live. I want to hear what they talk like, at least those who have an exotic different look. I want to meet someone, a pretty girl, who I fall in love with, even though I've only a puerile idea of what couples in love do. I just want love.

We stop at a town, I think it's called Cambridge. Thought Cambridge was in England. It's got oak trees, and people on the platform are eating pies. I'm always hungry, and it's connected to my nervousness. Hamilton starts announcing itself in residential sights and traffic. Then we're passing through the city and then the railcar is slowing down. We're in another town – no, it's a city. Not like Rotorua which is striving to achieve city status of a 20,000 population. This is big smoke stuff, 50,000 at least. Train stops. This is it. Time to get off.

Grab our duffle bags and head for the door. Except the guard is blocking it. What the hell? No, it's okay, he's got his hand extended.

'See ya, boys. And don't be too sad at the funeral. Happens to all of us.'

And I step off feeling the opposite at how I judged this kindly man. Come to think of it, he could get into trouble for not picking up that we were two runaways on his train.

But this is Frankton station in Hamilton. We've got separate forward tickets for the country's capital, Wellington, hundreds of miles away. An impossible dream. Someone will nab us. This can't last.

So we may as well try the pies here, seeing as we're soon going to get arrested. They do taste nice. Love another one but we've got to watch our money until we find work in Wellington. Actually, the plan is to work our passage over on the inter-island ferry to Christchurch. In Christchurch we are going to make our way out to my grandfather's farm by walking over the Port Hills. I had a landmark of three fingers of pine trees coming down Grandad's hills to aim for. We'd camp in a kind of cave I knew there and pinch our food from Grandad's as well as Uncle Will's until the day Grandad came up shooting rabbits whereupon we'd reveal ourselves and beg him to lend us the fare to go to South America! Where in that vast continent, I hadn't planned. My idea was to tell Grandad I couldn't stand living in the same house as my brother Nick as he knew that Nick hit me and made my life miserable. When the truth is Nick had nothing to do with it. I was just running. I would tell Grandad that this was my chance to go and start a new life and that soon I would be back, a different person, successful and changed. I'd pour out everything that had happened in those growing up years that I'd been afraid to tell him earlier.

Railway platforms are made for writers. But not twelve-year-olds running away from home on stolen money. It's lonely and smells of urine and the empty railway tracks seem to head off into a dire place, not where freedom reigns. Freedom from what and whom anyway? Who am I running from, when my mother's been gone nearly two years? I honestly don't know. Not even now. Adventure seems the main reason. I just liked the idea of a big adventure. And I guess that aching desire for love.

We have a long wait, I don't know how long. But no cops appear. Just a fat mother in an emotional, despairing state with several little kids crying and grabbing at her dress as she struggles with a heavy suitcase and a railway employee stands watching them with institution-alised folded arms, and indifferent, heedless eyes. Soon the platform's transformed, to a buzzing activity of people waiting to meet arrivals or get on. We're safe now, swallowed up by the crowd, the noise, the echoing cacophony of locomotive squealing and clanking to a halt. On we go. Find our seat numbers, too nervous to say anything. We're either onward or we're not.

We're onward. I can't believe this, I can't believe it, it is so exciting and so illicit. It is like victory over something, over impossible odds. Might be that I'm addicted to this at a young age. No, that can't be. I'm no daredevil, not in the physical danger stakes. I just like illicit thrills. I have always liked breaking the rules.

I remember how fat the china cups and plates were at our first food stop, Taihape station, the middle of a high altitude farming nowhere, and us having another railway meat pie but this one with gravy and peas and a dollop of spud – I think. We don't stay on a high, not with his mother and father to worry about. We've bought time by tricking our way out of school with notes signed by his unwitting mother on both our behalf, the details of which I do not recall. My father won't be worried, not till about six o'clock tonight, as we could be playing anywhere till late, he's never minded that.

Reaching Wellington at eight o'clock at night is a reminder that we'll now be on the official list of police informed by parent and parents that we're missing. I especially have no idea of the anxiety this is causing my father. It does not occur to me. Of course I know he'll be pissed off, but to me it's not that much of a big deal. I'm quite big for my age and I can look after myself.

Till we get out and are left standing there, confused, without a plan, in the cavernous Wellington railway terminal. And so many people seem either drunk or weird, not to say dangerous. So this is the big city! And we haven't stepped outside the station building yet. Hardly out on the wide steps and gazing in awe at the city when we're approached by a man – a pervert, for sure. Pick them a mile off, even at our age. Well this guy's surprised when I swear at him and back up into a defensive stance. He sneers the way they do, with a promise that one day they'll be back, and he scuttles away.

But now my mate's been hit smack in the face with reality. 'Al, I think we should ring home....'

Uh-uh. Why would we do that? Our friendship starts dividing right there and then. He wants out and we haven't even had our first night. We start walking, sulking with one another. Some fuckin' dream.

Desperation and emotional seething soon brings estranged friends back together though. We try cars for an unlocked door, looking for blankets. Cars had them in those days, I guess because the heating units weren't reliable. Blankets we found very quickly, just as we found lots of cars unlocked. We discover an empty building site with concrete rubble somewhere up on the residential hills. We set up camp, with our blankets on the grass and over us. Fortunately the rain has stopped and the stars are out.

'Spectacular, eh?'

'Are they?'

'Yeah, they are.'

'Are they?'

'Yeah, and they're better than our rotten Rotorua stars, so there.'

All of a sudden I've rejected my home town, place of my rearing. And this city, half-wrapped around a harbour moving with slow lights of a big, departing ship, looks like a dream all lit up. I'm happy. My excitement starts up again, but not so for my companion. He urges me to find a public phone and ring his parents. But this bully will not let him.

I need this guy. I need him more than anyone. So I crawl and placate and I reassure him half the chilly night – as we haven't stolen enough blankets – that tomorrow he'll be all right, tomorrow we'll go down to where the ferry leaves from and we'll get a job. And when we get to Christchurch we'll get a bus out to Halswell and then we'll walk across farmland to my grandfather's place. Grandad will understand. He won't send us back. He once told me a boy should have a sense of adventure, and how quickly life goes, so you must live it to the full.

Daylight takes away my resolve to go down there amongst the capital city populace and ask for a job working on an inter-island ship. It's alive with traffic. The buildings are bigger than I remember them travelling back from Christchurch many years ago with Dad, who was down on work business that coincided with the end of the Christmas holidays with Grandad. We sailed on the ferry, I had my father to myself, didn't have to share him with anyone. I was six. It was the happiest time of my life. He was so smiley, so chatty; I seem to remember being lifted up to see things at every turn. We had a sleeper cabin. It was heaven. We went to the Wellington Zoo. I saw a tiger with a hole in its snout, from a disease. A giraffe. A monkey doing a rude thing to itself, or why else were the people laughing and the mother grabbing her children away from the sight? My father, I'm pretty sure, would have grinned. He was a liberated thinker after all.

But this Wellington I didn't remember. Where would we work? How will we pass off as sixteen? Make ourselves fifteen, can we pass for that? Probably not. I hear if you rub charcoal on your face it makes you look like you shave. Oh yeah? Yeah. So what do we rub on to make ourselves look taller? Let's roam around in the meantime.

Breaking into houses, since we're hungry and out of money and I'm succumbing to misery too. It only vaguely occurs to us that our stealing was wrong. It's just part of the adventure. But the police will be out looking for us – in Rotorua, that is. Who would think we got all the way down here, first to Frankton, Hamilton, seventy miles away and then over 350 miles to Wellington. We find a lot of unlocked houses, though only coins inside. But enough to buy pies and a soft drink.

We're warmed up by the food and by the success of our house burglaries. We're not ambitious, just kids wanting to have a feed, though if we find a house with lots of money it means we can buy our ferry tickets and not bring suspicion upon ourselves by asking for a working passage. Striding down this hill, eyes out for the next house, when suddenly we're both grabbed from behind, turned around by a very strong and very angry man who's demanding to know what happened to his birds. Birds? I look at my mate, he looks more like a sheep than a bird. He denies, of course he does. And I don't know what he's denying. Till finally he owns up.

'Mister, it was me who let your budgies out.'

And it's Mister who gives me an enormous kick up the backside, and gives my mate several of the same for being the guilty party.

'I'm calling the cops,' he says. So this is it. Over. Because of some stupid budgies my mate had let out of their cage. But for some reason the guy changes his mind and instead gives my mate another kick for luck and tells us to get the hell out of his neighbourhood.

Where the day went I don't know. Only that it was long and boring. Another night out looking up at the stars, except it clouded over and drizzled the whole night. Not a wink of sleep, cold and wet and both wanting to go home now. But try the ferry passage first.

In my gruffest voice I asked this likely looking figure of authority down at the wharves, 'Excuse me, we're looking for work on the inter-island ferry to Christchurch. We were wondering…'

Sure, the guy was very friendly. Come this way. We followed him to an office, he invited us to sit down, said he'd have to interview us, but first excuse him as he had to make a phone-call to his boss to give him the good news that two young workers had turned up, just when they were needed. Ten minutes into the 'interview' which we were failing at hopelessly, in walks a big cop.

'Would you two boys be from Rotorua by any chance?'

At the cop-shop, details are taken down, photographs taken, our belts taken, and shoelaces. Twelve-year-olds must commit suicide too. Naughty boys, don't we care about our parents and how they feel? Better to own up to any crimes you committed. But no confessions forthcoming. We're in trouble enough. Though later my mate owns up to breaking into a house or two and we are both officially informed that 'investigations into these serious crimes will take place.'

My mate's parents are driving down to pick us up. It's a six-hour drive from Rotorua, the cops are going to teach us a lesson in the interim. Some time in the police cell, until our lift home arrives. So I have my first taste of a police cell at age twelve.

Not that such places are new to me now, but your first impression sticks. It's concrete etched with names and obscenities and erect cocks and dates and police helmets scoured angrily into the concrete with a fist crushing down on it. It stinks. Of urine and vomit and disinfectant and shit and the stench of defeated men. And it's damp. This is where the dream ended up. The two runaways who'd sworn to join their destinies all the way to living in South America (I think I'd picked Paraguay out of my school atlas) are now not talking to each other.

Time goes by interminably. My mate starts sniffling. Then he's crying. And blaming me. Fuck this.

'Shuddup, you sissy! Stop crying!' That's the house rule at 29 Matai Street talking.

Which makes him worse. He's yelling that I *made* him do this, I *made* him steal money from his parents' money tin. And he's right. There wasn't money to steal at my home. Dad's salary got paid into a bank account, and he only carried a small amount of cash. It was my idea to run away, and he was the weaker of us. But not this weak – I *hate* people who crack up when things turn to shit. Still do now. So I punch him. He throws one back. I give him two more and just then the door bursts open.

'You!' The big cop points. 'You're staying right here and your mate is coming out in the warmth with us. He's getting hot food and you're getting it cold, if you get it at all.'

The door slams and locks after my mate. Now I've done it. I think I messed up.

eight

Back at school we're either heroes or outcasts. What's more, he and I are permanently estranged. What we did is outside anyone's imagination and so they're either in awe of it and want to know all the exciting, breathless details. Or it's way outside of what is acceptable to those kids who have been taught to get on with their lives, and we're bad eggs who should be avoided like the plague.

Our class teacher shows she positively loathes my escapade and me with it. She bawls me out in front of the class as setting the worst possible example to my classmates. I have brought shame upon my school, upon my family, 'Or those family members who have a sense of shame.' She knows only too well who she is referring to, my two older brothers who have passed through this school, and my mother whose reputation still lives on, long after extracting herself from our home.

What can I say? I ran away. I was in a police cell. I'm a disgrace. I know that. But if only a single person would ask me why, then maybe we could get the process started of getting to the bottom of this. Sure, I did it for the adventure, but it runs deeper than that. I can feel it, I dream it, it's what keeps me in this constant state of being unsettled, primed to lose my temper, to walk out of a class, to hit someone. Someone please talk to me. Inside this angry boy is someone else wanting to get out – to escape from the prison of his own mind. I need help, but I don't know how to ask and even if I could, I'd probably not be able to articulate it. Kids have feelings before they become thoughts.

Adventure distracts you, it takes your mind off yourself. So does defiance of authority, for they are both total involvement. You don't stand up to teacher authority half-pie. It's either all or nothing. So, this woman has me out in front of the class and now wants me to explain myself to them.

'Why should I?'

'Because I am ordering you to. And you owe it to them.'

'I didn't run away with them.'

'No. But you ran away with their right to pride in their classmates and their school. Go on, tell your friends why you did this to them.'

Stupid, blind woman. What would a bunch of eleven- and twelve-year-olds know about my fuckin' life?

'Go to hell!' And out I walk.

At home Dad is finding it hard to talk to me. And he's no sulker. He hates sulking, all our lives he's drilled it into us that sulking is childish. But I know he cares for me and soon he'll be over it. And he is and he does talk to me about it, asks me a wide range of personal questions, am I troubled, is it my mother, is it sexual, is it to do with him, could he be more affectionate? This is a good man, a good father, trying his best.

But it's hard to talk to your father at twelve, or at twelve with a huge chip on your shoulder, or whatever it is you call a troubled childhood. I shouldn't be so hard on myself. I'd love to tell him, Dad, that I ache so much it physically hurts, it turns my gut into a painful knot. Except I don't know that what is troubling me is a lack of confidence. I know it's a lacking, but I can't specify it. It feels like a hole in me, a hollowness, a place that's been gouged out and that at any moment someone will notice it and say, 'There! That's Alan's problem: he's got some part of himself missing! He's wounded.' Or something.

Uncle Tupu came around especially to confront me about my running away. Since I spent a lot of time at his house, living as one of his children, he had every right to. He asked my father if he could talk to me alone, and as Dad respected his brother-in-law he said go ahead.

We go out to the wash-house; it's concrete sinks and blue rinse in hessian pouches placed along the windowsill. And maybe some quart bottles of Dad's home-brew beer tucked under the sinks, though three bottles is his maximum to drink on any one occasion, unless it's a party. I never saw Dad drunk. Uncle's breathing is agitated. He's just looking at me, his mouth is twitching. He says, 'I've a damn good mind to hit you, boy. Don't care if your father is here or not. You're my nephew. I love you. I expected better of you. Say sorry, boy. Or I'll thrash you like your father should have done.'

'I'm sorry, uncle.' And I am. To him. Because his mana, and the love he's given me, is owed apology. The teacher who has refused to have me back in her class is owed nothing, she has no mana, and most certainly no love. I understand the difference between some men's outlooks, that they see the world differently even when it might be the same event.

I am not afraid in this moment of my uncle. I have been afraid, terrified of him many times. Not now though, for he is here to tell me mostly that he is a loving man who is not happy with my behaviour. He even tells me he was going to borrow his mate's car and come down and get me himself. Don't you try this again. No, uncle, I won't.

Big sister's not happy with me. Tells me it made it look as though I was running away from home because of how she treats me, of how she runs the house. I am so shocked to hear another's point of view I'm almost in tears. I stutter that I didn't mean it to reflect on her and that she's a good sister. Which she is. But she's not through yet, and proceeds to inform me that whenever we do things there are always other people affected. Her. Dad. My brothers and other sister. Our uncle and aunty at Whaka especially. And why don't I just use these brains I've got and get on with making a go of my life instead of all this mucking around and worrying everyone to death?

Why, sister? No confidence, sister. No self-esteem, sister. I start to realise that at school in the next few months. I'm out of one class and into another and that's not going well either, my male teacher finds me difficult to deal with. I answer back, I challenge his teachings, I yell at him, I tell him that if he so much as lays a hand on me – meaning the strap – I'll hurt him back.

It was from then on that school – or the rules at school – fell apart. It was as if some door had been opened and it was part of the plan to enter this house of confusion and a growing anger at what, I did not know. Only that I was angry. For some reason this burning attitude didn't affect my schoolwork so much. Perhaps because even angry boys still like the feeling of coming first!

I fought with teachers – physically. I had a set-to with the deputy-principal in the middle of the playing field one lunchtime, before half the school. He quite rightly wasn't going to let me make a fool of him and soon had me in a headlock and marched me off to the headmaster's office.

I deserved what I got there. And the headmaster was frank in telling me he knew of my home background and how he understood it hadn't been easy for me, as he'd had my two older brothers and their behavioural problems to deal with before me. But he did have a school to run and so he wouldn't hesitate to expel me if there was another incident like this. Any fool could understand this reasoning, and so for a period I settled down. I had been getting into more and more fights, and to be fair, other boys, especially Maori, were feeling their fighting genes stirring within them and neither side minded the confrontations. But at the same time I was increasingly aware of this fear of certain fellow pupils, or teachers, and social situations. I became a chronic blusher.

I took a real shine to one of the teachers, Mrs Ngatai, a very attractive Maori who spoke straight to me. One day, seeing me misbehaving, she marched up; but instead of a telling off she gave me an invite to her home! Her husband, Harry Ngatai, was a teacher at Rotorua Boys High where my older brothers were. He was a powerfully built Maori, yet a gentle man who welcomed me to his home. His wife Nuri's tactics worked wonders with me, at least where she was concerned. From that point onwards I wouldn't hear a word of criticism of her from any of my peers. I stayed at the Ngatai home on a couple of occasions and ironically, her brother Terry Morrison, also a teacher, is now a friend of mine.

One school lunchtime I'm on my own, because everyone's avoiding me as I'm in a foul mood. I happen along beside the assembly hall. There's a play rehearsal going on inside. I swagger up to the door, master tough guy, whole school knows who I am. Except no-one up on that stage rehearsing their play notices me here. They're intent on what they're doing. I lean against the wall, keeping up my act, wearing a part-sneer in case these kids think for a moment that I am actually interested in what they do. What, acting? Puh!

Yet it isn't long before my voice of truth is telling me this: they're what you can never be. You don't have the real courage that's required to go up, present yourself and your practised lines, and perform in front of people so they might approve or disapprove of your performance. The voice of truth was telling me I only performed driven by anger. And if I had such courage then why couldn't I get up there on that stage and allow the school's will to give me thumbs up or down? I was afraid of my own voice, that's what truth was now bellowing in my ear. And every one of those confident, acting voices was bellowing out echoing confirmation: *this* is true courage.

I knew several of these kids. Nothings, I used to think of them. They can't fight, they're very average at sport, I beat them acad-emically. Yet here they are, almost as if they were glowing, and in command of the world. Not afraid of it. Confronting it, even if in the guise of acting out another persona. This is fronting, Duff, and you know it.

So I walked out of there with my head hung low and from then on I knew I had a personality, or a born or made disposition, that was always going to steer me away from true confrontation. It was like I had come upon my betters and would never be the same again. And the only quality that separated us was confidence. Self-confidence.

My chronic blushing started around this time too. I'd blush at everything. Every tiny little social incident sent me into a state of hot flushes. I would end up running from a class in a fake outbreak of anger at something when the truth was, I couldn't stand the feeling of having a burning face and being so hopelessly inadequate.

I railed against the world, my teachers, other students, any figure of authority. The truant officer picked me up once in my street and as he slowed at an intersection I leapt from his car and sprinted for my life, only to be caught from behind. His name was Mr McKinnon, a prominent rugby figure who wasn't having any of my nonsense. And he proceeded to whack me a few times and then marched me back to his car and drove me to school. I deserved the whacks and bear him no malice.

I sought out my ilk, the lost boys, the considered troublemakers, the rebels of the school. Mostly they were Maori. I got to hear their sordid life stories, how cruelly they had been treated by abusive parents. So we were outcasts of the same ilk, except I had a father, an uncle and aunty, who loved me. I had a paternal grandfather and step-grandmother who showed me that there is a wider and better world. Whereas these kids, most of them from the rural Maori settlements outside of town, had nothing and knew nothing.

I still loved rugby enough to be a team player, though I was probably the world's least conscientious fitness trainer. Since most of the rebellious types were Maori, they were also good at rugby, so we didn't notice the contradiction. We weren't really aware of how our low self-esteem made us appear, these pictures of sour-faced little shits who spoke in mumbles and laconic bursts of anger and smart-arse talk, who spent our idle hours getting up to mischief or picking fights. Then it was going into town and shoplifting. Smokes, mostly, as I'd got the habit something strong. But anything would do, as long as we scored what we thought was a victory over life. I think inside, though, that every kid like this knows there's something wrong. He just doesn't know what.

●

She's meant to be gone from this house, it was her decision, she had an affair with another man and went off to live with him…yet whose familiar voice is that issuing from our kitchen?

Kevin's gone, he's at high school in Wellington, or maybe he's living at Grandad's and having his year at Christchurch Boys High School like I was to. I've got two more brothers, and we share the top room, single bunks. Of course we've seen her from time to time, at Whaka, at one of her sister's, even at her rented place. But at home, our home, at night, no.

Is she drunk…? Yes. Is she angry at Dad…? Yes. So nothing's changed, nothing. But what reason would she have to be angry with him? She left him for another man whom she now lives with. Why doesn't she leave poor Dad alone? And why doesn't he put an end to this once and for all and give her a taste of her own violent medicine? Oh, shit, here she comes.

'I want to see my children. Don't you dare try and stop me. I'm their fuckin' mother. *Chooool-rinnn!* It's Mummy! I been missing you!'

Yeah, but we haven't been missing you, so piss off.

'Hello! Sorry to wake you. Mummy just had to see you. How are you. Ohh, haven't you got so handsome, my son!'

We're all quite handsome. Or so most people keep telling us. Except I feel far from that description and right now all I want is for this maternal visit to end. Come and kiss us then. We'll hold our breath so we can't smell the beer. Get it over with. We don't believe any of this I-love-you bullshit. Love doesn't work like that. You can't walk out on your kids and come back like this, drunk, and expect a heroine's welcome. Love is consistency, it's an undying fire of loyalty and devotion. And when it's our father's version, it's affection and duty of the highest order. Go away, Mum.

Dad, poor Dad, returned to the past he doesn't want to know about. He's spent the last couple of years having to be both parents to us, and now she's back, the cause of all his and our troubles. He's standing in the doorway there saying nothing, letting her have her visit. He's always been far too reasonable. Fuck her.

Dad puts up with her ravings about how she's missed us, till she gets onto the separation and how it's not her fault and did we know that, has our father made us aware of that? For fuck's sake, leave us alone. Your words are stolen from someone who has a conscience. And we don't believe this woman has a conscience. Sorry, Mum, but we didn't and I anyway don't. Not even now, all these years later.

We should know the pattern, the drill off by heart, she's not happy unless she's turned the molehill into a mountain with her on top screaming and shrieking and threatening down from it. This is a nightmare come back to haunt us, when we thought it was all over. Dad has said he won't put up with it, he'll call the cops if he has to. Just leave us alone now, he'll call her a taxi.

'So call the fuckin' cops! Go on – call them. Call them! Call the fuckin' cops! You just go right ahead. I don't give a fuck!'

We're out on the street. It's cold, winter. We're standing out in our pyjamas to an old familiar sight of our mother putting up yelling, struggling, scratching, grabbing, punching resistance to police arrest. The neighbours are out too, or at the very least out their windows or trying to hide behind just-opened venetian blinds, and there, over there in the tiny parting of curtains. She's back. Kuia, eh. Kuia Duff's back. The Queen of Matai Street has returned to claim her territory.

When you grow up with one of your town's most notorious women as your mother, you become inured to attention, and coping now as a well known writer is easy compared to this: your neighbours, your peers, in witness of your mother at it again. Like I said, it breaks your fuckin' heart. Maybe that's another reason I ran away. I don't know. Fuck it. I don't know. I mean, like they say: get over it. And if you can't get over it, then put it behind you. But that's not easy. Not easy at all.

●

Intermediate school ended to my teachers' relief and my looking forward to going to my Uncle Jonny and Aunty Betty's in Tauranga for the Christmas holidays. My uncle was a keen fisherman and a diver. He loved a beer just as he loved a scrap from time to regular time. It was here that I experienced cruelty from my Maori peers and older Maori kids for being a half-caste. It wasn't physical, but of course it hurt to be sneered at and ignored by kids you just wanted to get to know.

Whilst on holiday we got word that my Uncle Tupu had succumbed to bowel cancer. A huge man of over eighteen stone, we were told he had wasted away to about eight stone. Tupu Raimona was only forty-three, a Whaka giant brought down in his prime. We went to Whaka for his tangi, as large a funeral as Rotorua has ever had. It went on for four days, as hundreds became thousands coming to pay him tribute. The women in black dress and with garlands of fern in their hair performing songs and poi dances in tribute to Tupu. The air shook, like our most famous geyser, Pohutu, as men roared as they did haka in homage to his memory. They sang hymns in Maori, his war mates sang Italian songs, the elders chanted ancient waiata, with gusto and abandon and unabashed love that Maori express so well in their grief, their respect for their departed ones. They say that the speeches were magnificent, both those in Maori and those in English, that men found an eloquence from the upper reaches to pay finest tribute to Tupu Raimona. His war compatriots wept openly as they sang the songs they had all sung together.

In keeping with a person of mana, scores of illegally hunted pigeons turned up on the plates of the elders at the Whaka community dining-room. Seafood arrived by the half truck, freshly gathered mussels, pipi, kina, snapper. Pakeha paid tribute in large numbers too and the Returned Services Association, along with representation of the Maori Battalion, as always, were there in force to farewell one of their comrades. He, like many of them, had gone to the Second World War as a seventeen-year-old, and come back a man long before his time. They had a different maturity to them, a quiet dignity. And eyes that had seen too much.

Uncle Tupu's death threw me into confusion. So much was un-resolved. Here was a great man whose ordinary side I had seen and lived with, and yet whose violence I had witnessed. Why did he die before all my questions could be answered? I still dream of him now, and he is gentle and older, his compounded wisdom giving me advice. In my eyes on balance he was truly a great man.

The following year, 1964, was my first of high school. Rotorua Boys High. The first day and I was sitting in the back with my Maori cousins and the considered 'wild' boys from the Maori settlement Ngapuna as the new entrants' names were read out for their allocated Third Form class. In those days they had grading, from A to I. My name got called out for 3A and when I got up a lot of my Maori mates were disbelieving and told me to sit down. But I had to keep walking over to my new set of classmates, some of whom I had gone through school with over the years, the 'clever dicks', the 'brain boxes.' All of them Pakeha, except me.

At lunch break I sought out my mates to discuss, as I thought, our respective new experiences, only to find they were, almost to a boy, hostile to me. It hurt more than words can say and I was confused at why they should have suddenly stopped talking to me. It was the Maori distrust, disrespect, whatever the hell it is, of those who have an intellect. On the second day whilst in a make-shift rugby team one of my Ngapuna mates hit me high and hard in a tackle. I jumped up and whacked him and we were brawling on the sideline. I wasn't putting up with the silent treatment and the physical stuff on top of that.

The peer pressure was considerable. I beseeched my father to arrange for me to go down several classes, if not to the lowest H or I levels, then at least to 3C where Mark Takarangi was and a couple of our other Whaka mates. But Dad told me not to be so stupid by discounting myself. I insisted, though. So, they let me sit intelligence tests, which I felt I was deliberately failing but not making it too obvious. I must have higher intelligence than I thought, for they gave me a pass on the test regardless! So 3A for me it was.

Socially, I was well into the realisation that I was somehow inferior. I was not comfortable with my classmates – for the short time we were in class together. For there was a major incident. I had failed to turn up for a science class in about my six or seventh week. It was a genuine poor sense of direction in being unable to find the class and so I sat it out in the toilets and general hanging around until the next class, which I had made a point of locating. The next day the science teacher called out the roll and at my name demanded to know where I was the day before. I told him I'd got lost. He said not to lie to him. I said don't call me a liar. He said not to be insolent. I said, he said, and next thing he came up and grabbed me by the shirt collar. So, I grabbed his shirt collar back, and refused to let go until he did so first. Which is how we marched ourselves, down long corridors, out on to the compound, up the main steps to the headmaster's office and the assembly hall, holding onto each other's collars for dear life!

The headmaster had a massive sense of his own power and a paranoia that every tiny act of youthful attitude was a threat to that power. I was not the first pupil he was going to run head on into. He naturally wasn't too pleased at seeing one of his senior staff in my grip, and he thundered at me to let Mr Halliday go, which I did. He was the boss of the school after all. In explaining that I had genuinely lost my direction for the missed class, the headmaster wanted to know why I hadn't enquired at the office. I said, 'How the hell was I to know?' for I heard in his tone and anyway could see in his face, with that thin moustache so symbolic of his rigid outlook and the authoritative way he saw the world, that he was never going to believe anything I said.

"'Hell?'" he said as his face went red. 'You come into my office and have the nerve to *swear* at me!' And he went for his selection of canes.

I asked what word of my sentence was a swear word. He answered, 'You know only too well. "Hell" is a swear word.'

"'Hell" is not a swear word.'

'Oh yes it is. In my books it is.'

'Why don't you look it up in your dictionary, sir?'

But he was way past the point of reasoning and so was I, I guess. For I had seen his fundamental weakness, which was seizing on whatever he could just as long as he thought it gave him the upper hand. He got madder and madder and bellowed that hell *was* a swear word, in the dictionary or not, and to ready myself for suitable punishment for this insolence.

So, I gave him a spewed forth mouthful of what real swear words were and I proceeded to walk backwards out of his office as he screamed at me that I was expelled. I stood outside his office window and yelled the words at him over and over. And then I walked out of the school grounds as if I had taken and defeated a giant! Me, a thirteen-year-old taking on the headmaster of such fearsome reputation. Indeed, he disappointed me for losing his cool and using such an exposed argument.

Negotiations went on for several weeks between my father and the headmaster as to my being accepted back. Dad was not impressed at this small headmaster man turning a minor incident into one of major issue. Years later, when I had a younger brother at the same school who was expelled by the same man for having long hair (it was just over his collar) my father attended a school meeting and stood up in response to the headmaster's thundering speech that every good person must join forces to stop this insidious lowering of social standards, namely long hair on male pupils. Dad suggested from the floor that it sounded like the man smashing the barometer on hearing the storm coming.

So Dad was more on my side than anything. Though he was very concerned that my education was being disrupted. Finally, I agreed to take my six lashes of the cane, but only because I was in the athletic team and was anchor for the 4 x 110 yards sprints and the 220 yards, and I was hot favourite for the singles of the same events. Those canes were the most painful experiences of my life. He laid into me as though I was his mortal enemy and when I stood up at four he said in the quiet voice he should have used in the first place, 'Bend back over, you coward.' I bent over and took the last two. I checked myself in the toilets afterwards and I had huge welts. But I knew I had won the war.

School was not the same after that. I had got myself a huge reputation of being Master Defiance, and when you're acutely self-conscious that isn't the position you want to be in. I still stood up to teachers who I felt were silly about minor matters. Teachers in the fifties and sixties were more concerned with their authority than trying to engage us in a learning exercise that we could all take joy from. The idea that knowledge is joy was foreign to all but a few in those days. Some kids need a little more understanding and sensitivity shown them than others. The few enlightened teachers who did get through my bluff found a child hurting like hell. They found a kid who would die for them, who never ever gave them trouble, not a squeak, once they showed they cared enough to try and find out what was troubling me.

Not that I poured my heart out to them, I wasn't like that. But I did confide that things hadn't been so good in my home before Mum left and even though she was several years gone I kept feeling as if she had never left, but was still there presiding, dominating over all of us. That much I did confide in understanding teachers. And all I asked in return was an empathetic ear.

My father's woes with me were not over. I met up with a bunch of misfits, one of whom was my schoolmate, a boy called Arthur, a Maori who was tall and gangly and had a drunken, abusive father whom I had witnessed in violent action at Arthur's house. Soon I found myself a member of a gang calling themselves The Rebels. I was sworn in as a member at this deadly serious ceremony in the town park, Kuirau. Thermal steam hissing around us, a vast spread of grey mud throwing up frog eyes of air bubble all over the surface, as the leader handed me my pale denim shirt freshly painted with my number, 23, with ROTORUA REBEL written above that. An alliterated statement that Alan Duff belonged somewhere!

Our leader decided we were going to set up temporary head-quarters in Kuirau Park, just until we could plan a bank robbery or something equally criminally spectacular to build our own clubhouse. We set up tent in a shelter of bushes where we couldn't be seen. It was poorly erected and leaked when it drizzled that night. We stayed up talking bullshit about what we were going to do when we became the biggest gang in the country, or at least Rotorua, where we'd acquire guns and of course knew plenty of places we could steal rifles from, all the hunters I knew. Though the thought of being caught by a hunter stealing his precious gun was beyond imagining.

Kuirau Park had a thermal bath available to the public, but a foot-bathing one, not for full soaking of bodies. It was under cover and was tiled and had seating around the edges. But we used it as a bath, having to lie flat down on our stomachs or backs; it was wonderful. We also swam in a natural pool formation out in the open, which was deep and at perfect bathing temperature for reasons I do not know. I would later come to the same open air natural thermal bathing pool with my brother Kevin and his wife just for a soak and chat.

In our discussions on who was going to be who, our leader, a scruffy, scrawny, unshaven, uncouth piece of white trash if ever there was one, who wore the number 1 on his shirt back, said that my numbers 23 stood for second or third in command. I fell for it. Not least that between his number and mine there were not twenty-one other members of our motley collection. We had six.

I wanted to go home next day, but peer pressure took hold. And you start to think, well I'm in the crap so I may as well go all the way. I'll never forget the poignant sight of seeing my father late at night wandering the park looking for me. That forlorn, faithful father calling out his son's name. How I wanted to call back, even if just to reassure him I was safe and to go home and leave me be.

The next couple of days I went to the Hindu greengrocer to book up raw peanuts in the shell, my favourite, and fruit for the boys – on poor Dad's account. He wasn't happy with the greengrocer for letting me do this, he told me after. Someone had seen me in the park vicinity and three nights later I saw Dad again. But still I couldn't come out of my hiding-place.

On the Saturday morning, he was in the park and this time I just called out, 'Dad?'

He turned and looked at me with the most controlled expression. That hurt me more than if he'd got angry. He said, 'I've been looking for you.'

I think I muttered sorry and we headed for home. He didn't yell at me. He just asked me quietly what on earth was going on in my head, why was I doing this not just to him and my concerned older sister in particular, since my life-hardened, mother-hardened other siblings didn't really care, but doing it to myself. I had no answer. Or not one that set the bells of truth off. I only know that I had this vague idea that somewhere there was an answer for me. But answer to what, I wasn't sure.

My gang association resumed the next week. The leader called me a sook for giving myself up to my father. I didn't like any bad or insulting association to do with my father. I threatened if he said that again we could fight it out. He was about three years older. I saw then how leadership can be an illusion, for he started to negotiate. A leader shouldn't do that in these circumstances. And I saw then the coveted number 1 on my own back as a distinct possibility. We didn't fight, but we both knew he'd lost face.

I'm in the main street hanging out with two other Rebels. We're studied poses of turned up collars and Elvis sneers with our swishback hairstyles and kiss curls, legs apart, thumbs hooked into the front of our trousers, sneering and glaring at everyone on a Friday. When I feel my ear grabbed – what the... It's my Aunty Baby! And is she mad.

'Get that damned stupid shirt off right now!'

'Aunty, but I can't. I haven't got anything on underneath!'

'Then get on a Whaka bus right now, get to our house and get one of your cousin's shirts on. I want to see that shirt burnt by the time I get home!'

'I haven't got a bus fare.'

And you're hurting my ear! Not to say completely ruined my image, which I had earlier been prepared to do physical battle for. She thrust a bus fare into my hand and marched me across the street to the bus-stop, still holding on to my ear. I had too much respect for her to wrench myself free. But I knew my gang membership was over.

Just before she shoved me on to the bus she said, 'Your uncle hardly cold in his grave, and you're doing this. Smarten yourself up, boy.'

This same strong person was the woman leader of a delegation from Whakarewarewa at the première of the film *Once Were Warriors*. I stood at the top of the escalator as the Whaka crowd rode it up. I was leaking tears with the emotion of it. Then my aunty got to me, gave me a big hug and told me, 'Stop crying! Wipe your tears and show a better face!' She even wiped away my tears and kissed me. I'm proud to say I established a memorial scholarship in her name at the school she was teaching Maori at and where she died whilst teaching a class.

But adventure called me again. I'm planning with my cousin, Koro, to run away, and this time for good, some place where we'll find our dreams. So we chose the east coast town of Wairoa, with a population then of about a thousand. We didn't have Koro's late father, Tupu, around to instil fear in us. But we did have our doubts as to whether we should really go through with this, me perhaps less so. I seem to recall we both visited Tupu's grave to say goodbye and probably sorry before we left. On the side of the highway leading out from Rotorua we bragged about what we'd do and the girls we'd pick up. Koro had been to Wairoa before, for a tennis competition. He knew people there, they'd look after us, find us a job. A car pulled up and we were on our way, and not a thought for his mother or my father.

We stayed the first night in Murupara, a forestry town in the middle of nowhere, bedding down on a shop building site and having a thoroughly cold, miserable time of sleepless glimpses at the stars through a windowless space. We hitchhiked in short lifts through the Uruwera Ranges, bush-clad and mysterious. We could hear the voices of Tuhoe tribe warriors, 'children of the mist' from the past, behind every tree as we tramped along a dusty road. At the settlement of Ruatahuna we found kids who only spoke Maori. Luckily my cousin spoke it too so he conversed for a while with them and later informed me that they had commented on his skinny 'half-caste' mate and was he sure I was in the right company, meaning was I tough enough! They also expressed disbelief that we were first cousins and he told them that I'd been adopted as a child from the Korean War, if I recall correctly!

Finally got to Wairoa and it was getting on dusk. Nowhere to stay and just a few coins to buy some pies and a soft drink. Washed in the public toilets, slept on the river bank, huddled under some coats we'd stolen from an unlocked car. Slept soundly after that long, dispiriting series of short lifts and long walking stretches.

Next day met up with some girls, Maori girls. Spent the day with them. I fell in love, of course. I guess every female was my mother but a potential lover at the same time. Yet I recall being so disillusioned at the girl's level of conversation. She was thick and very country. They arranged a job for us, to start next day working on a building site for a Maori contractor by the name of Smith. He would provide accommodation in work huts.

Our bathing facility was to be the Wairoa River, but the bank was too steep to get down safely so we washed in a public toilet urinal. Then got shouted to the pictures by our new girlfriends. Sat in there doing the old hand-creep that takes an eternity, but found gold! Who cared if she said stupid, inane things!

Our giant of a Maori boss worked our rings off having us push barrows of cement up planks all day long. We were so tired we felt like vomiting. The girls were waiting for us at the end of the day but we were too exhausted to be interested. Fell asleep early in our cosy beds in our tiny huts. This went on for three days, and we were starting to enjoy the physical exertion. He was going to give us some pay the next day. We were walking down the main street of Wairoa feeling quite grown-up with our sweated days when a cop car pulled up.

'What's your names?'

'Koro Raimona.'

'Get in the car.'

'And what's your name?'

'Sonny Thompson.'

'Are you sure it's not Alan Duff?'

'No. It's Sonny Thompson.'

'You're not from around here. How do you know this guy? He's a runaway from Rotorua. You better not be lying to me.'

'I'm Sonny Thompson. Honest.'

'Okay. On your way. And you, Koro, get in the car.'

I watched them drive off and never have I felt so suddenly lonely nor so rueful of telling a lie in my life! I trudged off in miserable wonder at what I'd do now. Then the cop car turned up again and the cop jumped out.

'Sonny Thompson or Alan Duff? Which is it to be?'

'Uh, Sonny Thompson – sir.'

'Okay. So it's Sonny Thompson's arse I'm going to kick back at the station for lying?'

'It's Alan Duff.'

'Pleased to meet you, Alan Duff. You're still getting a kick.'

Actually, he didn't kick my bum. I think he was in some admiration of me for sticking to my story. We were taken back to Rotorua in a Child Welfare car where we were handed over to the custody of a house that acted as an interim for wayward boys until the Children's Court decided on our fates. It was but half a mile from my home. Dad visited me every day. Naturally he wasn't happy with me and for the life of him could not get out of me why I had run away again. I didn't know either. Complex reasons I guess.

I heard the magistrate utter the words sealing my fate.

'Alan Duff, you are now a state ward. Meaning you shall be put into the custody of a suitable boys' home and not returned to your home until the authorities there consider you are fit to take your place back in society.'

nine

How awful to be a parent who loses his child to the custody of a child welfare home, to have a magistrate declare his child as 'not being under proper parental control' and deem that child a ward of the state. My father asked the magistrate if he could say something on his own behalf as regards his child not being under proper control. He was granted permission and he told the children's court gathering that he resented the wording, as I was under 'as proper control as can be reasonably expected of a sole parent, who even like parents who are together, cannot maintain twenty-four control over their child nor can they determine their behaviour… only influence it.' If I seem to recall those words with too much accuracy, it is only because I know how my father structured his sentences and we have anyway discussed what was said that day back in 1964 many times in my older adulthood.

The magistrate did not like his authority being challenged by this articulate man whose gentlemanly manner and dress did not suggest a parent who wilfully had no control over his child. He chided my father and suggested that perhaps he was speaking about another child and not this one of proven social problems standing in his courtroom. So that was that. I shook my father's hand, I was teary-eyed, only too aware of the heartache I'd caused him. Thirteen-year-old Alan Duff destined for the Hamilton Boys Home, 67 Mount View Road, Melville.

I was taken there in a welfare car, driven by a Maori welfare officer, Mr Tapsell. He had given me the option of either being handcuffed, or giving my word that I wouldn't try and jump out of the car. I gave my word. I felt like shit. Home suddenly came back to me as something to be appreciated. Why the hell had I run away this last time? And why didn't my cousin get the same treatment as me? I worried that I'd be beaten up by mad, older boys from rougher backgrounds. I'd heard stories that the big boys in these places rape you, and that the staff made you scrub floors on your hands and knees from dawn till *after* dusk.

Huia Tapsell talks to me all the way in a firm but kind manner, urging me to make the most of my custodial stay and see if I can't fulfil the promise I have shown academically and at sport and make myself into a real young man, someone to be respected and eventually admired. I can still hear these words, just as I can see the white centre line of the road bringing me closer to this unknown fate. There were so many well-meaning people along my troubled way; but it just convinces you even more that you can't undo childhood's damage, nor can you adopt self-confidence, or change until you wish to change. I had some way to go yet.

I'm taken inside and we walk along a highly polished grey linoleum corridor. It smells of floor polish, fresh ironing, disinfectant; I can't see a soul, so my footsteps seem to make a louder echo. Then a group of boys come round the corner my way. They're in shorts, they eye me up and down, and I notice only one is older than me, two are about the same age, and one looks hardly eleven. They say hello, too. This is a dangerous place?

Mr Tapsell takes me into the office of a man and introduces him to me. The man tells me he's one of my housemasters and not to be afraid, but be concerned. The difference, he explains, is that I have nothing to be afraid of, but everything to be concerned about if I think I'm going to cut up rough or misbehave or disobey any of the home rules. So that's made quite clear and he has warm enough eyes. He has a Dutch accent and he's tall and handsome with striking blue eyes and obvious powerful muscles under that casual shirt and tie. I'll meet the boss of the place, the manager, Mr Johnstone, later. Maybe tomorrow.

I'm slightly reassured. Mr Tapsell is heading back to Rotorua, so he shakes my hand and wishes me the very best. I feel like I've lost my only connection with home as I watch him leave the building. I start thinking about escaping. The next few hours are a blur, of being shown ablution blocks, the gymnasium, the laundry, the kitchen, the two wings, the dormitory I'll be sleeping in until I'm allocated my own bedroom – but that's a privilege not a right. We have no rights in here, the matron informs me. She's a Miss, and old and in my mind fits the unhappy spinster stereotype, which I later find out was quite wrong.

Each morning we assemble outside on a concrete compound for dress inspection. I'm introduced to every boy. They range in age from ten to sixteen. It's embarrassing being the centre of attention. I don't feel like I fit even with other misfits. I have a week to learn how to fold my bedding into the standard bedroll. After that if it's not up to scratch, then it's a loss of privileges. I'm confused. My brain doesn't operate like this, in a prescribed way. I can never remember formalised knowledge. So I intend to run away at the first opportunity before they discover I can't abide by any of this myriad of rules and set ways of doing things.

The manager is coming in especially to say hello to me. How complimentary. I'm standing waiting outside his office. The wing I'm looking down the passageway of has wooden doors to single rooms and then a steel grille door. I wonder what's behind there? Along comes an inmate, my age, a dark-skinned Maori, muscular legs, and easy walk. He stops and looks at me, his eyes widen, he opens his mouth, I'm trying to remember why this face is so familiar.

He says, 'Who am I?'

'Cassius Clay?' I answer. I remembered the great heavyweight boxer's image from a television screen or on the cover of a magazine.

'You know?' He's really surprised.

'Yeah.'

Then bang, he whacks me one in the mouth. And off down the passage he marches, laughing.

'What was that for?'

'To show you what Cassius is, ya wonk!'

I figure out on the spot that 'wonk' is an insulting term. Is my mouth bleeding? What if the boss asks me what happened? I know I can't tell. Any boy would figure out that rule amongst their own kind.

I'm not bleeding. But I do have an image of this boy's face – how could I not. Later for him.

The manager is a shortish man with a bald head and narrowed eyes, in his forties, maybe late thirties. I've seen eyes like these on card players: they read into your very soul, so don't be telling them lies unless you know you're a better liar. And I'm not, not with this man. He's power in the first instance. But he's friendly.

'I know of your grandfather,' he says. 'Not many wouldn't. He's a well-respected man and one of the country's finest minds.' Not a bad start. 'I have also been reading your file up at my home. There aren't many like you who come to this place. But just before you think that's going to give you an easier ticket – you're wrong. At every turn I'll expect more of you. Virtually every other kid here comes from horrible backgrounds, as you'll find out from their own mouths. I am aware your own home background was not the best, or one parent wasn't. But whilst you're here, we can only deal with what we've got in front of us. If you mess up, I'll punish you, or my staff will. If you knuckle down and make a go of it, we'll help you all the way. But don't you ever show me disrespect, let alone think you can take me on. Or...' No need to say he means there is a physical consequence and yet I find myself immediately liking this man, as severe as he looks. (My judgement proved right. Though we hated it when we knew he was on duty because he stood absolutely no nonsense.) 'Dismissed.'

Fair enough. Nowhere near as bad as I thought. I was still going to escape first chance I got. This time I'd lose myself in Auckland, the biggest smoke. They'd never find me. Learn the ropes in the first few weeks. Check out the best times and places where escape is possible. But quickly realised in the sheer extent of how they have your time controlled, all worked out to a tight schedule of activities. Though one of my first private tasks was to find that boy who'd punched me and hit him right back. Which I did and I won his respect on the spot. Let him know I'm not going to be bullied. Can't stand it, something snaps in me.

Hear this term 'King Pin', which is top dog. Find out it's a fifteen-year-old by the name of Doug. I had to see who he was as quickly as

My parents, but not as I remember them.

Jesse, my grandmother, whom I hardly knew.

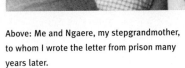

Above: Me and Ngaere, my stepgrandmother, to whom I wrote the letter from prison many years later.

Left: Grandad, as I remember him.

alan duff

At 'Spylaw' with Ngaere's mother, when
I was four.

Me on the same visit to Christchurch.
That is not a dunce's hat.

Dad, about to head off to the war, with his father, Oliver Duff.

Me, brother Nick, and brother Kevin. Quite cute, hm?

Above: Grandad and me. If only we knew.

Left: Kevin and Nick at Christchurch airport.
The boys had just arrived for the holidays.

Dad with Josie, Kevin, Nick, and me, on the steps of our state house.

Carol and my brother Kevin at their wedding, with Carol's mother in the background. I was best man.

At Christchurch Boys High. That's me, second row from the back on the right. Sullen? Surely not? I was only fourteen!

Seated: Uncle Roger, Dad, Ngaere. Rear: three male Duff cousins, Ian, Robin, and Gowan, presumably with two spouses.

Aunty Baby and Mum looking poised and affectionate.

Celebrating the launch of *Once Were Warriors*. On the left are Nick, Josie, and Mum.

Above: Paula with our daughter Katea in Barnes, London, 1979.

Left: My wife Joanna and me at my MBE award ceremony, Government House.

Guess who that is with me? Could it be Robert Redford?

My son Quentin's proud moment and me basking in it at his
swearing in ceremony to the law. Oh, the ironies, the twists
and turns of life!

possible, as I figured that since he was at the top of the chain, how he was would indicate to me where I might be able to position myself. Well, he was built like the proverbial shit-house, was Doug. Muscles everywhere, he was a heavy shaver and he had official manager's permission to smoke cigarettes. A virtual adult therefore! A half-Maori, he was more than his fearsome reputation; he looked like God to me. Boy, if he was the best, then I hoped he was far better than the next ones down or I didn't stand a chance. Doug's first introduction to me was at the Friday evening canteen shop, when we bought small items of sweets with the paltry wages we got for our all-day working tasks, me, like every new inmate, a cleaner and on the lowest pay. He accosted me just before I went to make my purchases, my first.

'I'd like a chocolate bar, Duff.'

He had his sycophants around him. They gave me the necessary expressions, from snarls to urgent nods, that this was how it was. I bought the chocolate bar and gave it to him. To my surprise he looked at it and then me and handed it back.

'Just testing you.'

So I'd passed by giving in? Or maybe he was just in a good mood.

I worked in the kitchen for a while, under the beady, thickly-lensed eyes of a woman who is memorable for her ignorance and the sheer scope of her superstitious beliefs about witches and Maori goblins. She had strange remedies for everything from sore stomach to emotional needs. She made every boy who did not go along with her prepos-terous beliefs and adamant statements suffer. Boys like me, who couldn't help challenging her. She poured scorn on me, told everyone I was a liar about my famous grandfather and my father being a forestry research scientist. Even when I sought Mr Johnstone's help in enlightening her, she hissed at me in private, 'I still think you're a liar! And God hasn't told me otherwise!'

She held God up like he was her big brother and had granted her permission to cause anyone who acted or spoke against her as much suffering as she could invent. For an ignorant, unread woman, she sure had a creative mind in finding punishments. But she did make the best porridge we'd ever tasted. I remember one of her worst qualities – she was a prize-winning sulker. A woman in her fifties and yet she packed sads like a five-year-old.

Most of the male housemasters were good too, especially the only Maori one, who was a short, stocky fellow with a cheery smile and considered a soft touch by the boys who loved him. But the Dutchman turned out to be not at all nice. He was one of those intolerant, fundamentalist Christians who smile and talk of a loving God through their teeth. We all hated him. He was a violent man, a complete hypocrite of his avowed religion. He beat boys for the smallest reasons and then affected a most innocent attitude when he occasionally went too far and it came to the attention of the manager, Mr Johnstone. He lied and he used his religion to put his hand over his heart and swear on his Lord's name that he was not guilty of the charges a boy had levelled at him. Upon being found not guilty he'd seize the complainant at the first opportunity and hiss in his face, 'Don't you ever tell tales on me again! You'll never get me!' No, we never did. But I hope something or someone has since.

We're in the dining-room, the rules are quite strict but mostly it's meant to be a pleasant social experience just as long as the boys don't talk too loud. But on his shift, this Dutch housemaster imposes a rule of silence at the first excuse he can find. One evening we're on a silence ruling when one of the boys has an epileptic fit. His hand shoots out and the stainless steel milk jug crashes over and spills its contents. The housemaster is immediately on his feet demanding to know who made that noise, whilst one of his young charges is convulsing on the floor.

'Come on, own up! Who made that noise?' The fool can't see the boy on the floor, not till he turns towards that table.

Bringing the fit under control is the first priority for everyone. A spoon is wedged in his mouth to keep his tongue from being swallowed, his eyes could not be more distant and less human as I stare at my first witness of an epileptic attack. What a delicate balance it is for some between the real world and one where the brain has catastrophic seizures.

When the boy has been taken to the sick bay, the housemaster returns and reminds us the rule is still silence. One of the boys calls out in protest that it isn't fair after what has happened that we can't talk about it. He's distressed and he's been scared by the fit, as are most of us who haven't seen such a thing before. 'Sir, some of us are scared and want to talk about it. Please, can we?'

A reasonable request. But the housemaster is not taking this crap and he's up off his chair again and over to the boy's table. This is a Rotorua boy, a fifteen-year-old.

'Stand up.'

The boy stands up.

'Say sorry.'

'Sorry for what, sir?'

'Say sorry or you'll be sorry.'

'Get fucked.'

The housemaster grabs him and drags him down the corridor where he starts punching shit out of him. I jump up and yell he can hit me too. So he races back and drags me down the corridor and meets my request.

He punches us both all the way back to our rooms. We know not to throw punches back, as at fifteen this boy is of an age where he could be brought before a court and sent off to borstal training. And I understand that punching back would be going too far, as if we haven't already by yelling and swearing at the housemaster that he's a bully and why won't he listen to reason.

Hamilton Boys Home had a cell block, but I never spent time in it – only once on cleaning duties. I remember the smell of desperation from all those angry, troubled, tormented youths who had been in there. It was a holding-place for older boys, mostly, on their way to other penal institutions, usually borstal. Outside we could talk with them through a high window. To be in there was to be a heavyweight, a hard-core criminal to be admired by us embryonic ones. It was where they put Home inmates for punishment in extreme cases, that is for violence beyond the pale, or for escaping.

One inmate who was there in my time used to dream about visitations from tattooed Maori warriors commanding him to run. This boy was from a backblock Maori settlement where his first language was Maori. He spoke English in a halting fashion and sometimes an interpreter had to be found, as there were several fluent Maori speakers amongst the inmates. We could hear him chanting waiata to himself inside his cell; he lived, we knew, in a totally different conceptual world. I had a deep desire to know him, how he thought, what he thought. But I only ever got a smile and brief exchanges of words with him because of the language gulf, and he disappeared out of my life like so many of the boys I lived with there, never to be seen by me again, not even now, thirty-four years later.

I had a good mate in the home, Mark. He was from Whaka. A cheerful guy who could turn anything into a joke. He'd not had a very good life. His father was not a true Whaka local but lived at the foot of Tuturu Hill in a forestry house way back, a half mile, deep in the trees. Mark was my best mate then. An exaggerated friendship caused by the circumstances, and a common bond with Whaka.

Most of the boys lived in single rooms, with a dormitory at the end of each of the two wings for newcomers or those who preferred to have the company of up to nine others. I had a single room. We were locked in each night and the day started at 6.45 a.m. The routine was regimented but I think necessary, for we had virtually all come from ill-disciplined backgrounds and were mostly volatile and ready to erupt at any time. Housemasters were in charge of us, both male and female. I remember just about every woman housemaster as kind, especially one, a Miss Bolfen. She and I talked for long periods and she was an avid reader of my grandfather's 'Sundowner' column in the *Listener*. She respected my intellect for what it was. We had something in common. She'd discuss with me what Grandad had written, a book she had read, an interesting article, a film. I soaked it all up; we laughed a lot. It felt like a secret relationship, pure and of the mind and soul only. I ran into her a few years later in Christchurch and she was even better fun, and so was I, without the restrictions we had on us.

I was one of only two boys from the home attending Hamilton Boys High, as a third former. I was most unhappy there, I knew no-one and felt nothing in common with anyone, not when I had to return each day to a totally different life of rules and regulations and duties and an unnatural environment, of fighting to preserve a dubious place in the pecking order, or just plain exploding in frustration and anger at the different situations with equally volatile fellows.

In my second week at the school I was confronted by three boys who informed me they knew I was a boys' home inmate.

'So what?' I said. 'How is that your business?'

Well, because silly boys make it their business. I beat two of these boys and the third didn't want to know. I loathe bullies more than most types and I never met a one who could match his intimidation with true fronting ability.

Most lunch hours I spent alone in a gully adjoining the school. A creek ran through it and I'd sit staring into the waters or else lying in the grass with my funny thoughts and the birds for company. I realise now I studied my surroundings in a broad brushstroke way, rather than in any intricate detail. I was completely contented there and though I'm sure I was noticed entering the area, no-one ever dared to come across to me in my secret hiding-place.

I had a fight once with an outside boy whose mother worked in the kitchen. We were coming home after school together and got into an argument, then a fight. He was the double New Zealand boxing and wrestling champion. I kid you not. And I beat him. On cloud nine I strutted back to the home, to be confronted by Mr Johnstone, who dragged me into the gym and said, 'Tough guy, eh? Punching up one of my staff's children.' Someone had seen the fight and reported it.

'But, sir, he's a champion boxer and wrestler,' I protested. But in vain. He punched me all over the gym, telling me how fighting was for losers. Then I realised he wasn't hitting my face, just short sharp blows to the body. And when he had finished and we were walking out together, he turned and said with a wink, 'Good on you. He's an arrogant little shit.' Funnily enough I saw that boy's name on a list of boxers that Bob Jones had handled in his days of boxing promotion, though I'd be sure not to brag about my past effort in case he showed me the trained version of the man!

A teacher found me in a classroom one lunch break when it was spitting with rain and you weren't supposed to be inside. He marched me to his office and told me I was getting 'six of the best', meaning canings. For just that? I told him where to get off and I'll never forget him saying, 'Get out. You've got the guts of a grouse!' I wanted to turn around and smash him, since it was he who was of that timid bird's description. But I couldn't, or my punishment from Mr Johnstone back at 67 Melville Road would have been unbearable, not least that I feared his disappointment as much as his physical anger.

●

The Hamilton Boys Home made one of the biggest impressions on my life. Perhaps thirteen was the right age to have impressions stamped on me. Maybe the observer and crude analyser was coming out, for I seemed to go through a series of often quite startling revelations. I was finding the artist, or something, in myself. A mind announced it existed. I had an opinion on everything and being pretty tough with it, few were brave enough to call me what I must have seemed, a big-mouth.

I loved the singing too, and hearing the talented Maori voices and guitar players around me brought out a musical joy. We'd gather down in the recreation room and sing our hearts out to one of the boys, Bill, on the guitar. I saw this guy's name in the newspaper many years later having committed some serious crime, just as I was to see many other names of boys I had shared my life with appear on the newspaper court pages, including one who shot off his own arm in a bungled armed bank robbery.

The boys' home brought out my physical abilities as we had all sorts of compulsory sport – basketball, table tennis, hockey, softball, rugby, and a gymnasium game called scrag. I was one of the best table tennis players and good at rugby too. But scrag I loved best; it was a game where the ball carrier charged at the opposing side until he either scored or was stopped. A game of strength and determination. But unofficially, it was the fights that sorted out our pecking order. I was one from the top, my superior being a Waikato boxing champion from Mangakino, Henry Payne. I ran into him thirty-four years later at an address I gave to primary school principals in Whakatane. He was still the nicest guy possible.

My eyes started opening to other things in the home, like the fact that all of us state ward inmates were afflicted with the same emotional problems, and that most were Maori. From troubled backgrounds every one of us, we were a cauldron of anger and childhood hurt ready to spill out. At any given time one or more of us could break out in fists or tears. So many of us were destined, fated by our childhoods I think, to serve borstal sentences and from there prison sentences. Many craved to 'graduate' to borstal and then to prison, with dreams of being big-time convicts. Anything, as long as it made us feel adequate.

We shared tales of our childhoods, mine tame in comparison to most. There were stories of a foster mother who would get a boy to urinate on her whilst she lay on her back masturbating; of a mother burning her children with cigarettes; of a father, an uncle, a grand-father who 'was dirty with me', since none could speak specifically of the sexual abuse they'd suffered. Stories of hidings and thrashings and beatings and whippings and jug-cord lashings and kickings, of torture, of unrelenting verbal abuse and lives of being screamed at, made to feel like nothings. Of boys remembering being beaten up by their father from a young age, and how they laughed bitterly when they told about getting a further beating for crying with pain. The vast majority of these sordid tales came from Maori children. We were our own micro society in that home, a residence of sixty-six beds; we had half-wits, an eccentric, two epileptics, a boy with a reputed IQ of 150, two rapists, a gay boy, and every one of us surging with the hormones of puberty and manhood, all of it overlaid with a culture of violence. Yet there was that other Maori quality of love and spontaneous wit and humour. So it wasn't all bad.

One day I get a letter from my mother, a nice letter. She names a date and time when she's coming. I'm surprised at how excited I am. I feel as if I can show my mother off, as she's still an attractive woman and she has a lively, confident personality, not afraid to crack a joke, make an irreverent but good-humoured remark in front of anyone. Surely she wouldn't come drunk?

I wait and I wait. The manager tells me not to get my hopes up. But I have and I won't be dropping them. I am convinced. 'She'll come,' I tell the man who only thinks he knows wiser. But she doesn't come. I am in my locked bedroom that night staring out my window at a sliver glimpse of stars and I cry. This memory found its way into *Once Were Warriors*, with the character Boogie waiting in vain for a visit from his family, doomed by Jake's diversion to a pub.

My mother does show up – two days later. Drunk. Got waylaid, she slurs, trying to cover up her state. Every kid in here knows what waylaid means: it's unable to walk away from a booze session. She creates an ugly scene. I calm her down. I can smell her. Everyone can. God, the depths booze plunges people to. Can't wait for her to leave. Just go back to your piss-up party, Mum.

Some time after that Mr Johnstone called me into his office to inform be I had earned my way home. Oh joy! Joyful but uncertain. I'd made mates here, and yet freedom was what we all dreamed about. Saying goodbye to the boys, to the staff, the kindly Miss Bolfin especially, and Mr Johnstone, whom I had come to respect greatly, was an emotional experience. Only a few weeks later I caught a bus from Rotorua, then another to Melville and walked down Mount View Road, a free boy this time, to gift Mr Johnstone with a paua-shell ashtray.

The reality of the prodigal son returning to his last year's residential home, though, is that you are not welcome. Everyone wonders why you've come back. I must be thick-skinned not to see that *no-one* comes back, especially not to give the boss a present, no need to crawl to him now. But that's what I did.

I also paid a visit to my mate Mark who had been fostered to parents in Hamilton and had a job in the labour force. My bus back to Rotorua wasn't leaving till 6.30 that night, so I had time to say hello to Mark after work. I hung around the boys' home half the day to kill the time till just after five o'clock. When I made my difficult bus and walking trek over to Mark's foster home at the address he'd written me, his foster mother refused me permission to see him; told me she knew who I was and that she had forbidden him to associate with any of his former 'bad company'. So that was it. I got a brief glimpse of a hapless Mark and my Hamilton visit was over. Like they say: you can't go back.

ten

Dad had visited me at the Hamilton Boys Home as often as he was able to borrow a friend's car and drive the sixty-eight miles from Rotorua. I was always glad to see him and felt awful that he had to bring himself all this way for an undeserving son. He was unflinching in his support of me and I felt so proud being visited by a father who was a research scientist, whilst most of the other boys either had no father or they did but got no visits from them, and they were invariably workers. My time in the home ended around Christmas of 1964, about nine months of rather epic experience for me.

I got a holiday offer to stay in Christchurch with my Uncle Roger and his second wife, Myrtle. Roger offered to have me for the next year, I could go to school at Christchurch Boys High. I was mad keen to accept and discussions went on between Dad and his younger brother and it was decided it might be just the thing I needed. When I was living with Uncle Roger and Aunty Myrtle, I remember my aunty looking at some photographs taken on one of our moa bone digs and she remarked, 'And here come the photos of my handsome nephew,' as she pulled out photographs of me.

Me? I looked around, expecting to see someone else walk in, perhaps one of her brother's sons. It never occurred that she might mean me. No-one had ever said such a thing about me, not my father because he'd think it encouraged vanity, and certainly not my mother. I just couldn't believe it.

'Did you mean me?' I asked.

'Yes, of course,' she said.

I shook my head. You can't mean me. I'm ugly, I'm ugly, I'm ugly. Words that had gone on in my head for as long as I remember. But yes, she did mean me, she even got up and came over and kissed me and said it again.

'You are a very handsome young man.'

Well, whether anyone thinks I'm handsome or not now means very little. I'm going on fifty, and vanity has a more pathetic hold on my ego. I am happy if someone says the smallest thing nice about any part of my physical existence. But when you're a teenager it is absolutely vital to your self-esteem how you think you look to at least those who love you. It's what I observed first of my wife's middle-class relations, they were highly encouraging and complimentary of their children. They spoke to them as equals and assumed them rights in conversations that only my father had given me, his family members, and middle-class people in general.

My uncle and aunt meant their best by me and it was not their fault that things didn't work out. I clashed with Myrtle and she clashed with the whole world.

My Fourth Form year was a contrast of being one of my best and my troubled worst. I was the school junior sprint champion, third in the 110-yard Canterbury Championships (the only sprinter without running shoes), played rugby for the Canterbury Under-15s, and had good mates, most of them middle-class and white. But I also had fisticuffs with my uncle, got caned by the headmaster for drinking beer on the school grounds, did three weeks in the Christchurch Boys Home, and had a tumultuous time having a part-requited love affair with a woman in her late twenties.

At school I got a reputation almost immediately, after I fought a bully-boy two years older in front of hundreds outside the school gymnasium. And won. Being one of only five Maori amongst over a thousand pupils made me a curiosity. Kids would follow me around during break periods and ask me to say something, as I had a pretty marked Maori way of speaking. Ironically, when I returned to Rotorua a year later, my cousin Koro remarked how toffy I sounded!

One thing about the school I did not like was the compulsory military training. I was very much against it, maybe because I had a resistance to taking orders, let alone blind orders. Dressing boys up in thick winter uniforms in the middle of summer and practising to be soldiers was not my idea of fun or training that might be good for us.

The prefect system is something else I resented too, of being told what to do by my fellow school pupils, many of them clearly crawling goody-goods. CBHS students had to wear the school cap at all times travelling to or from school. I wasn't wearing mine on one occasion and heard a prefect bawl me out. I dropped my bike and walked back to him and demanded he not shout at me. But he shouted even louder. So I ended up being caned for an assault on this Upper Sixth-former. But no prefect ever bawled me out again, and I did wear my cap to and from school.

We had a fierce rivalry with Christ's College, considered more upper-class than us. The rugby field was where we sorted out who was better than who and I don't recall playing in a losing side against them, though at the time I was only dimly aware of the social differences, something certain Cantabrians find more important than the rest of us.

The music of the time was the Beatles, the Rolling Stones, the Kinks, and these rock stars' hair and dress were all the rage too. I followed not a jot of it, preferring my American black music, English crooner Matt Munroe, P.J. Proby, Nat King Cole and I still rather liked my pre-puberty idol, Elvis Presley, though he didn't last much longer after Fourth Form. There was many an enjoyable session had in our kitchen with Chris Blain and me singing 'You Will Never Grow Old' and 'Born Free'.

Chris was the son of a doctor. To me their house seemed a mansion and their social lives so full of confidence and social ease, not to mention jolly good fun as I witnessed their parties if I was staying the night, and saw everyone laughing and singing, people doing musical items on the piano or singing solo. Ex-All Black captain Pat Vincent was a regular party visitor there, as well as a teacher at our school. Their idea of fun was strange at first to me and I was always expecting it to turn ugly and yet it never did. I remember the moment of suddenly realising that these people were perfectly content and they were not ever going to degenerate into abuse and brawls, and so that made me feel this deep trust for them.

I and another mate, Graham Harrison, had a holiday with my Maori classmate Pete Woods up at the Conway River where Peter's father taught at a country school. Near the Kaikoura Coast, we put down pots for crayfish and came back the next day to find them spilling over with eighty or more crays. They were the days when you gave them away, or donated them to the local gymkhana. I met the double VC winner, Charlie Upham, who lived at Conway. A real live hero in the flesh, and so quiet and reserved was he. His biography was on our bookshelf back home in Rotorua. At Conway we went possum shooting with .22 rifles, this trio of classmates who were all in the same school rugby team, with two of us destined to play for the province. I was in the team more for my speed than for being a gifted rugby player.

There was racism in the school, of boys who had been raised in exclusively white environments and had a negative picture of all Maori, or simply none at all, a vacuum which was filled by an unfair stereotype. I didn't help that image with some of the fights I got into, though always they were with older and bigger boys. But the racism was mostly mild and hurt me on only one occasion, as I recall, when I went with a mate to his house and his mother completely ignored me except for giving me nasty looks. The fact that she was so very attractive for some reason made it worse.

I still liked fighting. It was a physical test, a mental test. Part of me still has the fighter alive and I make no apologies for what nature has made me. It is only something to apologise for when it hurts others – and I don't mean the opponent who willingly enters into a contest with you. It is in many men's nature to fight.

My oldest brother Kevin lived in Christchurch. I saw a lot of him. He came and watched my rugby games for Canterbury. When we played Otago at Lancaster Park he said he'd buy me two bottles of beer for each try I scored. I got very drunk that night trying to down six quart bottles of beer.

The relationship with my Aunt Myrtle fell apart. We fought as if we were lovers. I had a teenage crush on her, which I turned into ugly verbal attacks. She was known as a chronically unhappy person herself, so we were a natural clash. My crush turned to intense and unreasonable dislike and I goaded and taunted her to the point of despair.

I had a good relationship with my uncle. He was obsessed with his work and was proud of his achievements. I got exposure to such a diverse range of people in this country, thinkers, politicians, writers. Roger Duff knew Chou En Lai, and had met Mao Tse Tung. He was respected in the United States and many other countries for his contribution to anthropology. He spoke fluent Maori and I discovered he had somewhat of a fixation with all things Maori; he showed me superb pencil drawings of his studies of traditional facial and buttock tattooing done when he was a teenager and he had Maori friends the length and breadth of the country. His were the dignified ones, those who had been raised with their culture or else had an education. He was always rather bemused by my tales of what our Maori relations were like back in Rotorua, for I don't think he got near that heavy-drinking, violent kind of behaviour, perhaps because he didn't want the romantic notion destroyed.

Towards the end of the year I grew more and more aggressive. Sullen, sulky, angry, at what I did not know. My behaviour got right out of hand one day when I got drunk out of my brain. My uncle quite rightly phoned my father to inform him that I was out of control and he was handing me over to the custody of the child welfare. Three weeks in the welfare home shook me up enough to say sorry and I wouldn't play up again. Dad had to fly down at great expense for the discussions on my future. These poor, concerned, well-intentioned adults couldn't know that I was heading for borstal.

It was a funny old year, but on balance I think it did me good. I was exposed to different outlooks, to the unfailing kindness of my uncle and aunt, my grandfather and step-grandmother. Christchurch Boys High School was a good school with fine traditions. It had a long line of illustrious former pupils, and was one of Christchurch's oldest-established schools. Whilst there I certainly took a pride in being a pupil, wearing my blue and black colours to most places. I came away with the words of Charlie Caldwell, the school headmaster, who told me, 'Whatever you do in life, even if it's only a taxi-driver, be the best at it.' It would take a while for that to sink in, but I have never forgotten it. I just feel a little sorry that the taxi-driving profession should be the late Mr Caldwell's lowest benchmark! I was destined to a long, long growing-up process, one that was going to make me different and eventually take a turn for the better.

When I returned home, Dad was vehemently against me leaving school. We argued over it all through the Christmas holidays. But I was adamant; he said I'd live to regret it, the usual parental wisdom, which even sensible children don't always hear.

●

Rotorua, 1966. We're hanging around outside a dancehall down by the lakefront. Every kid wants to be part of the action, which is either inside there, where the lights pulse red to the music, rock and roll, and where the girls are, or outside here, showing how you can fight, since the talk we have is neither social engagement nor anything meant to communicate other than basic animal signals, like dogs sniffing and tail-signing each other. Do you know so-and-so? Yeah, do you? Yeah, he's my relation too. We must be related then, eh? Yeah, mus' be. Shake on it, cuz. We exchange information about what girl is easy and who's a waste of time or just a cock-teaser, who had a fight last week, last month, last whenever, and who won and how. Oh yeah? Yeah. That right? Yeah, man, it's right. Real banal, basic stuff. There is a lake right there, with Mokoia Island sitting majestically in the middle of it, as if we can see it, or any of the beautiful scenery we are surrounded by in our seething states.

It costs an admission price to go inside. And even when you do have the entry price you can't stand being in there too long if no girls are attracted to you. It becomes you on a lonely island surrounded by happily inter-connecting boys and girls. You notice that it's not necessarily the best-looking boys who get the girls, either, but the most confident. The dancers, the rock 'n' rollers. The ones who we say love themselves. We mean it disparagingly, when truth is, self-love is what we outsiders lack.

There's a hundred unwanted boys wanting sex, less like me wanting sex and love, and not a one you can see who'll make your dream come true. If just for one night. Every boy knows that a girl lets you know with her eyes but so far I've only seen hostility or heavily signalled yawning disinterest. So I've gone outside again, with a need to show my physical prowess at least. Most of the kids are Maori. This is a Maori town when it comes to dances or a fair in town. Most don't have parents who care. Our parents (my father exempted) are at parties, getting drunk out of their minds again.

A mate picks a fight. I get a flash, a moment of honesty where I know these guys are innocent. I happen to know one of them and whilst he's not a mate he's not an enemy either. A year or so older than me he just wants to go inside there and try his luck with the girls. But honesty in a coward doesn't last too long and in I go, joining my mate in assaulting these three guys. Down they go. And up our egos go. Aren't we tough? Are we men before our time or what? Did you see that? Some beautiful punches there, eh? And the chorus of onlookers, of witnesses to your startling fighting powers say yeah, man, you fullas were good all right.

I can remember the strut coming into my walk. I understand why young males from messed up backgrounds find fighting so intoxicating: it's uplifting, almost like someone is telling you that you're alright, you're someone who's worth something. Your confidence balloons. You hear yourself talking fifteen to the dozen, you want this feeling to last forever, of being victorious; and not over those poor victims bleeding and limping off into the night they'd had such excited dreams of, but over that aching that's been inside you forever. I know this because I've discussed it countless times with young men and grown men. Winning a fight makes you feel, perversely, almost as if someone does love you after all.

The night seems to confirm itself with a fast ride in a sports car with a cousin's mate out to Whaka. Though I was terrified at how he turned corners since we were perched up on the top of the rear seat of this open top convertible. But better to die in unprotesting silence than let anyone know you're afraid.

A shop had opened in Whaka maybe a year ago, a takeaway place that sold really tasty food and was run by an especially nice married couple who had a way with the local boys, who understood their teenage seethings and could handle each of us just right. They installed a jukebox and when the Righteous Brothers came out with their all-time classic, 'Unchained Melody', this machine was going to get my coins as long as I had money in my pocket. I loved this revelationary style of Negro-influenced white vocalism. I played that song over and over and thought I could sing it almost as well as them after so much practice. And the fact that they were white boys, these American brothers, astounded and impressed me further. For it gave the rest of us mediocre, non-Negro (as they were called then) singing talents some hope that at least a few could reach the standard.

Out at Whaka I found some of the boys outside the shop, which had closed. Sitting on a wooden seat in the dark, we have a bit of streetlight to go by, the thermal noises of a geyser going off, steam hissing up through a fissure somewhere, maybe someone's singing at a party over the bridge. I like the company of these boys. We've known each other a long time now, played rugby together, dived for coins in that river gurgling by not far away, sat around for hours of a day in our choice of hot thermal baths and talked and laughed. We didn't fight each other much either.

I'm boasting about the fight outside the dancehall and my mates are sort of impressed, but we both know I'm more troubled than they are. They have pretty good mothers after all, most of them! Their mothers whisper about mine being drunk and violent and a slut to boot. I've got a log fashioned in my mother's image on my shoulders. Some would say I still have. So they listen with less of an impressed ear at the shrill voice recounting the fight, blow by blow, to them.

I start eyeing the shop as a further way to show I'm different and better than the rest. Someone dares me to break in there. I move around the building and when I get to the back, feel this sudden rush of power. Hear a voice telling me that if I can get into there then I have proved myself.

So, one after the other I remove the toilet louvre window panes. Up I clamber and then I'm in. I remember a feeling of doubt but then excitement pours in and you feel invincible. What exactly is my purpose I no longer know, as if I did in the first place. In the dark, like this, it is a completely different place. That voice tells me I shouldn't be here. Just as another tells me this is exciting.

I get to the front of the shop and there's the jukebox – a Wurlitzer,

I guess – standing aglow in the dark. 'Oh, my love, my darling. I hunger for your touch' are the lyrics from 'Unchained Melody'. I have this crazy desire to play the song and look, there's the till. I'll get some coins and play it and won't everyone outside be so impressed. That crazy Chow, they'll be saying in admiration. Chow is my nickname, given by my Aunty Mary, who upon seeing me as a chubby-faced baby said I looked like a Hinamana, which is bastardized Maori for China-man, which became Chow.

First, I stuff packets of cigarettes down my shirt, about twenty I think the police charges read. Then I try and get into the till but can't. Out to the kitchen to get a screwdriver, back out and trying to lever open the till drawer. The boys are waving at me through the window. Oh, aren't I the boldest one around! One of them is waving frantically at me and I figure he must want me to get more smokes. I indicate my shirt full of them. Can't get the till open.

Out to the kitchen again, look around. May as well make a sand-wich, and I'll toast it, just like the delicious toasted sandwiches they, the proprietors, sell us. There's the toasting machine, I think I'll have ham and cheese. Into the fridge, find the ham is sliced, two thanks, and there's a large block of cheese. Take it out, go to cut a slice off when the door opens. It's a cop. And another cop. They see the carving knife in my hand.

'Put that knife down, kid, or you'll be in worse trouble.'

The knife? What are they talking about? Oh, this knife. Jesus Christ, I'm done for. Over a year later, when I come home from borstal, one of my mates tells me he was waving me a warning that the cops were on the way. But what is worse is, they are followed by the couple who own this business. Looking at me with the most hurt expressions.

The wife says, 'Alan, how could you do this to us? We've been good to you.'

And her husband says, 'We treated you as someone special. Like our own son.'

What can I say? I mumble I'm sorry but it doesn't ring true, or why would I be in here. The cop asks, 'What were you doing just now, not making a sandwich, surely?'

'Yes, sir. I was.'

The owner's wife says, 'We live just up on the hill. If you were hungry you could have knocked and we might have been grumpy, but we would have gladly made you something to eat. We really liked you, Alan.'

I'll never forget those words: 'We might have been grumpy, but we would gladly have made you something to eat,' when that's not why I am standing here in their shop, unlawfully and traitorously on their business premises. I'm here because I'm lost, I'm fucked up.

God, now I am feeling so bad. I didn't know they had liked me so much. I didn't think that any adult liked me, not like these hurt faces are saying they did. I thought a few cared for me, like Dad and Uncle Tupu and Aunty Baby and a few others. But never that anyone actually liked me as in loved me. No-one. And the thing is, it would take me another thirty years before a friend pointed out to me that I was closed off to true friendship because I was closed off to love, or trusting myself to others' love – mature love, of friendship and trust.

The husband: 'Just tell us that you didn't steal from us. And we'll forgive.'

One of the cops goes out to the shop front and calls out, 'He's been trying to get into the till.' Yeah, to play the jukebox, though I'm sure I would have taken more money if I'd found it. But not my prime intention.

The other cop said, 'And what would that be underneath your shirt?' As he walked over and patted me there. Out I came with the cigarettes, the couple now staring at me in total betrayal, at an unthinking, heartless fifteen-year-old ingrate, a thief.

At the cop-shop there's two more charges awaiting me, of assault. The victims have laid a complaint and now I have breaking and entering to add to those charges. Long-suffering Dad, if it's no longer his departed wife it's one of his children, as I'm not the only child of his falling foul of the law and authority. We've all but two begun the process of social upheaval with the world. Here he is, tired-eyed, bristles on his face, sitting in a police station interviewing room with me and he's asking, 'Why? Why are you doing this to yourself?'

And I can't answer. It looks like this is to be my fate, always offside. Dad begs me to think about myself, my life. I've already refused to go back to school, Fifth Form, this year. We've had countless arguments over it but I would not budge. I got a job briefly out at a forestry camp in a place called Wairapakau. I thought I was going to be a big tough tree-feller, but they put me on a road maintenance gang with another, older Maori guy who spoke hardly at all and treated me like shit. Three miserable weeks I lasted only to be called into the boss's office and told, 'We're dispensing with your services.' I think that was the first euphemistic term I ever learned.

After that I tried working at another forestry camp at nearby Waiotapu. It was release-cutting, which meant we had to slash away growth around young trees not long planted. It was thankless, back-breaking work and the camp we lived in was full of rough, crude men who drank heavily and seemed to have keen eyes for sensitive souls like me. They'd say things like, 'Your mate reckons you're a bit of a brain box. You look like a skinny weakling to me.' One old bloke accosted me with, 'We hear you've been telling everyone lies that your old man is a forestry research scientist?'

'Well he is. It's not a lie.' So get fucked, I was tempted to tell this grizzly old white man sitting on the steps outside his hut, his sole home and in it his pitiful worldly possessions, nearing the end of his working life and with yet another quart bottle of beer in his hand, telling me I was a liar. Funny how the working class so often refuse to believe another world exists outside of their immediate surroundings.

'Listen, boy, don't be telling me. I've been in the forestry game my whole life. And I've never heard of your old man. So don't be running around making yourself look big. Or you'll get big all right – big kicks up your arse and then booted out of here.'

I reckon there are times when violence is justified. I should have chosen this moment as one of those. Funny thing, young though I was, I didn't feel scared of them. As if I knew that they were just life's losers, resentful at anything young and hopeful. I didn't last long at the job. One day I looked down at that road out of there, put my slasher down and said to my childhood neighbour mate, Kohi Kiel, who was working alongside me, 'I'm leaving.'

And I walked down that rutty slope with its loved little budding pine tress all nice and cleared of those naughty weeds and choking growth by our calloused hands and slasher tools and I was laughing and laughing.

The opposite of now, with Dad looking at me in the cop-shop wanting an answer as to why I kept getting into such trouble. But there was no answer to give.

Well, the magistrate in the court had an answer. Borstal training. My father asks the cop if he can take me to have some lunch before I am taken away. The cop is aghast. 'Mr Duff,' he puffs himself up. 'Your son is in lawful custody. And you want to take him for some *lunch?*'

I remember muttering, 'You call the food you've been giving me lunch?'

And the cop just grins at me. 'Sonny, wait'll you see what you're in for the next little while.' Then he adds, 'And it might be longer than a little while too.' Ominous, but I missed it at the time.

Shake Dad's hand. Fathers look terrible when they're helpless to do anything to save their child from a certain fate. Dad mumbles that he'll visit me as soon he is allowed. Then he turns and walks off rather abruptly. To cover his emotion I am in no doubt. I am certain that Dad had no idea of what borstal was, and though I thought I did from the tales I'd heard in the boys' home, it was very much different to anything I'd imagined.

For bureaucratic reasons I was held over at the Hamilton Boys Home for a few days. The manager Mr Johnstone's face when I came in said it all: Alan Duff, you have got some learning to do yet. Mr Johnstone wished me well and said he was sure I wouldn't let anyone push me around in my new place of residence, but not to get caught up in that cycle of behaviour. I was soon to realise that it was a warning, of another world to come. But I missed the real meaning in his words.

We shook hands goodbye and I never saw him again. I was told a few years ago that he had died. I'd tried to track him down after I wrote *State Ward*, since it was about the boys' home, but couldn't find his whereabouts. It was like a father figure had gone.

For some reason I have no recollection of what vehicle drove me to Waikeria Borstal. I think it might have been in an unmarked police car. Borstal, though, I'll never forget.

eleven

Borstal was not what I expected. It was a gaol, a men's prison, of iron grilles leading into a main wing where before me was cell door after cell door on the ground floor, a steel landing and more of the same doors on that level. I'm fifteen years old. The inmates were men to my eyes, the majority Maori, and big and mean-looking and giving me the newcomer the evil eye. Escorted by a warder to my cell, which was unlocked and had my cell-mate lounging just inside the doorway. He was Pakeha, had muscles everywhere and was adorned with tattoos. Turned out he was from Rotorua as I squeakily introduced myself after we were left alone.

He told me, 'Lucky for you, I know your older brother Kevin. He's an alright guy so you must be okay.' He was nineteen and doing his third borstal lag and looking forward to doing 'real time in a real prison'. So what the hell was this? Fifteen and I'm in prison? I want my Dad!

The day before, the Rotorua Court had sentenced me to a period of borstal training, from zero to two years. The zero was for those suddenly found innocent or who might be found to have a personality type or a medical condition that made the inmate unsuitable for incarceration. But there were no tales I'd been told of anyone getting out on their first day.

My first meal in the place was lunch, a bowl of soup and two bread rolls, one of which a bigger guy tried to grab. We tussled over it for a bit before he relented. I felt the eyes of the long line of the table at me for any sign of weakness. Suddenly the rules were men's rules.

I was put on cleaning duties, like every new inmate. The discipline was harsh and the officer warders yelled at everyone. We had an exercise yard and we had to do exercises under the control of a very fit Maori warder by the name of Mr Thompson. Someone got insolent with him on my third or fourth day there and he whipped the young man in front of our eyes with his fists. This was 1966, before liberalism.

My head spun with the noise of opening and closing grilles and heavy cell doors and the eruptions of voice of both inmates and guards – 'screws' we called them. Fights broke out all the time and were quickly and brutally quelled by the screws. I stand not in judgement here as I realised instinctively that these inmates understood only one thing: fire with fire. Show weakness and they'd be all over you.

My first real test came over a boiled egg at breakfast. A guy wanted it and naturally so did I. He'd snatched it from my plate and I had to near break his fingers to get it back. He stepped me out, meaning we went to the room where the cleaning gear was so we could fight without intervention. Out of nowhere he hit me with a hard object. I saw he'd grabbed a wooden hand-brush. Blood poured from a deep cut by my left eyebrow. But he didn't win. By the time the fight was over everyone was lined up outside their cells for clothing inspection and then a brief lock-up period before each went out to his allocated job. A screw asked why I was bleeding and I said it was a bust pimple. No sooner we were locked up than my cell door opened and I was dragged out. I saw they had my fight opponent.

We appeared before the chief officer and then what they called a visiting magistrate, who ordered we serve a week in solitary confinement on No. 2 diet. It is unimaginable now that any fifteen-year-old of mine should be doing a week of solitary confinement. And yet I think it was one of the seminal events in my life that made me. Nonetheless, I can think of other ways of making my children!

A cell is a cell. A solitary confinement cell even more austere than austere. We had four walls that ran with condensation, an enamel toilet pot, squares of toilet paper, and that was it. Within an hour of being in my cell the door opened and in came the diminutive chief officer, a hawk-faced Pakeha, accompanied by a warder I'd never seen, either

Maori or Pacific Islander and a mountain of a man.

Chief officer: 'What're you in here for?'

Huh? As if he didn't know. 'Fighting.'

Whoommph! The big guy punched me in the stomach, doubled me over. He yanked me up by the hair.

'Say sir when you address me. What're you in here for?'

'Fighting, sir.'

Whoomph!

'That's for fighting.'

Whoomph!

'And that's to remind you who's boss around here.'

Whoomph!

'And that's in case you forgot the first time.'

And they left me in a sprawled heap on the cold concrete floor.

The routine was you got a mattress and blankets to sleep on at 9.30 at night. At 5.45 a.m. the sound of grilles unlocking was your alarm call and you had to be up and out of bed with your bedding made into the bedroll they had taught us. If you weren't ready then you'd get a biff. You carried your bedding into a storeroom, where you got at least to see your other solitary confinement inmates, there being six cells, and even the guy you'd fought with was now your friend since you were in this boat together. A boat going nowhere, bobbing on a cold sea, as your day stretched out in front of you with every excruciating minute slowly ticking by. No reading material, no form of tactile stimulation, just the cacophony of your mind experiencing this for the first time. It was hard the first two days but then they made a mistake.

We were invited to donate blood. In return we'd get a couple of cigarettes and a cup of cocoa and some biscuits. I remember my sense of betrayal upon giving blood and returning to the cell to be given two cigarettes, a piece of match strike, and a single match. Two smokes in a row turns from pleasure to nausea for most. That's what they did to us. But the mistake they made was to let us go to a library selection. At first one of the screws insisted that we only have the choice of nursery rhyme books, till one of his colleagues told him to take it easy. I selected the fattest book I could find, the author was Taylor Caldwell. I have no idea if he or she is a good writer, let alone what gender. I only know that as soon as I started on the first page my solitary confinement was effectively ended, as I got taken out of there and into the world the writer's words created. Freedom! And victory; for they had dealt me the winning card hand without even knowing it.

I read and read this book and when it was time to collect my bedding and lights out, I couldn't wait for morning to come so I could get back into my book. The meals were three days of No. 2 diet – breakfast of cold porridge, a teaspoon of sugar, half a cup of milk, and two pieces of toast with a fat dripping spread. Lunch was a bowl of foul soup, a bread roll and half a cup of milk, slices of cold meat, and mashed potato. Dinner was several pieces of bread with fat dripping spread and a whole cup of milk. My recall of this is almost certainly flawed, but it would be close enough. On the fourth day we were entitled to normal populace meals. Of course I got hungry and of course had times of self-pitying misery. But mostly that novel saved me. At the time, I wasn't to know just how much.

We had a game we played of having little rolled balls of toilet paper which we had to jump and pop in the air vent holes, twelve of them. We could call out to one another through our doors. Someone would start the competition and away we'd go, six sets of jumping and landing legs times twelve. It was always the same person who called out, 'Finished!'

At our daily shower we all but one managed to confer about this consistent winner. Soon after a game was called, except this time all but one just stood and listened. Sure enough, we only heard ten landings sound. So we were ready with an eruption of boos and threats that we were going to get him as soon as we got out, since to cheat in these circumstances was, even to us youthful low-lifes, the pits.

I finished the novel the day I was released, reading the start of it again when my cell door opened and I was told my punishment was ended. I read another paragraph as my way of saying I had kind of won.

Back to my cell I found I had another cell-mate, a big friendly Maori. With brains too. He was from North Auckland, I forget where. He could sing and dance and tell jokes like no-one's business and we got on famously. The standover merchants were always doing their rounds for victims who could be parted with their tobacco issue and sweets. They never touched us and I think it was because of my cell-mate. Though I'd not for a moment have given in to them.

My cell-mate got hold of some home-brew, made from fermenting pumpkins and potatoes he told me, and obtained from the kitchen workers who hid their still up in the main kitchen ceiling. My friend kept tossing back glasses of this brew and soon he went from giggling to ugly. He picked the double bunk – I wasn't on it, fortunately – up off the floor with ease. I feared he was going to nut off and attack me. But the noise he was making soon had screws arriving and they carted him off for drying out in solitary, 'the Digger' as it was called.

I took a television crew back to Waikeria Borstal in 1993, nearly thirty years after I had been there. I remembered my cell location and I also remembered 'the Digger'. It was the strangest of feelings, of power, of triumph over life, to be in a position to bring documentary-makers back on a journey into my past. An inmate serving a solitary confinement spell overheard me and the television crew talking. I spoke to him through his door. He knew who I was and he amazed me by saying he'd just finished reading *Once Were Warriors* and he thought it was a good book. That was the strangest feeling, as though I was talking to the fifteen-year-old version of myself.

Not long after I arrived as a borstal inmate I was taken to the psychiatrist, a Dr Parker, who asked me various questions and then asked me to give my first impression. 'Confused,' I said.

'Oh, that's a very good answer,' said he. 'Anything else?'

'Yes. Could I ring my father?'

'Why is that?'

'I want to tell him I think I'm in the wrong place.'

His fixed smile fell away then. For some reason he thought I was trying to make a fool of him or was just getting smart, when I meant no such thing.

'You're in the right place, all right. This is a place for bad boys, like you. Like all of you. I have read your file and you ought be ashamed of yourself, of letting down your illustrious family name. I urge you to seek God's forgiveness.'

'God? But I don't believe in God.'

At that he jumped to his feet. His face had turned scarlet.

'How dare you!' he thundered. 'How dare you come into my office and tell me *you* don't believe in God. How would you know what you believe in, a mere fifteen-year-old boy? Now get out of my office!'

I have a thing about religious fundamentalists, especially one who has an eminent qualification in psychiatry. He should know better and be wiser and kinder. But then so should even troubled fifteen-year-olds, when I think what I was in borstal for.

The toughest boys in this borstal display themselves like dogs prancing amongst all the other dogs with wagging tails or tails between their legs. Practised facial expressions, swaggering walks. Like Jake the Muss in *Once Were Warriors*. Wake up angry, go all day angry, go to bed angry. Most of the tough guys are Aucklanders. They have the advantage of the big city aura over the smaller town tough guys, the rural area would-be tough guys. So they, the non-Aucklanders, spend their time trying to figure out how to climb that ladder. It's written in the silence of their permanently grim faces, those etched-in scowls. I've seen friendlier pig dogs up at the Kiel's house.

All new inmates are cleaners, no matter who you are. You find your own place in the pecking order. Pecking order is everything, since it affects you at mealtimes, in the shower-block. If you're a nothing you invite others to thump you, for no other reason than you're at the bottom and they are not. Maybe it's their warped way of expressing how glad they are that they're not at the very bottom. Some inmates have jobs outside the building. The borstal is sited on a large area of farmland, running its own cattle and sheep, and with a substantial vegetable growing area, which I will later work in and rather like. The inmates work normal hours outside, from 7.30 a.m. till 5 p.m., have early breakfasts, and consider themselves above the rest. They're reputed to earn high wages, several quid a week. They're all older boys, up to nineteen, maybe twenty.

There are fights all the time, most out of the eye of the warders, in the shower-block, the cleaning storage rooms, wherever budding angry young men can find to settle their differences the only way they have been taught – with their fists, and anything else that will achieve victory. The fights here I can see are for keeps. They hit harder, and use the boot, the knee.

I want a way out of this hell-hole. Try to use my supposed higher IQ, which is said to be on my file. But it means nothing here. Nor do they tell you what does count, what will get you out of here in the shortest possible time. You only know that you will be assessed by certain people at certain times. And the psychiatrist has not given me a very good start, so I'm informed by one of the officers. His recommendation is that a longer, rather than a shorter, period of time here would be in my best interests. Not a bad summary from a three-minute meeting. Thanks, Dr Parker.

You get to know the hierarchy very quickly. There's a guy called 'Sharkie', who's meant to be one of the toughest and a dead certainty to do time at 'the Mount', that is Mt Eden prison in Auckland. There's 'Hotstuff', named after the facial tattoo permanently etched down one side of his face of the comic-book character of the same name, a devil replete with grimacing expression and three-pronged pitchfork. There are youths built like the proverbial brick shit-houses, and mean ones with dangerous eyes, oozing hatred. Tattoos are the order of the day, everyone either wants one or is in the process of putting one on. This is a needle with cotton wound around the end to soak up the ink and you tap out puncture marks to follow the pen design. So many of them are sentimental: 'Mum' inscribed in a heart, when you can near guarantee the youth had a rotten mother. A girl's name. A gravestone with someone's name and the cause of death etched forever in skin. Buddy. Died Car Accident, 1964. Rest In Peace. I had a tattoo, and had it removed by a skin surgeon when I went to London many years later. I never liked tattoos, not from the day I had it done, nor on anyone else.

One morning a warder calls up to an inmate to take off his jacket since it's not cold and the jackets are only for cold days. For some reason the youth's reply, in a Liverpudlian accent, sticks with me. He says, 'Wha'? An' walk aroun' in the bleedin' nude?' I think it was his self-confidence, of being able to speak out like that in front of the entire borstal populace that made the memory stick.

After a few weeks I'm surprised I've settled in. Get a letter from Dad giving me 'official' permission to smoke, even though, he says, the legal age is sixteen. Dear Dad, so much out of touch. I am not in his custody, I belong to this institution. They let me smoke. I buy the prison issue plastic bag of tobacco with my first, lousy, pay. If I ever did time again, smoking is the one weakness I'd leave out. Just makes you desperate all the time, and for such a dubious pleasure.

There's been some trouble, in Auckland's Mt Eden Prison and a whole lot of adult prisoners have been transferred down to Waikeria. They've set aside a wing for them, and everyone's excited that their heroes are going to be living in the same building. Manned guard-houses have been erected overlooking the newly adapted wing, and we can see the guards through our cell window – they're armed, with rifles. This is exciting beyond belief. This is movie stuff and we're in it.

A Mt Eden contingent arrives and inmates are escorted down the walkway past the iron grille to our wing, which is crammed with hero-worshippers staring in awe at these hard-faced versions of what they, the youths, will become. They call out greetings, someone cheers, someone recognises an infamous face and greets him by name. The face turns and spits at the youth and growls at them all to, 'Fuck off, punk.'

Bubble burst. Hero spat in your face. Yeah, and fuck you too, mister. Get you one fuckin' day. The child, the youth, the man, they're all gonna get someone one day. Get everyone except themselves. To grow up, that is. But we don't see it. Those who didn't get spat on talk in excited disbelief at setting actual *eyes* on not just one but several convicted murderers.

''Magine that, murdering someone. Oh yeah! Just point that fulla out and *I'll* murder him! 'Magine doing life imprisonment, man. Oh man, oh man, think of the status you'd have. And who would dare fuck with you? What would you have to lose, of your remission time, if you had a fight? Why would anyone fuck with a lifer? Oh, to be that big.'

twelve

Borstal is borstal. It isn't so much interesting as demanding of your emotions as each and every one of the troubled inmates tries to exact his toll on part of your soul. He challenges you, with his eyes, his attitude, his every sly trick in the book to get a reaction from you so that his existence is acknowledged by whatever weight he wants to put on it. He fights you physically, abuses you, tries to make a fool of you, does make a fool of you, humiliates and taunts you, steals from you; and it's like a game everyone understands they're in, they have no choice. It's not the game of being incarcerated, but the game of the life you inherited, of being an emotional fuck-up before anything, of having inadequate social and intellectual skills. Even when you consider yourself to have a good mind, it doesn't have any sway in a place like a borstal. After all this is just a place where childish men still think being physically tough is everything, a training-ground for the next step up on the penal ladder, prison.

He wants your ear, your heart, your sympathy, your trust, your mistrust, your hatred, your love – all at once. He can never be satisfied, no matter what full aspect of yourself you might give him. Some you give an ear to, others you give your fists. They all get to have a chew on your soul regardless. They befriend you and then proceed to see how many people they can set up against you by lies and cunning. Childhood mess-ups getting revenge for their childhood. Low-life re-enactment of their parents and other adult role models they grew up with.

In the papers over the years I have seen the names of some of these teenagers who as adults committed heinous crime – murder, rape, armed robberies where innocents got shot, grievous bodily harm. I could have stood at one end of that borstal wing and pointed out who of those young men was going to grow up to be a total bad-arse. Evil has a way of showing itself even amongst a whole lot of pretenders.

From different cell-mates, from intimate conversations in there, I heard more of the stories of childhood that I'd heard at Hamilton Boys Home. Horror stories. Most of them were Maori, especially where gross violence was concerned. But just as many had tragedy written all over them, and so they fell too.

I had numerous fights. A lot of us did. They were vicious and you learned to adopt an immediate killer attitude or else you'd get the shit beaten out of you. Unless, that is, you were happy being bullied and being a lackey to everyone, which I was not. The contradiction of violence is that the same thing that condemns you to growth-less immaturity and causing others unnecessary suffering can also save you and help you keep your self-respect when you live amongst this kind.

I have a clear memory of feeling inadequate in the presence of a group of toughs who came from Panmure in Auckland. They were heavily tattooed, and swaggered around the place as if they owned it. To my eyes I thought they had self-confidence, as well a certain glamour. I guess I wanted to be like them, even though the leader was one of those evil types whose name I would see many years later in the paper receiving a lengthy sentence for a violent armed robbery that went wrong. If they came near me, or I happened on to them, I'd feel clammy and uncomfortable, as if my mere existence wasn't worth a shit. I now see that my reaction reflects a sense of worthlessness I have always had.

I was chosen to go to Hillary House, an open-style separate part of the borstal for those youths thought to have promise. When I informed a guy I had got to know well about it, he spat on the ground and called me that name: 'Wonk.' I was a goodie-goodie and from that moment on not worthy of respect or even talking to.

I attacked him. I wasn't having this. He was supposed to be my friend. We fought out in the middle of the ground floor and like the true coward he was, he didn't put up much of a fight. But it got me brought before the boss of the whole place whose title I forget, maybe it was the superintendent, who told me that normally the fight would have cost me my place at Hillary House, but since the reasons I gave him were understandable, he'd give me one chance. And do you know that same person tried to provoke me into another fight on the day I was going to Hillary House, anything to keep me back. It is a quality common to all losers: they want you to go down with their sinking ship.

Hillary House, named after Sir Edmund Hillary I guess. How ironic that as I wrote this I have attended Sir Edmund Hillary's eightieth birthday dinner by invitation from the Governor-General, the venue being at Government House. How ironic that the wording in the invitation should be, 'as a New Zealander who has made a significant contribution to this country' that they should apply to me. Not that borstal boy just turned sixteen back in 1966, surely he was never going to elevate himself that high? I remind myself of where I was and what I was, in gratitude that I didn't go the same way as that boy who tried his utmost to hold me back. I wonder where he is now, what he is.

Hillary House was run totally differently. The main borstal was old and had grey brick and steel, and lock-and-key and cells. But in Hillary House you had your own room with a desk and the place was new and clean. It had recreation rooms with large windows, a dining-room the same, classrooms that offered a wide variety of courses, and staff who talked to you more like equals. We even had optional military step-marching taught us by a rigid, but very nice, ex-British Army military man. We learned the slow march, and did the step that the Queen's guards do. It was quite fun once you got the hang of it, and yes you did feel a certain extra pride in yourself. The food was better, we could have more showers, better everything. I was never going to go back up to the main borstal.

I took a course in motor mechanics. Didn't really like it, but someone in authority persuaded me a trade would serve me well when I got out. Sat exams and scored highly, but I had no enthusiasm for how a car works, not then not now. The staff were better, more friendly, more helpful, and they were willing to talk to you about a concept you had never heard of back 'up top' as they called the main borstal – your future.

Music by this time had grabbed me as a true disciple and I couldn't hear enough of it. I wanted to learn music, but then again I didn't tell anyone as it might make me look a bit sissy. Odd how that feeling stuck for years. When I was writing *Once Were Warriors* whilst living in Central Hawkes Bay, and my wife was running the Pukeora Home for the Disabled, I was coaching a pretty mediocre local senior rugby team and having the odd game. But if any of my players turned up to go for a training run or for a beer, I'd see them coming up the drive and I had a blanket ready to throw over my typewriter, and I'd take off my classical record and put on a pop LP. I was thirty-eight then. I didn't want them to think that I, their (very ordinary) coach and rugby mate, was really an aspiring novelist who used to dream to himself of the big time and who got a lot of inspiration from classical music like Mahler, Rachmaninov, Schubert, and Chopin, and Russian choral music.

At Hillary House I hung around the best singers in the place, always Maori, who were usually the best guitarists too, and I could listen or sing along with them for as long as we could get. I would get in such an emotional state if I heard a piece of music on the radio in the kitchen I worked in, I'd start walking around in silent exclamation, jabbing my finger at everyone to shut up. One day I heard Stevie Wonder singing his version of 'Blowing in the Wind' and it was the most revelatory display of singing perfection I had ever heard. The teenage black American genius was doing stuff I never thought possible with the human voice. Whilst Stevie Wonder is a genius in his field, he stood on the shoulders of musical giants before him, like everyone does.

I'm walking around unable to believe my ears. Stevie is accompanied in parts by a singer with an older, deeper voice. At the end of the song I express my disbelief, I'm jabbering in astonishment, can't stop myself, which must have irritated a Maori guy for he called out, 'Shuddup!' I walked right over and punched him on the nose. And kept hitting him until he apologised for what he'd said about *my* music. For it felt as if he had insulted my very soul, my own inner being. Maybe it was a reaction to all those years of being told to shut up whenever I tried to express myself to Maori relations, the adults that is.

It was the first single record I bought when I got out. And I still listen to it, on a Stevie Wonder CD collection now, and after a thousand and more times of hearing it, I still have the same sense of astonishment and admiration at the heights a singing voice can reach.

In the summer I got a job working in the gardens. I loved every moment of it, the hard physical toil of picking tomatoes, weeding, barrowing manure, digging and bagging potatoes. I loved seeing the corn sprouting and the huge marrows on the ground; onions dug up and spread out to dry. One of the screws in charge was the happiest man I ever met. He was kind to all of us, content in the job he loved best, and so glad to see not just myself but quite a few other boys converted to this simple joy of seeing a fecund earth reward hard labours.

I was always the last to knock off work, and none dared called me a crawler as they usually would. They were both scared and anyway knew that I just loved the work and the pleasure of being outside. Suntanned and muscles developing, I put this hard work to good use when we had an athletics day of the combined borstal, Hillary House, and the building opposite us which was the Detention Centre, for short-term young criminals who had to endure three months of harsh discipline. We'd witness them standing outside to rigid attention for an hour at a time, running on the spot for another hour, or on hands and knees through their plate glass windows polishing floors.

Once we had a cricket outing to Tokanui Mental Hospital. The psychiatrist in charge was a Maori, one of the illustrious Bennetts. He was the man responsible for getting the law against Maori women drinking on licensed premises overturned after an unsavoury incident in Rotorua where he and and his wife were hotel guests but only he could lawfully be served an alcoholic drink. We were visiting this hospital to play a team of patients at cricket.

It is imprinted on my brain, the ghastly sight of a huge Maori woman, hardly twenty, standing on a bank overlooking the cricket pitch and hiking up her dress to reveal nothing underneath as she proceeded to leap up and down in mad glee, the spread of old brick buildings behind her. The wafts of the insane on the breeze, of bad hygiene, of the odour that madness gives off is like nothing else.

There was the middle-aged Pakeha wicketkeeper who muttered vicious obscenities behind us as we batted. Yet whenever we turned to remonstrate he would give this huge smile and laugh hysterically. There was another, a middle-aged white guy, who when in bat stopped halfway down the pitch and sat down and started talking to his ghosts. It was like a surreal movie to my eyes. I realised that fate deals some people a most awful hand. We were about to leave when one of the patients approached me. I recognised him: he was from Whaka. Never have I seen more plaintive eyes as we greeted each other and he immediately spilled forth with the plea that he was put in this place for nothing, when he had been previously an inmate at another boys' home and the reasons had been disciplinary. I knew him reasonably well and he hadn't seemed anything but sane. I got the call to get on the bus back, so we shook hands and that was it. I don't know if he was kept there unjustly or not, nor of his ultimate fate.

One athletics day I got to taste sweet success against competition that was mostly boys older and stronger than me. There was a guy with a fearsome reputation by the surname of Tua, a large, powerfully built Maori who was expected to clean up in most events this day. Except he didn't. I did. I even beat him at the shotput, though he won the discus. I won the sprints, I won the 440 yards, and the long jump – but not the high jump, and the hop-step-and-jump – and I anchored several relay teams to victory. It was the most glorious day of my life. I felt ten foot tall. Found I could go up to anyone and converse, be they toughs from 'up top' or officers or even a couple of the wives of staff who had come out to watch the events. Nothing and no-one scared me.

I got a whole heap of treats as prizes accumulated for my winning events, Christmas cake and tobacco and tailor-made cigarettes and sweets and chocolate bars. Then I got more goodies for over-all winner of the entire day. Gave most of it away. Couldn't get to sleep for hours that night as I lay in bed wallowing in it. Wrote a letter to Dad to boast of my achievement and he promptly wrote back to say how proud he was of me and perhaps I should give some thought to applying that talent to other aspects of my life.

There were of course fights at Hillary House. Though you knew the consequence was immediate return to 'up top'. Still, young men will fight regardless of the consequences. I had a fight in the kitchen one day that changed my perception of yet another young man, from the bush town of Murupara, whom we all assumed was one of the toughest amongst us. I was serving food from behind the hatch and a little Pakeha did the set-up by giving lip and when I reacted his big Maori friend was around my side confronting me about 'getting smart' to his mate. I was so angry at the set-up I cleaned the guy up in no time; watched his eye swell, then the other, as I peppered him with punches. It was suggested that this victory made me the top dog in the place. The thought did thrill me, a mere sixteen-year-old, of course it did. But I was no standover merchant, and I hated bullying. I also knew that inside myself I could never wear this mantle comfortably. Much too sensitive, I could easily be upset by a cruel, personal remark regardless of the fact that I could physically take care of the person. I had my blushing problem too, so that whenever the attention went on me for any reason (with the exception of that winning athletic day and I don't understand why it should be the exception), I would be reduced by an acute self-consciousness that still afflicts me, if to a lesser degree, today.

One morning I walk into the kitchen, say good morning to Mrs Fry, our boss, but she is grave-faced and she asks me, 'Are you any relation to Oliver Duff?' Yes, he's my grandfather. 'To tell you the truth, when you mentioned that a while ago I didn't believe you. I'm afraid it's bad news.' And she pushed a newspaper over to me.

Oliver Duff had died peacefully in his sleep at his farmlet cottage in Landsdowne Valley, Christchurch, aged 83. He left a widow, Ngaere, and four children, Gowan, Roger, Theo and Alison. (And a grandson had an inordinate fixation about you, Oliver, who had no idea he had been blessed by your literary genes, but certainly inherited intelligence. Yet I was in here, a penal institution, shaming that man's proud name, or so I believed at the time.) I just felt this special closeness to my grandfather. I had long been aware that I used his illustrious name to boost my own stocks with whoever I wanted to impress, but at the same time was also a youth who had done nothing himself to earn anything even remotely similar, or just a hope, of respect.

The boss and the minister, Manu Bennett, now Sir Manu, were happy to make arrangements for me to fly to Christchurch for the funeral. I was anyway due for release in the next few weeks. Well, I don't know what happened, maybe it was tension or grief, or just my natural aggressiveness, but I got into a fight with a boy over the dartboard, and that put paid to my funeral trip. The authorities couldn't be seen to be not punishing me for fighting, when the normal punishment was return to the borstal and your release date put back.

Dad visited me soon after the funeral and apologised for not thinking to let me know. I still feel somewhat of an emptiness at not being there to at least say farewell to one of this country's finest literary, journalistic figures, and to show my grandfather my love. He had OBE after his name for services to New Zealand literature and journalism. I now have an MBE for services to New Zealand literature. I accepted the award in honour of my grandfather's memory – I was worthy of the literary inheritance he gave me. I also accepted because it is a constant source of irony that I, a former guest of one of Her Majesty's prisons, should be described on my award certificate as 'Her Majesty's trusty and beloved servant'.

So my release, whilst it felt wonderful, was tempered somewhat by an uneasiness that I had let Grandad down by not having the self-control to hold my temper. But it was hardly going to be the last time.

thirteen

All those dreams of going home to the big welcome, of Mister Tough Guy who's done his borstal time. Who else has? Only me. Praise me, admire me, envy me. (Love me. Give me self-confidence – please!) The reality is, you've been dropped off in a town called Kihikihi, the nearest to the borstal, by a screw who shakes your hand and says he'll see you again no doubt, with an all-too-knowing smile. And he drives off, leaving you alone to wait for your bus, first to Hamilton, then on to Rotorua. You're free and yet you're as scared as when you first arrived in that place some ten months ago, if not more so.

Scared of what, though? You don't know. Only that you feel vulnerable, hear every passing vehicle as a startling noise, a possible threat, see every face that calls in to this little country store as looking at you, and knowing. You see meaning in those faces; they are what you are not and never will be. You realise you've been kind of safe and insulated back there, surrounded by your own inadequate kind. This is real life, these are real people, and you're not sure you're going to cope. If I had found somewhere to cry, I'd have gone and let it all out.

This is not how it's supposed to be, not a soul to proclaim your newly-freed state to, your joy. No bustling town or city shopping centre of normal citizens to throw yourself back into. Any moment there'll be tumbleweed blowing down this deserted stretch of tiny town street. Or else a delegation of pointing, yelling locals, telling you to get the hell out of their one-horse town. At last, here comes the bus.

A fairly long wait at the Hamilton bus terminal. I know the town quite well from my previous stay here, yet I sit for some time at the terminal, assuming I need permission to go wandering. Waiting for an order to do something. Then it occurs to me that I'm free. I'm free! I go for a walk through the city. It isn't very interesting. Drab, unimaginative architecture, and grand reflections of Kiwi pragmatism everywhere. Even a newly released borstal boy can intuitively see this. I only want to shout out to someone that I'm free. I'm free! But then again, am I?

Back to Rotorua, where my father is waiting at the terminal for me. I pray like anything he doesn't expect me to be doubled by him on his ridiculous bike. It would be just like him, and to stem my protests by asking me, 'What does it matter what other people think?' He had no idea; he didn't understand that to this son the world consisted of countless judging eyes on him. Thank goodness he's walked into town, is of course glad to see me. We go and have a bite to eat somewhere, and he lets me order what I wish. We walk home, talking all the way. We've always talked, no matter what age I've been.

Home feels strange. The same, but different. The kitchen has the same old formica table, the same chairs sitting by the L-shaped windows looking out at the hedge and the neighbours' houses beyond. Dad's books, our books, are where they always were. The bathroom is still the bath with no shower attachments, and that little profile drawing I did of Davy Crockett's head in a racoon hat with tail is still on the wall outside the bathroom. I can't smell my mother, nor that accompanying array of pungent and sweet odours of her cooking – those pots of boiling pig bones, brisket bones, fish heads. Yet for some reason I'm thinking of those very smells that have been absent for several years. My siblings still remaining at home are my youngers and they greet me awkwardly. Nick is in Christchurch in his first year at university, Kevin is married and also living in Christchurch. Josie has her own home.

I woke during that first night home thinking I was still in my room at Hillary House, and was groping around to see where the sound of snoring was coming from. It was my brothers. Up in the morning, and it's so quiet compared to what I'd known. I went into town. Feeling self-conscious and not at all the returning young ex-con hero, or whatever notion it was that I was supposed to feel. Wanted people to notice me, ask me where I'd been, or acknowledge and praise me for being now a fully fledged borstal boy. Yet another part of me wanted to turn around and flee back home.

In town I approached a main street intersection and saw a mate of mine who called out a greeting. But I suddenly became so afraid to face him I turned and walked the other way, back home. For several weeks I could barely leave the house. My mates the Kiel brothers from up the road were amongst the few who called in that I could face, the others being Mark Takarangi, my close mate from Whaka, and my cousin Koro. Even then I could hardly find words to converse; it was as if I had suddenly realised that I was on the outer margins. Not just because of the borstal sentence, and before that the boys' home, but me the person. The flawed, frightened, besieged personality that was Alan Duff. I reckoned everyone could see inside my soul and see what I was. What saved me from going completely mad was listening endlessly to music, not least 'Blowing in the Wind' by Stevie Wonder and practising singing it in near perfect imitation. I'd get hot and cold shivers, go into the bathroom and stare at my face till it changed to this caricature, this grotesque, seemingly truthful image of what I truly was – some kind of gross misfit. I masturbated till the damn thing near fell off and fell deeper and deeper into this mind abyss.

I was officially out on parole. Weekly reportings to a probation officer, a nice Maori man, and sometimes an equally amiable Pakeha woman. My difficulty was in the circuitous route my shyness had me choosing to get to this town office location. I had no idea of what I wanted, this inordinately seething youth of sixteen. Then my oldest brother Kevin rang and suggested I should come down to Christchurch where he could get me work, and I could live with him and his wife. I was on that train to Wellington and the ferry to Christchurch in a flash, with borrowed money from Dad, and the lie that the probation people had given me permission to go as long as Kevin could confirm he had full-time work for me – which Kevin did, but by phoning Dad, not the probation officer.

It was heaven. I got on well with my brother, though he did have a few of his own troubles, one of them being he acted like a man of thirty, not of nineteen or twenty. Yet he displayed outbursts of childish behaviour that gave him away, especially when he drank. Not that I'm judging those outbursts for a moment – he was entitled to be his age. Except he was never his true age, not emotionally. Our mother had taken that right from him by the burden she put on his shoulders of having to take responsibility for us, his younger siblings, whilst she indulged herself in her drunken, violent rages.

I had seen quite a bit of Kevin and his wife Carol when I was in Christchurch at high school. I had been best man at his wedding. My sister-in-law was a sweet person and I settled in immediately. The job Kevin had arranged was as a labourer at McKendries Concrete Products. It was hard work and involved a lot of heavy lifting, but I enjoyed it enough. What's more, I enjoyed the freedom from not having a probation officer to report to every week and hearing the same old lecture which we both knew was just going through the motions.

Have you ever seen a probation officer? They are world-weariness epitomised. They realise that no-one can change the young persons they have to deal with. They've known little but disappointment. Even the tiny handful of people they vested time and energy in, thinking they at least might have hope, turned out just as bad as the others. One crude line of my poetry keeps coming back: 'How could I fight a damage unknown, when childhood's murderous seed was sown?'

The boys I had gone to school with were all still at school. I thought we could pick up the friendships where we left off, but both sides found it uncomfortable. I was a working man, earning a wage, going to the pub with my big brother. They were still in shorts, and anyway going in completely different directions to me. A few close ones stayed close, though.

My two work-mates were Maori from the North Island and they treated me well. When I told them I was actually here against my parole conditions, they used to tease me by yelling warnings during the day that the cops were here! My first Thursday payday – which was the following week – the Maori guys took me to the pub where my brother joined up with us. This is six o'clock closing, with not long to go before the country's most monumental social change of licensing hours extended to 10 p.m. God saved us from becoming a nation of flush-faced swillers! But there I was, wallowing in being in a pub for that one single hour on a Thursday after work, tipping beer after beer down us, with the sole object of getting drunk quickly. Now, I like to get half-drunk a little more slowly.

I recall my changing accents depending on who I was with. My Maori work-mates I aped, just as I did with any Maori. With non-Maori I spoke differently. I guess it's from growing up as neither one nor the other.

I saved money during my stay at Kevin's. Then the probation office sent someone knocking on my door. I had broken my parole conditions and I was very likely to be returned to borstal. It seemed so unfair, though I knew I had deceived them in coming to Christchurch. I paid my own way back to Rotorua and when I appeared before a magistrate I presented my savings bank book as evidence that I had been a good citizen. Saved by my savings book, as the magistrate decided to give me one last chance. I asked to go back to Christchurch, but he said I was to stay in my father's custody.

The probation officer arranged a job interview for me at Rotorua Sheetmetal & Insulation, where the work ethic was introduced to me in the form of my self-confident English working-class boss, Terry Fitzgerald. It was a job, a place, and a people that would have a lifetime influence on my thinking.

Insulation is what is required on any form of heating to prevent and lessen heat loss. That's boiler-houses and pipelines. Commercial cold usage pipelines also need insulating to keep the cold in. In both instances a material is wrapped around the pipe or vessel, be it fibreglass wool or polystyrene foam, and metal cladding is fixed over that to protect it. Since pipes go in all sorts of directions, including 90° bends and 180° ones too, and reduce in size as different pipe diameters are required, the size of the insulation also reduces. The pipes have finishing points at, for instance, valves, which require the cladding end to be fixed onto a cone. The bends have to be marked out using set mathematical calculations, which are not too complicated once you learn. It's rather satisfying to see the finished product, of rolled and riveted segments joined like a crayfish tail wrapping around an insulated pipe bend. This was basically our job.

I arrive with the attitude, you better treat me right or I'm out of here. So I refused to make the boss and his partner a cup of tea in the first week because they didn't say please. Well, the boss soon fixed that. He made tea himself and kept me working during the tea break. When I protested he said I could either accept his way of doing things or piss off. I accepted, if sulkingly. He told me early in the piece he had the answer for stroppy boys like me: hard work. 'Duffy, I'll work you so hard you won't have one of your arguments left in you come Wednesday of any week. And within a year I'll have you worn out by the Monday night, so the rest of us get some peace around here!'

Terry was a great boss and one of the most significant influences on my life. He taught me the work ethic and led by example. Of course when a group of his teenage workers got together we used every trick to skive off work, but ever so surely I was becoming a lover of hard work. I became one of Fitzy's best, and could install calico-covered fibreglass pipe section on to any job lot faster than anyone going. Except him. He wasn't going to let 'his boy' beat him, not yet!

I was earning a wage, being forced to understand the work ethic when part of me was wanting to stay the irresponsible, lazy child. But having to work with older, mature men, many of them Maori, who took their jobs seriously and did not abide slackers, was good for me. We worked hard and drank hard, that's how it was. I have only fond memories of those days, of working and socialising with real men, honest men who work with their hands.

I'm still not seventeen and we have a job that will take two days in a town called Whakatane. Do a twelve-hour day, check into a hotel which to me is the height of luxury, shower and change 'into decent clothes' the boss has ordered, because we're going to have a few beers in the lounge bar then we're dining in the restaurant. Oh, this is pretty sophisticated stuff for the lad. I've cracked it here. We have a great night, don't know how the boss manages to find a level of conversation with me. Only know that he seems to have enjoyed our night. We go off to bed and he asks if I would like a nightcap. A nightcap? No, I'm not cold. But where do I find this nightcap in my room? I search under my pillow and he is standing in my doorway laughing his head off. I join him in having the nightcap, I think it was Drambuie, and I really enjoyed it. Back to being Master Sophisticate.

I saw the world of big business, without really understanding what it was, only that the pulp and paper mill at Kawerau was a huge, sprawling, smoking, steaming, machine-running complex producing our paper. We were there for the massive boilers that needed to be re-insulated. Half-mile-long steam pipes that had to be lagged and clad in metal whilst they were still going; one touch and you knew all about it. We worked up in ceilings, in high temperatures, and extremely tight spaces getting pipes insulated, dragging a small plank across ceiling beams and trusses to lie on and get those pipes covered. But it was satisfying, you knew you'd done a fair day's work for a fair day's pay.

I spent days that became several weeks spreading a black oil-based waterproofing substance called Flintcoat over our calico-covered and wire-netting wrapped pipes. I had never till now seen the sight of hundreds going to and from a twenty-four-hour-a-day shift cycle as I did at the Kawerau paper mill. Saw trade unionism and how it had gone too far, with inflated pay demands and gained conditions and payments out of all proportion to their productivity output, and failing to recognise the first principles that he who risks his capital deserves the greatest rewards. A worker after all has nothing at risk except their work time in any given week. I was quickly being educated by my boss to understand that employers had to make money too, that the smaller employers like himself put their houses on the line for their business and yet are first victims in the process when a business fails.

Under school classrooms, on your back in the dirt, insulating the pipework to keep those young bodies above me warm. Crawl in with not even sitting-up room at 7.30 in the morning, come out at lunch break and finally out at five or six o'clock at night, or longer if the boss could get the flood lights hooked up. You hated it and you thought of every trick, every lie, form of false sickness, a death in the family – anything to get you out of it. But with your boss cunningly dropping you off at the job, you had no-one to lie to. There were just those endless stretches of pipes to lag and a hard, stony, lumpy ground to drag yourself over as you reached up in the tight space and put on another section of pipe lagging, sloshed the joint with glue, rubbed it down flat, on to the next.

To lag the bends you had to cut segments of the tubular fibreglass section, so they looked like wedges, which of course gave you the inner and outer radiuses of the bend. If there was a class above you it was interesting listening to the exchanges, to the rattle of thirty or so chairs at end of class, to girls' giggles and boys' muttered cheek. If there was an empty class above me I'd sing my heart out, imagining myself to be famous one day. But my writing became my way of being the singer that I wasn't. My old work-mates of those early days tell me that even then, at seventeen, eighteen, I would tell them I was going to be a writer one day. For some strange reason I cannot recall having this desire.

What I wanted most of all was confidence. I had long known it, but by seventeen it had become a burning obsession, one that turned in on itself and made me so self-conscious I could hardly face any group of more than a few people without feeling panic-stricken and numb with shyness. How it killed me inside being like this, and how it has taken its toll on me for years and years. I've attacked it with lies and aggression and dope and booze and bluff and crime and sheer calamitous behaviour, and nothing worked. I gave myself to the age of twenty-one, when by some preordained miracle my shyness would disappear and this new Alan Duff would blossom. I counted down every day, since most days there was an incident of acute embarrassment.

So many of the fights I got into came about not from my hot temper, but from either feeling hurt at being humiliated, or covering up that most awful, giddy sense of shyness. It's like the world's suddenly grabbed you and is shaking you in taunting contempt, and you want to lash out at it in fear, then anger, that you should be afflicted with this inexplicable reduction of self. Or you wake up feeling awful, feeling such a low person you can't go out and face anyone. Not even the losers you live with. The only way to stop this feeling is to take it out on someone, pick a fight, win the fight, feel good, feel like someone. It lasts several days that feeling of the victorious.

After work I'd often go out to Whaka to catch up with my old mates, many of whom were still at school doing Sixth Form. I'd have to wait till after dark before I could face them, for I couldn't stand them looking at me, couldn't stand arriving and getting off the bus to a group of them sitting there at our usual gathering-place waiting to laugh at me, the furious blusher. And being Maori, they generally did not seem to suffer from blushing, not unless their darker skin hid it. They'd laugh at this neon face glowing scarlet red. So I started waiting till dark before I caught the bus, or I'd get off the stop before, or maybe two stops back. Thus I made the first fatal step a lot of shy people make – you look upon the entire world in terms of what threat it might offer your shy existence. It becomes nothing less than a curse, an ever-closing noose around your neck, and I would wish it upon no-one.

I could feel I myself moving to the outer. I hated this inexorable backward shuffling of myself, unable to prevent this shifting further and further away from the world of social intercourse that I was crying out to be part of. I felt neither Maori nor Pakeha, just a wretched loner who had this 'condition', this state of mind that put him in a panic at the very thought of trying to move to more stimulating, more person-ally achieved social company. I was screaming inside to be part of the wider world, knowing that I had something to contribute, and yet feeling so worthless. Whenever I did make what to me was a mon-umental effort to join the wider world, just one look turned me into dust again and I floated off like dust, into the background.

I just stood in the shadows, aching to be part of the normal world, but every time I tried it was unbearable. So many times I literally fled at the sight of people. What a curse it is to be forever on your guard against embarrassment, shyness, and self-consciousness that is ready to swallow you up at any moment, knowing every social situation is a potential bomb that could go off in your face. That's why alcohol seems the answer, because it appears to give you the confidence you lack.

But you still end up finding your own inadequate kind. You seek and find relief, a false comfort in being with others who are like you. Except mix this condition up with alcohol and you have anger spilling out, and with it that other false promise of being drunk – you're Superman. Superman who not only wants to fight the world, but thinks he can conquer it while he's at it. When, really, he is just another undignified, violent sight of messed-up youth throwing punches and having punches thrown back at him by equally messed-up human beings.

We brawled, we argued, we started fights over unbelievably pathetic things. We went at each other exactly the same as our parents and aunties and uncles and adult cousins had done, and our grandparents before that, and our ancestors before them, slugging each other, screaming and yelling with hatred, caring not for who we were affecting, since the afflicted don't know how to care. I can look at this because I had a father who did care, who used to ask me in his open-mouthed, ceaseless astonishment, how we youths could behave in such a violent way. Especially me, since I had grown up with a mother he'd have thought would have turned me off violence for life. Sorry, Dad, not how it works. Reality. And one which more Maori than anyone get as their behavioural legacy.

And here we were, the young imitators of what we had grown up witnessing. If you have a dispute, settle it with your fists. If someone looks at you the wrong way, hit him. If he's said something about you, hit him. If he's said something about one of your relations or your friends, hit him. Hit him for the smallest reason and question not. Just glory in it, that you hit him before he could hit you, or you hit him harder than he hit you. If it's your girlfriend and she upsets you, hit her. Teach her a lesson. Teach everyone and anyone a lesson for daring to challenge you, hurt you, wound you.

I am not a coward now nor have I been for many years. But the accusation remains and shall stay as a lifetime pronouncement that Alan Duff has been cowardly and lowly. It is inexcusable, not least that in my case because I had a father who was vehemently against violence. I'm sorry to say his teachings took a long time to reach all but two of his children. One fact is certain. There was hardly a house of a Maori relative that we children went to where we didn't witness violence. Domestic violence and violence against children. And violence between the adults. But we have to break the cycle. Violence is cowardly unless used in self defence.

fourteen

I worked for Terry Fitzgerald from age sixteen till nineteen, the last year of that self-employed. When I was seventeen I had the good luck for someone in the Whaka Senior A team to pull out of a rugby trip to Fiji, and they asked me if I'd like to take the player's place. So in 1968, the year after I got out of borstal, I was having my first trip out of New Zealand – to play rugby, my beloved game.

I went away for a fortnight in the company of men, most many years older than me and far more rugged. I had an insatiable curiosity for my fellow man (and woman) and in hindsight this rugby trip had quite an impact on my perceptions of the ordinary – and yet extraordinary – mainly working-class rugby man. It showed me that the basic New Zealand rugby man is a good person, a 'decent bloke'.

Having a Fijian uncle and first cousins who were half-Fijian, I naturally felt an empathy with the Fijian people. We played two games on the island of Kandavu, a remote place with generator-driven electric power and very basic living conditions, where I came close to drowning whilst snorkelling when I got caught in a rip and had to be saved by one of our prop forwards who never let me forget it for years afterwards!

At a party in Suva after losing a game against the Fijian Army I was standing in the sitting-room of our Fijian host when I saw some photographs of… Could this be right? That was my Uncle Abe and his wife, my Aunty Margaret, Mum's sister, and there in another photo I saw the smiling faces of my wonderful Fijian cousins! Turned out our party host was none other than the brother of my Uncle Abe.

Our last game was in Nadi. I marked a guy who went on to represent Fiji and he so cleaned me out with a cheeky, dazzling display of running and side-stepping and three tries, I felt like giving up the game on the spot! They caned us.

Waiting back home in New Zealand for me was my girlfriend, who would later bear our two children. We lived with my father for a while and then got our own flat. My de facto relationship was typical of two youngsters who ought not be living together. We were parents when I was nineteen, she was seventeen. We'd gone out together for two years. From totally different backgrounds and of totally different personalities, we were never going to work out, not if we'd met ten or fifteen years later. Not ever. And if there hadn't been children born of this relationship then it would not get a mention. Except for me to say sorry.

I tried to set up a business making chillybins in a garage with a mate. We were a hopeless team, me the determined but shy individual who was never going to go out and sell our product even if we did have a saleable finished item instead of these crude constructions of foil-taped bits of polystyrene. My partner, an oddball ex-bikie, was tall and skinny. His cheaply attractive wife had joined them to the Seventh Day Adventist Church. I remember when the church ex-communicated them when they found out they were 'living in sin', and my mate's wife telling how the church elders grilled her for several hours on every explicit, lurid detail of her sex life. Did she *really* commit the act from behind, as dogs do? How? Describe this to us. How these pervert hypocrites must have enjoyed grilling this hapless woman.

I'd always wanted to work for myself, to decide my own destiny from my own efforts. I thought Auckland would be my best option for a new life, starting as an insulation contractor, but maybe getting into other things that were hinting vaguely there at the back of my mind. Maybe I'd join a band as a vocalist.

With a pregnant wife, and me the shy young man with dreams too big for such a personality, we set off for the big smoke... in a New Zealand Road Services bus. Once we found a base in Auckland we had a son, a beautiful son. I was there at his birth and whilst he'll read these words with understandable scepticism, he was the love of my life. I had work in the insulation business and we had a very nice rented flat at St Heliers. I intended going out on my own as a contractor as soon as possible. One of my first priorities in acquiring this new way of life up here in sophisticated Auckland was to enjoy a few of the finer things, like red wine. And as my income was limited until I got contract work for myself, there was only one way to get the money to buy the wine: work. I got a job cleaning offices at night, demeaning work and most unsuitable, if it hadn't been for my obsessive desire to be socially upwardly mobile! I didn't last too long at this charade, but did acquire a taste for red wine.

I'd always wanted to sing. So, I put an advertisement in the paper inviting interest from anyone wanting to form a band. The response was enormous; already I felt giddy at the prospects. This is me! I felt. Offering myself as lead vocalist I got a band together. And the minute we started our first rehearsal I realised this was all I wanted to do, be creative, make music. Being an insulation sheet-metal worker wasn't me – this was. The band was going to cure me of every ill, from the shyness to the deeper down troubles that used to haunt my every nightly dream and have me grinding my teeth in my tormented sleep, cure me of my aggression.

●

Music. It claimed me at an early age. It comes from my paternal grandmother and from the Maori side as a whole. Though I am not particularly musical, not in an original sense. I couldn't compose a line of song, and if I do have a good singing voice it is not for a moment original. Not like the American black singers. I just copy, but boy I love to listen.

At Whaka I'm outside the Geyser Hotel public bar on a Saturday. People are arriving, and not necessarily to pick up their husband or their father drinking inside that bar as the hour heads towards six o'clock. For once my mother and her card-playing, surreptitious drinking friends aren't parked on the grass islands in the middle of the wide road. Otherwise they'd be drunk by now, an embarrassing distraction from the singing started up in there, the Geyser Hotel.

'Silent Night. Holy night. Allllll is calm. All is bright.' A chorus of powerful men's voices ring out. Outside, the gathering nods and smiles and listens in awe. These are the Whaka returned servicemen, and my Uncle Tupu, I'm proud to tell anyone, is one of the lead voices. Hear that voice? That's my uncle. They've got five-part harmony going and their every sung line is perfectly timed. They bring a boy out in goosebumps.

'All is calm. All is bright.' So are the admiring eyes of all these people come here specifically to listen to this. People are mouthing along with the song, or singing it quietly, not daring to compete against it. A couple of kuia sit in the council-erected shelter on the road island, listening with closed eyes, their old bodies gently swaying. Ah, these are their boys singing. An old man stands rigidly erect, supported by his carved walking stick, his tokotoko. He has a grey moustache, and eyes that are bright. His posture is of knowing the magnificence of your own kind singing, expressing themselves in such glorious form.

A police car pulls up and several cops get out. They stand and listen as the song completes, and they join everyone outside – and inside too – in applauding. The singing has spread grins and happiness everywhere, and I the boy am in such a state. I am one word away from crying. None of us want it to end.

The cops go inside the bar, we can see the tops of their helmets through the high windows. Friendly hands pat them. We can see drunk men's smiles. Good drunks. Calmed, put at peace by the singing of men. Only a fool would cause trouble in there.

The bell goes. It's six o'clock, no more orders. Men will have stocked up beforehand. And it being Saturday, they have had since eleven in the morning, or whenever after that they arrived, to have their fill. They sing another song, in between gulping down their own last beers on these premises. I know the inside of this place. My uncle is barman. It has a long horseshoe shape of varnished wood and the beer glasses are filled with tap-guns. The ceiling is panelled timber, so the acoustics are very good. The room reverberates with the lines of an Italian song learned by these men when they were at war with those allies of the German enemy. Would make any Italian heart proud too.

When finally they have to leave the place, even the police can't stretch the time any further. It's twenty-five to seven, which is considered *really late*. Men emerge blinking at the sunlight, near to a man wearing a glad smile of appreciation. The singers emerge like returning heroes and the crowd lets out with cry and applause and begs them to sing a song standing up there on the concrete rampway. The cops make sure everyone is officially off the licensed premises so they're covered too, and the drinkers join the sober gathering looking up at the confident, smiling Maori men lined along the rampway. Most of them are big, powerful men, but some of them are going to seed. Not that they care and not that it matters.

They sing everyone's favourite, 'Come Unto Me.' Kuru Waaka leads off, joined by my Uncle Tupu. Their voices and that of a man called Teddy Keepa are the most prominent ones. You can hear them above the others. These are proud men, former warriors now turned their talents to voice expression. They are men of love, just as some can be men of darker passion, of angry fists, of mindless, unseeing violence. Not now, though. Not as they sing of God's love, meaning their love, meaning your love, my love, our love, all love wherever men and women and children gather. This is what they represent. That is what they're saying: 'Come unto me and I will give you love.'

I heard these same voices singing at funerals, at the tangi they held at the meeting-house over the bridge. The women, too, had voices that were every bit as powerful. I remember Mary Royal at my brother's and two first cousins' tangi leading a most poignant farewell hymn, how her voice rang clear of everyone else's and when she was joined by the masses her voice lifted even higher, just like Mahalia Jackson, as if nothing less would do. Bennie and Tatai and Mrs Murray had voices from heaven too. I have heard them at parties, in rugby clubrooms, in bars, in Maori meeting-houses, in the Whaka baths, at gravesides, walking along in the steaming thermal activity, these wonderful singing voices.

When we were both living at home my brother Kevin kept a Top Twenty chart, the hit parade line-up of mostly American entertainers. In those days Elvis ruled the roost. We loved him, we knew dozens of his songs off by heart. My brother adopted the sultry, sullen Elvis pouting look. And he acquired that straddle-legged stance of Presley's, and the kiss curl, and the turned up shirt collar. I thought my brother *was* Elvis at times. I mixed him up with reality. I'd come into a room and get confused at seeing him, wondering – and hoping – my true brother was Elvis Presley. Only problem was, I sang better than he did when it came to Elvis, as Kevin wasn't the world's best singer. We had posters of Elvis and Fabian on our shared bedroom walls along with Connie Francis and the actor Sal Mineo, whom my brother also bore an uncanny resemblance to.

My musical revelation happened at my Uncle Tupu's. He's bought a television set, the first in Whaka. Our telephone has rung several times to tell us. We can go out and watch it if we want. I'm on my bike that evening. It's a couple of miles ride. I love biking. It's free and fast.

Uncle's sitting-room is full – packed with his family and relations and neighbours, and I'm amongst the kids having to peer through the sitting-room window because I can't get in. Then I see this huge Negro woman appear on screen. She has a broad face and lips like large soup spoons, especially the bottom lip which is more like a paddle. She starts singing, with her eyes closed. And something immediately comes over me.

I push my way to the door and wriggle inside the room, all aglow with that soft, magical light of black and white television in our lives for the first time. And that Negro woman singing, Lord is she singing.

'Who is it?' I ask.

'Shush!' my aunty tells me.

'Who is it?' I just have to know, even though Aunty Baby might tell me to get out if I can't shut up. But for some reason she doesn't chide me further. We all keep watching. Witnessing, more like it. For me it is a witness of – and I cannot figure this out – myself. It's as if I am what I have dreamed. No, that's not it. It's as if I am finally being given an answer to some artistic question that has been in my head for years. Inside me I was saying, 'Yes. Yes, this is it. This is it. I know where she'll be going next, I can hear it coming. I understand this, the emotion, the reasons, the music.'

And sure enough, she starts climbing into this great flowering rising note. I'm so taken I want to scream and cry and run around in circles, I want to grab someone who might be able to tell me what it is I'm experiencing. It is what I imagine a religious conversion experience is like. Except this is reality, of hearing a gospel singer named Mahalia Jackson.

My uncle has a superb voice. So immediately Mahalia is finished I'm watching him. He too is numb with awe and he knows I love my music for he says, 'Pretty good, eh, nephew?' Oh yeah, pretty good all right. From then on, I've got my eyes peeled for when Mahalia is next on this miracle communication box. She's on every fortnight. I think I have that right. I only know that I will bike out to Whaka in the pouring rain if I know I'm going to see and hear Mahalia Jackson sing. A telephone-call from my uncle, or one of my cousins and I'm over there as fast as I can pedal. I wish Dad would buy a television set, if just for Mahalia's performances.

I love music so much I use people just to be in hearing of it. I remember a frail, nervous boy at my primary school, I think he was Jewish. He played the piano at school assembly one day. I befriended him immediately and found out he was bullied by other boys. So I offered him my protection, in return for me getting to go to his house to hear him practise piano.

Every snatch of radio issuing from someone's house was a potential capture of my ear. Passing a church on a Sunday, I'd stop and listen to the choir. Even the traditional Maori waiata chants, in half notes, out at Whaka, at funerals, on doorsteps, under Whaka verandahs, in the baths, they attracted my ear. I might be hanging around the meeting-house with my cousins and about to head to the river, or somewhere, when I'd be stopped by the sound of chanting from an old kuia, or one of the old men. I'd tell my mates I'd catch up with them and I'd stay and listen. I'd not understand a word. Didn't have to.

I remember the famous American singer, Chubby Checker, who made 'the Twist' one of our modern cultural icons, coming to Whaka. Our own famous singer, Howard Morrison (now Sir Howard), brought Mr Checker out to look at our thermal wonders. He wasn't as black as I'd imagined and I remember someone saying, 'Man, I've seen blacker Maoris in the river than him!'

The Kyle Isles once made an appearance at the Whaka community dining-room. I kept sneaking in and getting thrown out, but I was determined I was going to see them, especially the beautiful Lisa Kyle, who was a goddess to me. Whaka produced a famous singer, Ana Hato, whom I now I have on CD, and Dean Waretini was a popular singer in the seventies. The village had dozens and dozens of fine voices, as every Maori community has.

I sang with my mate and Whaka relation, Rueben Morrison, in the back of an old car wreck, or in the back of his borrowed father's car when we were teenagers. I did the same with another old Whaka mate, Mark Toa, in another car wreck up at his place. We all sang in the bath together, sat in the Down Bath changing shed and practised harmonies. Sang as we walked, sang in our beds together as a last goodnight to this simple world we knew.

At one stage while I was still living at home my half-sister Maxine and her husband Perry moved in to board with us at Matai Street whilst they waited for a state house allocation. I had an obsession to have my own guitar and get to play in a band. Perry was in a band called the Viscounts and one night they had a venue about eight miles out of town at Ngongotaha, which I begged to go to. But there was no room to take me in the van, not with their band equipment. So I hitchhiked. The hall they played in was all done up as they were in those days, with low lighting but a lit-up stage and everyone dancing their feet off to saxophones and electric guitars and bass and drums and singing voices belting out rock and roll, and the guitar classic 'Guitar Boogy'. I just loved seeing them up on stage singing into those fat microphones and being loved by the crowd dancing and joying to their music.

I wanted to be up there with them. I wanted the confidence to get out on that floor and dance. But I was content enough just being there in the presence of the music, the action. I tried to get a ride home, but there was still no room in the van. So I said I could get a lift from someone else and hung around till I saw the van leave and then I took off. I walked.

What I remember most of this night was the stars out in their full glory and me starting to jog and finding this wonderful rhythm. I felt as if I could run all night. King of the night road, running on air, hearing the music of that night in my head. I got about two miles from home when my kindly brother-in-law met me on a bicycle well after midnight, concerned about me. But I never lost that obsession to play in a band.

●

That first band I formed in Auckland broke up after a few months. We were just too incompatible. So I formed another one. Moved with my de facto wife and baby son Quentin from one rental house to another. I lived for the times we had band practice, which was twice, or often more, a week. Practise till eleven, midnight, I don't want it to end and…I don't want to go home. Not to a relationship, to fatherhood and responsibility. I want to be married to my music. I'm finding a voice, literally. But inside me a despair is niggling away in the background that I'm losing the battle with self-confidence. To hell with that nonsense, I'll just work harder, plunge myself into this role until it becomes me, totally me.

We were doing stuff that no-one else was doing – progressive black music from America, like Sly and the Family Stone, Buddy Miles, Stevie Wonder. I loved those American greats such as Sam Cooke, Aretha Franklin, Nat King Cole, Ray Charles, Ben E. King, the Temptations, the Spinners, Gladys Knight and the Pips, the Four Tops, Smokey Robinson, the Drifters, I could go on and on. And they're all American black. We got a few gigs, nothing too promising. And we had a brief period of having our own nightclub venue when we hooked up with a sleazeball character whose premises we could use for practice in Karangahape Road, right next door to a strip joint, which I never got to visit, that being of no appeal to me. This guy turned it into a nightclub, with an average of about twenty customers a night. But at least we had an audience and once we had a black American navy ship crew as our audience and they really appreciated hearing their kind of music, even if sung by a half-Maori, half-white vocalist. I'll never forget how well they danced, such pizzazz, rhythm, dexterity. They had an outrageous belief in themselves, which puzzled me, given what the world knew of their great suffering.

But the private me is falling deeper and deeper into turmoil. I don't really know what it is. I just feel so miserable, so mixed up. I feel as if I'm going mad. Maybe it's from wanting too much, what I can never have. Maybe I've got depression? Is that why I'm getting suicidal thoughts? At worst I'm the nineteen-year-old big baby, wallowing in myself, and don't see my own child, my own baby.

One day I say to my de facto wife I'm going to the shop. Keep walking, catch a bus, get off somewhere, phone someone. Can I stay with them for a few days? Yeah, sure. Don't turn up there, but at a downtown bar, as seedy as they get. Drink with my ilk, the lost and the wretched, till it closes. End up on a building site, drinking with a woman who says she has venereal disease otherwise it would be yes. She kisses so well. Tell her I don't care if I get VD, I just have to get it on. But no go and afterwards obviously I'm glad, and shocked at myself, the extent of my descent of caring not for myself. Stumble off into the night, many nights, lost, lost. This is not how it was supposed to turn out. And yet it is; it's exactly how I knew it would turn out. I have dreamed about this for some years. The dam broke. I couldn't hold it back any longer. Lost I am.

I take up with the band again, find solace there. Too self-centred to be worrying about the welfare of my de facto wife and our baby. The world is just me. Or it's madness waiting to grab me, I can see it and feel it. Let's do that number one more time, boys. When we've done it a hundred times, two hundred. We're all rehearsal and no live action. So we get sick of going nowhere. Where are our gigs, where are our names in lights? We drift our separate ways. I wouldn't know where my boat is anyway. This sea is vast and endless.

End up in another town. Another. Back home with Dad. What a state he can see his son is in. I'd made a late night phone-call to him some weeks ago, begging, demanding him to say he loved me. How puerile. What blackmail of your own father, demanding that he say what he doesn't like to express. Can't remember big chunks of those times. Not so much from drinking, but the fog of emotional turmoil.

Write to Dad's sister, Alison, good old Aunt Alison, artist, sculptor, she'll understand: 'I've found my niche. I'm going to be a writer.' Surprised I can spell niche, since I can't put it in the right context. A niche comes from experiencing all around the final activity does it not? Going to be a writer, eh? Easy to say. Takes a few seconds with a ball-point pen and the cost of an envelope and a stamp. Don't know where the voice comes from making a statement like that. I don't read a lot. Went through a stage of soaking up the American classics, but I am on this earth *feeling* it, not figuring it out in literary terms and forming new means to communicate, or even practising tried and true means of writing. I'm just this confused youth, supposed to be a husband and a father.

Except I do have this strange sense of rhythms churning around inside me, of trying to find their pattern, their meaning. And my dreams are cinemascopic, panoramas of unbelievable scenes in finest, most meaningful detail. I can wake up and recall so much of them. I wake up screaming inside to somehow capture these dreamscapes in words. But every time I try they mean nothing. Simply nothing. Just descriptions. Jumbled nonsense. So why do I have them, fantastic dreams like this? Later, quite a few years later, I learn to pull water from the well-spring of these dreams. I get experienced, sharpened at knowing how to take the meaning from them, to separate the dross out, the wheat from the chaff.

End up in Christchurch. Have a bad experience involving someone close. Betrayed him. No conscience, Alan Duff. No confidence, no conscience. But no excuse. You're a piece of cuckolding shit. Decide one night I might as well end it, can feel that dark descending. Take half a bottle of sleeping tablets washed down with several jugs of beer that I'd bought with the last of my dough. Go for a slow walk through Hagley Park one winter's night waiting for chemical sleep to claim me. I even lie down in the dewy grass expecting I'll not feel the cold. I don't know what's happened, I'm not even sleepy. Vomit soon erupts. Spewing out my death sentence. I'm going to live. Yippee.

Drift to another city, Wellington. End up with my old mate Mark Takarangi. Looking back on it, we're losers who don't have a notion that we are. All talk no do, or wrong do. We're conceptually lost, don't have the armoury, which is knowledge, which is application, which is everything we are not. Though at least my writing ambitions are out in the open now. Not that I was capable of producing even one informed, well-written article of, say, 800 words. You can't when you have lots to say on only yourself, your narrow vision, your inner woes, your limited and childish outlook. You're just a potential waiting to happen. But you've known bars all over the country with people like that: waiting for nothing, in truth, to happen.

Drift on again. End up back with my de facto wife. Don't know how she keeps accepting me back. I'm such a weakling, a pathetic excuse for a man. How have I fallen this far? Can't tell anyone why I am like this, as I don't know. I only have a feeling of being scared of virtually everything of the world. But briefly a bright light: my son Quentin, now two years old, recognises me after an absence of a year. Launches himself into my arms and holds on tight to me for a couple of hours. What has your father done, child? What can he say? Worse that he can feel it inside him, as sure as he knows anything, that this won't last, he won't last, the relationship with his mother won't last. Because I can't last.

Back in Rotorua, the talking sessions with my father at least confirm that I have a mind, a brain worthy of respect, as there's little else about myself I do respect. Start contracting again to Rotorua Insulation. Good to see my former boss again, he's a good man. Big life lesson at work: to be rewarded with exactly the effort you put into it. But still too thick to see that you must put effort into the management side of your business, not just hurl yourself at the job with pure physical energy. It's called boxing clever. I work so hard I'm never going to be broke, but I just don't apply the efficiencies to keeping good books.

One job I had took me up to Auckland, where my brother Nick was finishing his Masters degree in philosophy. We'd got on well together in our adult years and we arranged to meet up for a beer at a pub. He had brought along a book to give me. It was poetry by Gerard Manley Hopkins. He reckoned I'd like Hopkins, even though I said I was not a literary man, at least not in the formally studied sense. He saw more in me than I did, for upon being directed to Hopkins' 'terrible sonnets', written during his period of great internal, spiritual struggle, I stood there in this Parnell pub reading them in an increasingly stunned state. I would never have believed that twenty-five years later I would get to sit at Janet Frame's kitchen table and recite lines from one of these sonnets.

O the mind, mind has mountains; cliffs of fall
Frightful, sheer, no-man-fathomed. Hold them cheap
May who ne'er hung there...

These words leapt out at me, they echoed from the canyons, the chasms of the poet's mind to this like mind. His very last poem, To R.B. who was Robert Bridges, his friend, as Hopkins despaired that his muse might have flown:

I want the one rapture of an inspiration.
O then if in my lagging lines you miss
The roll, the rise, the carol, the creation, ...

Lord, my brother had opened my eyes. The lights went on. In the literary sense they did. I became instantly certain that I'd write one day, I'd be published. I read Hopkins every spare moment I had, at morning 'smoko' break, during the lunch half-hour, and at night. His words had me in a state of excitement, of enlightenment, and only many years later, when I was writing *Once Were Warriors*, did I realise that Hopkins' rhythms were echoing my own. Not that I compare myself to Hopkins as a writer; I just recognised the same creative beat we each are born with and knew about the despair he expressed.

From then on I started reading fiction and poetry, anything I could get my hands on. I'd come home on a Friday evening carrying several books purchased from Whitcombe and Tombs, along with classical LPs. And I was openly telling friends that I was going to be a writer one day, not for a moment thinking that there was a lot more personal growing up to do for quite a few more years yet. Looking back on it, I have no regrets at not being published earlier, and no regrets that it took so long to grow up. For I gained so many rich experiences along the way, was more down than up, but I gathered fruit for later years, had a greater range of paint colours to splash on my canvases.

William Faulkner was my major discovery in this period. I loved his rhythms, his sermon-from-the-mount style of delivery, his giving the reading world insights into the American Negro voice. John Steinbeck, Ernest Hemingway, William Burroughs each gave me some more literary and personal growth. I dreamt about being a published author. I didn't know then that it would take me eighteen years.

fifteen

By this stage we had two children, a son and a daughter. Family life back in Rotorua seemed to have assumed itself on me this time and I worked at being a good parent, and wasn't a bad de facto husband either. For a few years anyway. Start playing rugby again. Speed still there, just had to gain the fitness, find the discipline from somewhere. Work really enjoyable, making money and loving being my own boss. All I ever wanted was freedom, and to overcome the shyness.

My de facto wife played netball, very good netball. Tennis in the summer. Sport was a shared passion, but not so our intellectual interests. We played our respective sports for the same club, Whaka. Immersed ourselves in both sport and the accompanying social activity, especially the combined social forces of a Saturday night after our games. Rugby is great, social life at the Whaka Rugby Club even better. Tuesday and Thursday nights after practice at the Geyser pub with the boys is close companionship. I try and shut down my thoughts, my intellect. What writing ambition? It could not be less relevant to this thoroughly pleasant, physical way of life. Who cares about serious matters in this company? Though I can't shut down the observer in me, the eavesdropper, the fascination with damn near every character in sight or hearing distance. I play back each one's different way of speaking to myself when I'm driving alone, or working in some lonely spot on a vast building site where no-one can hear me. Every speaking voice is a musical instrument to my ear. Their dialogue, sentence construction, different emotional force, tone, personality, intellect, character. And I have to run a list like that because that's how I analysed them; no doubt a lot of it due to wanting to find out who and what I was in turn.

But the basic brief to myself was to be one of the boys at Whaka. I loved my time with them, the drink, playing pool, the constant laughter, singing, buying raffle tickets, and the simple joy of winning a meat pack, a tin of five dozen Bluff oysters to take home or share around with your football mates. Often we'd end up at a Tuesday night or a Thursday night party, with a $5 'put-in' to cover the beer and drums of pork bones and watercress cooking on an open fire, and we'd be singing and laughing all night. Just so long as I kept that mind of mine shut down. What a life, what insulation against internal pain. What wonderfully happy (and occasionally violent) people are my Whaka Maori people. This is what I am. I'll stay it for life. Be content, happy, joyous, occasionally volatile, just like them.

Saturday play rugby, drink at club, at pub after that, head for that jukebox and play favourite soul songs over and over. 'Have You Seen Her?' by the Chi-lights. Lose myself in it, loneliness becomes less because these people they can hear music, they do music, every Saturday night. Just gather around our netball team wives' and girlfriends' lounge bar tables, hear us sing, see us dance, this is a good life, who'd want any other? Nice and simple, Maori simple, Maori at their best. I'm not leaving this. This is emotional, social connection at its best, for me it is.

On Sundays go for a ten o'clock run up in forested hills, an hour to hour and a half, whole team, don't treat it lightly coach warns us or it'll be longer. Fit young men, bursting out of their skins, how I love being around physical men. What writer, what literary career in the making? This is what I am and want to stay.

Back at the club rooms, into the big thermal bath, hear the tales of last night's drinking antics, who did what, who had a fight, though not a lot of that and nothing nasty about our fights, not here, they're straight punch-ups, man to man. Always one fight for Sunday morning bath recall, but not many more than that. These are happy boys not fighters, they're singers and beer drinkers and merchants of humour, laughter abounds. Joined by our wives, girlfriends, children happily play in the big hall or outside, guitars go, people play cards, euchre, sometimes poker, for money, $2 game stakes.

Confidence not an issue here, the collective comfort wraps you all in the same big embrace. Just know the rules. They're simple. Be happy, be glad to be alive, don't analyse, don't argue about stuff you've read, these people don't want to know. Just enjoy, Chow baby. Might be all over before you know it.

Go to work Monday, do it hard all week, to your utmost, you have the incentive, you're paid according to your production, no more no less. Get to it. How I love the simplicity of this argument and if only more people knew just how simple. And how I love the simplicity of being a working man, a self-employed working man, a New Zealander, lover and player of rugby, a beer drinker.

Except at every site I go to I have a reputation for being opinionated. Yeah, the big-mouth. Look out, here he comes. Wants an argument. Too big for his boots. Too certain of his every argument, too articulate by half, what's he on about, why is he here amongst us, ordinary workers? Fuck off to university, mate, if you're so frustrated about every intellectual issue. That's what they used to say to me.

Read the newspapers, talk a lot with my father, love talking with him, he's quietly guiding me, steers me to different books that become another step in my enlightenment. At the same time I'm trying to live the lie of the common ordinary man. Can't keep my mind down, think about everything. Want to engage with someone, anyone. Every smoko time, whatever site I'm on, I'll find someone. The English usually like to debate, Maori not at all and my fellow Pakeha Kiwis are too laconic and narrow and anyway don't like talkative types let alone argumentative twenty-two-year olds who have an opinion on everything. Why don't I shut up or piss off and find someone else to annoy?

My boss will debate anything, except he's not really my boss, not officially, I'm self-employed. But he feels my boss and in a good way, a way of someone I respect, even admire, and I think he's gained a respect for some of my arguments too. For I don't follow conventional thinking, I challenge it all. Though of course the general working-class view is not so indulgent. These trade unionist dyed-in-the-wool types

I am genetically hard-wired to slam up against at first sighting, and they me.

I go on to sites and by lunch-time I have every trade unionist giving me the evil eye, especially the English ones who treat every question as a dire threat. On one site I go on to, a unionist has us removed before the day is out when he discovers we don't belong to a union. Of course we can't when we're self-employed. But they win, we don't go back, workers on wages and with union cards have to go and finish the job. And I know that it loses money because the workers don't have the incentive. Anyway working hard is actively discouraged on any site where there is a strong union presence.

Work in the same shared workshops with a lot of self-employed Maori tradesmen – refrigeration engineers, including a fine man called Hira Christie, and Terry Ngawhika, who wrote a stunningly tender book many years later himself, about the memoirs of a pig hunter. More of a man than most I ever knew is Terry, a loving father, a good husband, as tough as they come, but warm and genuine. Roofers, sheetmetal and insulation workers, welders, all with their own little businesses. That was Rotorua. It was a place where Maori – some of them at any rate – aspired just as much as their European counterparts.

Not that there were Maori merchant bankers ready to explode on the world. Or property tycoons, or any kind of business tycoon. But at least they were Maori with more pride in themselves, more self-belief, and for quite a few years I happily was one of this hard-working, contented lot. If only I wasn't born with the peculiar mind I have.

One Friday night I'm in town and stroll into my regular bookshop. Came out with two books on architecture, don't know why. As if no other books in the shop existed. They were on the architects Le Corbusier and Gaudi. Hurry home, feeling quite illicit about it, as if I shouldn't be doing this. Not me, the man who works with his hands, the former borstal boy. There's a fence around me and I shouldn't be on this side.

Every page is a revelation, of construction, form, lines and curves and tones I didn't know existed. Walk around the same as I do when I hear a song that blows me away, exclaiming like some religious encounter. I never knew such humans existed, or such constructions of their genius visions.

I race round to talk to Dad. Yes he's heard of them, of course he has. He's not big on architecture but he's broad on knowledge. I'm so lucky to have such a father, whom I can take any idea, any concept to, as long as it's not emotional and personal, and he'll sit there at his kitchen table and discuss it till late at night.

There is no history of exposure to architects and yet I feel as if I have met up with lost cousins. Something happens to me after these architect discoveries. I am left dissatisfied, aware of my inadequacies again, when I thought I'd left them effectively behind with the lifestyle and friends and self-employed job I had. And Stevie Wonder is hitting an artistic peak. I listen obsessively to him, to every instrument of his own playing, and marvel at his producers putting all the sounds of separate recordings together. I listen over and over to my Beethoven piano sonatas, my Mozart symphonies, Rachmaninov, can hum them along with the entire LP.

I bore everyone shitless by playing them songs I love, classical pieces that inspire. Except inspire me to what, I don't know. That writing ambition is just words, a handful of unconfident attempts. Though I am getting more and more verbally articulate. Even if most of my mates say (and not all disparagingly) that I have the gift of the gab.

Insecurity returns, just like an old, unwelcome person you thought was gone. My mind feels as if it's breaking free, into another dimension, I feel so estranged from my normal world. I start to not belong. I try to drop hints to some of my closer mates, that I'm going through something strange, unsettling. But they can't hear me. I'm just the same mate as I always was. Inside, though, I can hardly face the world, or not outside of work. Work you can lose yourself in, you have goals, targets to reach. At nights I drink beer and read and drive my wife crazy with not knowing what's happening to me. Think – God, how I think. Drives me crazy. The voice is screaming, 'I want out!' But out from what I don't know.

I start looking at old friends and acquaintances in a new light. They seem ordinary and yet on the other hand safe, inside that fenced area where everyone knows who and what they are. Safe, uncluttered of thought and emotion. I try and get back in. Immerse in the rugby, the drinking culture, the mateship culture. Parties, losing myself in the group singing. Go overboard in playing the part of: Look, me ordinary working man like you. No thoughts different to you, I promise. When inside it could not be more opposite.

Drink to excess. Have violent outbursts upon my de facto wife. Her very existence angers me in between times when I think I love her. We're not getting on as it is. Our children keep us together. Have to get that comfort back, that feeling of security, even as it dawns that it can never be for me. But what if I grab it with both hands, wrap my legs around it, sink my teeth into that way of life? Yeah, that's what I'll do.

Train hard for rugby. Have not a bad season. Revel in the social life. Immerse myself in being a simple Whaka Maori. My commitment to them is total, or so I think. For whenever an interesting looking person walks into our public bar, I'm over there in a shot, introducing myself, wanting to talk, to hear what his story is and, if he's foreign, all about his country, his culture, his secret to self-confidence. Oh God this state, this affliction makes you pitiful sometimes. Most of all I want to connect with not just intelligence, for there are plenty of them in my company, but informed intelligence; minds that hunger for knowledge, for understanding, that seek to find the pattern, the meaning in everything.

Must immerse myself deeper. Try rugby league for half a season, get smashed in my first game. Get picked for the Bay of Plenty trials, but that's it. This game is not me. Though now I rather like rugby league. Go back to rugby, have to get reinstated and what a carry-on that is, dealing with ignorant rugby stalwarts who regard any other game as if a threat to our very lives. Have to fill out forms, get on your knees and say sorry I'll never play that horrible game again, get a respected rugby advocate to speak on my behalf.

In the pub one Thursday night after rugby practice, have had a good month, made more money than I would working six months for wages. My brother Kevin comes in. We've seen a lot of each other. He's a drinker. And lost. I'm slightly less lost. We know what we are but just can't admit it, he less so. Can he borrow some money? Sure. He's my big brother, he's good for it. Give him some money, we have a beer, he's off somewhere. See you.

He comes back a few minutes later. Can he borrow my vehicle? I have a utility. Yeah, all right. He'll leave it at Dad's. That's fine. I chide him mildly about borrowing not just my money but the ute as well. He breaks into this most beaming smile. As if he knows he's a naughty boy and may be like that for some years to come. That's just Kevin. How he is.

I never see him again. Not alive. Two weeks later I get a knock on the door of where I'm staying and Honeygirl Morgan says she's got very bad news: Kevin has been killed. My brother is no more.

My eldest brother Kevin was my hero, my idol. Everything he did I admired – the way he walked, talked, played sport. At home he spent his time defending us from Mum's insistence that we come and witness her argument with Dad. At school Kevin fought to defend our family's honour that Mum's behaviour continually brought into disrepute. We all learned to do this in turn, but Kevin most of all, being the eldest. Kevin Duff was an exceptionally gifted person who had a formidable intellect and a natural sporting ability. He was in the top ten School Certificate marks for Maori students in New Zealand, which he sat for a second year in the Fifth Form, when he was not yet fifteen. He was a Bay of Plenty soccer representative, playing in men's teams when he was only fourteen. He was a cricket all-rounder, and he had matinée idol looks on top of that. I was best man at his wedding when I was fourteen. Growing up in Matai Street he had a close mate Eddie, whose father was the neighbourhood's sexual pervert on an awful, incestuous scale. Eddie and Kevin shared a common sense of being under siege on account of what their respective father and mother did. I think they saw themselves as Lone Ranger and Tonto (my brother being the darker one) against the world.

One of my younger brothers, Neil, insists that the undertaker remove the coffin lid so we can see him, say goodbye to him. We're all in shock. Six have been killed in a car crash near Maketu Beach where one lot have been drinking all night and were travelling back to Rotorua at eight in the morning and collided head-on with another car, killing the married couple occupants. An extended family group of two brothers and several cousins and a brother-in-law of mine, and the two killed cousins' father, my Fijian Uncle Abe, have gone by van to Tauranga to collect the bodies. God, four of them. My brother, my two first cousins, and the fiance of one of them, all killed. My cousins are teenagers. Everyone's injuries are so bad that traditional open coffins, as Maori custom usually demands, will not be this time. I am still angry at Kevin's death, the passing of this irresponsible, immature, lost soul, killed in a drunken car smash. The driver lived. My brother left a young widow and two young sons.

We have to sit and wait for hours whilst they try and remove the one-way screws of Kevin's coffin lid. The undertaker tells us he has had to do some cosmetic work on our brother as he is not a pretty sight and he's had an autopsy. Finally we are told he is ready for viewing, but we are not to touch him because, as one of older relations tells us, he's 'held together'. Say no more.

I take a long while to step out from behind my brother Neil to stare at Kevin. I can't face what he will look like. But it is only the familiar sight of his facial bristles still growing (he was a heavy shaver) that has me say to myself, 'That's my brother.'

And I drink in that sight of him in his last, aware that it is such a waste. It is as if he reaches out to me and puts my mind in a blazing light of truth that will yet not reveal itself for some years. It's as if he's saying to me that, somewhere along the line it will be my turn to look after him. His memory. Or the life that got wasted. And, as it turned out, the stories that got told in my novels.

I am looking at my dead brother and I keep saying inside: remember this. Remember this. Never forget this. Never. Then the lid is put back and he's gone. Gone. Part of me, part of any brother, any sibling, takes some of you with them. It took eighteen years before his name got into print in the dedications in *Once Were Warriors*. I think he'd be pleased to know that it is still selling steadily to this day, nine years after it was published, and he would have enjoyed the movie. I also established a scholarship bearing his name at his first primary school, Whakarewarewa Primary.

What a waste of a fine mind, a young man who, if he had been able to throw off the shackles of that childhood trauma, was sure to have made something of his life. Instead, at just twenty-five, father of two sons, estranged from his wife, he's another lost drunk soul become a road fatality mention in a newspaper. Killed, say I, by the life he had, the upbringing he inherited. His childhood got stolen from him. Ignorance was the thief as was heavy drinking and a culture of violence. No more now, leave him his dignity. He's gone. Though not so the life that helped kill him.

How fitting, what a contrast of the same worlds, that we should take our four young dead in their coffins to the marae of the married couple they killed, where we should witness culture and grieving so profound it stays in my mind as clear as my brother's face did. I can still see the old man who could hardly walk, but when he got to the speaking forum suddenly straightened and twirled his whale-bone ceremonial traditional weapon in brilliant sweeping arcs to emphasise his points of oratory. He gave a superb delivery, even though in a language I did not understand, but it was part-translated to me by an older relation. The powerful massed singing, the ancient waiata, the Maori ancestors and Maori gods being summoned to help their people through this grieving for six dead. Six coffins laid on mats in front of this Te Puke meeting-house.

And back at Wahiao, the meeting-house at Whaka, they gave our four dead a wonderful send-off. Such eloquence of oratory, such singing, such shared tears with the relatives and friends of the deceased. Then what ugly truth, what hideous confirmation of our legacy, that the after-funeral ceremonies should end up in violent, drunken chaos exactly like the life that they – we all – grew up with.Witness again displays of anger wanting gratification, as a man-child takes his problems out on my father. Some legacy – our mother's, not our father's – to be brawling after your loved ones' funeral.

sixteen

The relationship is over. I am before the court on driving charges and the magistrate is not happy, thinks I am in need of a sharp lesson, meaning prison. It's not in keeping with the offence, which is traffic, though I accept he can see what I know, if I was prepared to admit it – that I'm starting to spin out of control. Thinking on my feet, I tell him that I'm making a new start by going to England. He gives me periodic detention until the weekend before I go. Leaving my children was hard, but words are meaningless in these instances, just meaningless.

By ship to Britain. And as each port was left behind, so was the old me. Then London. What a town. Hit the pubs, the clubs, go to shows, get laid, go to museums, art galleries, everywhere lapping up a life I couldn't even imagine. Small town boy getting his eyes pulled open. Don't stop to even draw breath, not till the money runs out. Get work in my insulation field. After a week I ask to go on contract, which takes my staid English boss aback. 'What's wrong with wages?' he asks. Everything, I tell him. Let me be paid for what I do. He says I won't last. I say we'll see about that. We agree on contract rates for different types of installation of pipe insulation. In my first self-employed week I earn what would have taken five weeks on wages to earn. I have proved my point. The guys who have been wage-earners the whole time resent me. Who cares?

The contract is way out at Beaconsfield, involving a forty-minute train ride from London and then a walk through an English copse to this new army base. It's a stunning walk, right out of the pages of books on England, Robin Hood and his men, or breathless upper-class trysts in the dappled conceal. I see my first fox in this little English forest. Can hear the ghosts of this country's long, oft-violent history behind every tree. I love this walk.

At work none of my fellow insulation wage-earners will talk to me. I'm the enemy, and worse than that I, the foreigner, have become self-employed in just a week. I see that they don't like hard work. But I don't care, I just carry on.

The foreman resents me for doing what he's too cowardly and lazy to do, and he starts holding up my production schedule. My English work associates openly disapprove of me working through morning tea breaks and taking a short lunch break. You're supposed to stretch every break out to the maximum, just as a work day is to be endured rather than regarded as a challenge. If only they had figured it out, that I actually worked less hours and had the freedom to start and finish when I wanted.

One morning coming to work I am walking along this forest pathway when I stop and start looking at the plays of light, and for a sighting of that fox. Start forming descriptive sentences in my mind. I hear rhythms like Gerard Manley Hopkins' poetry. Many minutes pass and I hear a voice telling me that this isn't me, my destiny lies elsewhere. Not writing, so much as a different kind of freedom.

And so I turn around and walk back to the station and catch a train back to London and they never see me again on that job or any other building site in this country. I'm finished, so I think, with working with my hands. Still daren't give too much credence to that writing aspiration, not after some of the authors I've read, like William Faulkner and Ernest Hemingway and William Styron. I couldn't get near them. I want another form of employment altogether and something tells me it is a social contact need.

I want human contact. I want life, I want fun, I want whatever action is going. I want to learn from first-hand observation and increasing participation what this confidence thing really is, what the hell this confusing life is all about and why it so troubles me yet doesn't appear to trouble the majority of others.

Next day I'm employed as a barman at an Earls Court pub called the Prince of Teck. And love it. I'm well practised at being fast and efficient from my insulation work, so I am quickly appreciated. Might as well look at the rugby scene while I'm at it, someone takes me out to London New Zealand. But after practice everyone's drinking Kiwi beer and I don't see any locals and that's not what I came for.

The pub wages are pitiful and the publican's tight-fistedness blatant. He invites being ripped off, and we duly do so, giving our mates beers and nicking a few quid here and there. The pay for a seventy-two-hour week is £23, not even enough to live on without having to share a tiny bedsit with several others or, as three Kiwi bar staff did, share a room in the pub which is smaller than some of the cells I've been in. I enjoy the social contact, especially the availability of women from all parts of the world, in particular Scandinavia.

We're on orders to pour the 'slops' (that's the unfinished beer left in the glasses after closing time) into a stainless steel bucket. The brewery supplies a special filter for recycling these slops back into the kegs. Cigarette butts are part of what the filter stops getting into the keg. It is a disgusting English practice that we end up refusing to be part of – let the boss do it.

One thing I notice is there is a lot less drunkenness amongst the English than us colonial guests. And we are more easily bent towards sorting out our differences with fists rather than the English use of verbal cut and thrust. South Africans – Afrikaaners in particular – think they can muscle every dispute and disagreement into submission with their superior physical presence. But then Australians are a physical race too and so are Kiwis. I am only one of a handful of Maori, and we have between us a volatile cocktail when you mix it with a culture of high beer intake. There's a fight every few days in our wider social circle and half the time I'm in the centre of it. Reminds me of someone. A re-enactment.

A private hotel in the area is getting a bit of a name in Earls Court – strictly speaking, Lower Kensington, as it's on the other side of Cromwell Road – for being a place to go after-hours. These quaint English have a licensing law that closes pubs from three in the afternoon till 5.30 at night. And then they close at 11 p.m. For the hard-drinking colonials that inhabit Earls Court, this won't do, as we like to drink lots and for long hours. The private hotel bar has a simple 'guest' sign-in book for its after-hour customers and there we become part of a local legend, the Trianon Hotel bar.

It has twenty rooms for accommodation, taking in mostly oil and gas industry workers who come to London every six weeks for their fortnightly leave. They have bulging wallets and thirsty gullets and they're hard-doers, being mostly Aussie, Kiwi, South Africans, Rhodesians, and Canadians, along with a smattering of English who have opted for the more boisterous company of 'the wild colonial boys'. Their day starts around noon at the King's Head pub up the road in Earls Court. Then from three o'clock till about 6.00 p.m. at the Trianon bar, then back to the King's Head or somewhere else, and finishing back at the Trianon until the small hours, everyone blind drunk. But mostly happily so, even if fights were fairly common.

But so was lively conversation, for these were worldly men, hard-case characters who had travelled extensively and worked in strange and exotic places where oil is to be found, with tales to tell over the countless beers and whiskies they drank all day and night.

I got a job as a barman at this hotel. The pay was nearly triple what I was getting at the pub and the kindly boss gave me a hotel room to live in. So I became part of the place virtually overnight. And I wallowed in it, serving customers who were so different to any I'd ever met before, and drinking with them as long as I didn't get drunk on duty, a rule which I usually stuck by. Besides, we got too busy to be drinking a lot on most nights. I made a lot of friends.

One day two hard-looking men came into the bar and one ordered champagne, which we didn't have and so a staff member rushed out and bought some from a liquor outlet. They wore navy reefer jackets and the leader had a silk handkerchief in his breast pocket and the most confident blue eyes, along with a charming conversational style. He told me I looked like a fighter. Naturally I was flattered. He said he hired fighters for a job that was unique. 'Glamorous, oui,' he said in his Belgian French accent. 'Dangerous, of course. Highly paid, this goes without saying. Women, for sure. And bonus pickings, like abandoned banks, if you get lucky.' Right out of a novel. He said he was staying for a week or so and to let him know if I was interested in talking further.

I found out from my boss that this suave Belgian house guest was a recruiter for mercenaries for the Angolan war. Not me at all. I hate war. It's bad enough fighting the one with yourself. As it turned out, some months later, I was attacked by a mercenary who had fought in those very parts, a Rhodesian who menaced us all in our bar one night then finally made his move when I was shutting shop for the night. Unfortunately for him I'd been serving him double whiskies of his numerous ordering, whacking in extra shots just in case I needed him off balance. So he wasn't too much trouble.

One of our customers was the infamous prostitute, Christine Keeler, whose sexual antics with high-ranking Secretary of State for War, John Profumo, brought down the British Conservative government. The outraged public voted Macmillan's government out of office at the next election. Profumo went to gaol. I used to look at this innocuous woman and wonder how on earth this callgirl's shenanigans could bring down a government, wreck so many careers, lives. She drank in the bay window area and sometimes when the light was right she looked alluring and quite capable of being the seductress of men of power. Yet on other occasions, sitting in that same spot, she looked like most of the other patrons, a heavy drinker who was seeing her life out in the bottom of a gin glass.

The Trianon bar was patronised by a huge diversity of people, ranging from boxers and Rhodesian and South African mercenaries, to a Fijian who was a scrapper, and a rugby player and, we discovered, a homosexual. He lived with a white, upper-middle-class English lawyer by the name of Martin. They made the oddest couple and it was never overt. We had an American writer who had sold the film rights to one of his westerns, an outrageous character, hard-drinking, hard-doing, who I once saw get a broken bottle shoved in his face over an affair he had with the wrong man's woman. He laughed about it, said that was the story of his life and where else would he get his fictional, cowboy characters from, if not real life.

Drug dealers came and went, but they never managed to get in with the regulars who were drinkers plain and simple. We had a gun-runner to the IRA, a jolly nice bloke considering, who was later convicted and gaoled. There were all sorts of slippery characters drifting in and out, flying in from all over the world, of mysterious and certainly illicit origins. But it wasn't a place to be judging other men, just standing up for yourself and obeying the unspoken rule that you be a decent bloke, have honour, be a good mate, and pay your round when it came around.

A hard-core group of regulars made marvellous company and they ranged from an ex-paratrooper turned school teacher, to one of the gutsiest guys around who looked like a tough and yet spoke like a toff. He was South African, born and educated at a top English public school. I played rugby for his Old Boys club. He was a champion boxer in his youth and was always getting into scrapes with young guns who fancied their chances. He never lost to one of them. There was a local fish and chip shop proprietor, George 'the Fish', who died of a heart attack at an early age, a cockney who had the loveliest nature and a great sense of humour. One other South African was a boxing champion who had a violent streak that scared everyone, but behind that broken-nosed, heavily scarred face, I found a rather sweet and sensitive man who thought deeply about all sorts of things, and we'd spend many an hour in close conversation on quiet nights. Not once did he cause trouble in my bar.

Then our boss rented out the basement, 'Downstairs' to a bunch of likely lads, well-dressed larrikins and suave-looking wide boys, headed by an outlandishly self-confident Australian. It changed the whole place and many lives with it. One of our oil and gas boys lost his beloved Ferrari in cards to them, others lost small fortunes, their hard-earned savings. They changed everything, including my own life, though not for a moment are they responsible.

They'd come sweeping in, unbelievable apparitions of sartorial elegance, of studied gangster style, in the cold weather in their cashmere coats and cashmere jumpers, in warmer weather in silk shirts and linen suits. Saville Row tailor-made pinstripes, deep-pile velvet jackets, crocodile and snake-skin shoes, watches worth thousands of pounds, gold Dunhill lighters, solid gold bracelets, diamond rings you could build a house with the price of, and million pound smiles to go with the eyes that could, however, turn dangerous if they thought that was required. These larger-than-life, elegantly attired characters are what I saw and began to wonder what their secret was, from whence the self-confidence, where did they learn to dress like that. Who were they?

They came from 'Downstairs', where mysterious things went on that we only knew had to do with gambling. Rolls Royces and Mercedes and Jaguars would be parked along the street and the owners would usually use the basement entrance, though some came in the public entrance and popped into the bar for an early drink. They could not be more different to myself or our regular bar patronage, who were not exactly fazed or worried by these newcomers, being pretty tough men in their own right, if rather more upright citizens.

The Aussie leader would dominate. He'd stand at the bar in his fawn cashmere overcoat and spin a coin and catch it behind his back. He had an Aussie mate who spun cigarettes and caught them in his teeth. They walked and moved with swagger and attitude and fairly glowed with their can-do-anything aura. They had equally impressive Australian company, men who had warmth and mischief radiating from their eyes, who carried wads of dough, several hundred, a thousand or two, done up in what I found out was a Gypsy Roll, with a note folded around the ones inside to denote a hundred if it was tens, two hundred if twenties. They spent freely and generously, buying for the whole bar. Not one but several charismatic characters. Boy did I want badly to be in with this lot. I'd do anything.

An array of cockney characters came with them, a differently charming lot, more dangerous underneath the fast-talking, rhyming-slang wit, but no less fascinating for it. I wanted in and needed to know how.

But I was no gambler. It just didn't interest me. I thought it stupid and had never seen a successful gambler, not on horses which was the main activity down below, nor in the few London casinos I'd experienced. The other main attraction was the card games, which could go on all night and all the following day. No-one had a job, I never overheard conversations about bosses or careers, they all just came and went at hours that were random and none of them was short of money.

I got to know them from being regular drinkers at our bar, though they didn't like our main regular patronage who were too rough and rowdy for them. There were a couple of incidents involving fringe regulars who made the mistake of picking on one of these guys. Their smiling charm turned to brutal fists and head-butts in a flash.

I couldn't get near them. We were too different, and I guess in their eyes I had too far to come – from being a man who tended bar for them, to wanting to be their equal and their peer. Looking back, I was star-struck. But when I got to know some of them closer and got involved with them, the stars had gone out of my eyes. Indeed, if there was any star in our midst, it was me – though that would come later.

Got the writing bug out of nowhere, took off to Crete to start a novel I truly believed was just sitting there waiting to pour out. Had a pleasant time, got to see the ancient island of old Greek culture, did lots of writing. But no novel came out of it.

Came back to find the owner of the establishment had promoted me to bar manager, which was quite good news for a homecoming. Had a memory flash of my Uncle Tupu's joy at being given the same position at the old Geyser Hotel. But I was hardly ecstatic, not with seeing that those downstairs boys had widened their influence, drinking up in the bar with the rest of us, and getting on well enough with the regulars. Though they kept a certain distance and they went and did their main socialising elsewhere, to places glamorous and exciting, I found out – I actively sought to find out. I wanted in on what they were doing, since it clearly was to do with being smart, and I thought I was smart.

No use regrets. I made the decision. My personality was at a stage where I probably had little choice, desperate that I was to prove myself at something, anything. I went in with my eyes open and my morality shut down, period.

It had a slow and lowly start. One day the main man saying he had 'work' for me, which turned out a Saturday afternoon in an Irish pub in Paddington where he ran a bookmaking operation, and put me on as general hand, writing down bets! Was this it? Was this the secret to their success, making money from dumb gamblers? My mate got paid five quid for a Saturday afternoon of taking bets and I got a desultory two quid. I could have earned more working behind the bar. But hungry, ambitious young men will put up with everything to get in. To belong.

They drove around in E-type Jaguars and sporty Jensen Inter-ceptors and had wardrobes out of fashion magazines. Whatever it was they were doing to look like this, and have this lifestyle I decided I'd do, unless it was drugs or involved guns, neither of which looked likely.

But quite suddenly I let my thoughts of my children, Quentin and Alecia, get through my guard and I began thinking about them all the time. I started making regular phone-calls, and hearing their voices got to me, the part I'd shut down. Soon I had an overwhelming desire to be back with them in New Zealand and see if I could resume the relationship with my children's mother.

When I left London I thought I would probably never see any of my friends again. That dream of joining those flash boys had amounted to a single incident of indirect involvement, when one of them sold me some travellers cheques which I cashed. They bore an Arabic signature, a mess of squiggles and hooks and flicks that seemed impossible to match – doubtless why they were sold to me and on the cheap. Took a train to Edinburgh to do the deed. Why there, I can't remember. It seemed a good opportunity to have a look at the famous city whilst testing myself at this signature forging. Hours and hours of practice had paid off. Stayed the night in a hotel and hardly slept a wink with excitement at what I had done. In some ways I was now wondering if I should be returning to New Zealand after all. But there were my children, and I had long been denying that I was missing them.

seventeen

Being back in any old relationship is fatal. We struggled on for a few self-deceiving months and then it blew up. Back to square one. We parted again. And I'll never forget the face of my son in particular, looking at his father deserting him for the second time. And though we're very close now, nothing can make up for what happened back then. He has made himself into as fine a man as I know – a Christian, a good husband and father, and a lawyer.

I got work as assistant manager at a Rotorua hotel, which I rather enjoyed not least for the social side, of meeting tourists and New Zealanders who were guests; and I indulged in the free availability of women. In fact, lost myself in women.

Took up rugby again at my old club, but only Senior B grade this time. London seemed quickly behind me as I resumed the life of old in Rotorua. Then I was asked to transfer to a company motel in Paihia which needed a manager and found myself in a sleepy hollow of about a thousand people and little to do. At one stage I had thought about trying my hand at writing again, but I wasn't there mentally or emotionally. I was hell-bent on rushing towards my fate which I thought was my destiny. Hello Mister Lost, I'm back.

Go to Australia. Sydney, Melbourne. What the hell am I? Who am I? Why am I so lost? Find myself back in London. With a New Zealand girlfriend in tow. We're staying in a hotel in Knightsbridge. I don't know how we're going to pay the bill. Or what the hell I'm doing back here in this town. Seems I never reunited with my children at all. I only hurt them, threw their lives into disarray again. Why do selfish, self-centred people get to cause so much hurt?

My life is a mess. Stuck in a hotel I have no money to pay for, the world closing in on me so fast I think I'm going to go mad. Find I'm by myself, my girlfriend has gone for a walk. I am lying on the bed when I feel this twitch in my leg starting. Can't rid myself of it. Soon it's as if someone is inside my head screaming at me, trying to gain my attention and I'm ignoring it.

Find myself huddled on the floor in a ball, a foetal ball, shaking violently. Then I'm over at the window, trying to get it open so I can jump. I've had enough of living with myself, this self-loathing, confused man who can't ever figure anything out. Telling myself what's the point, this is how it's always been.

The walls are moving. The lighted street below looks so inviting, as if it is an embrace, the one I've been seeking, just waiting for me to 'come home'. That's how it felt and those are the words I heard in my head, embarrassing now that it is to recall them.

But the window didn't open far enough for a body to squeeze through, even if I'd had the courage – if courage is what is required to end your life. I doubt it. More like despair. So instead of myself I started hurling clothing out the window, my girlfriend's clothing. It's always partly a woman's fault isn't it? A weak man can never shoulder his own guilt entirely. Or maybe I'm throwing my mother out the window, that symbol of womanhood, motherhood, that has betrayed me, failed me. Or maybe I'm just a self-indulgent wanker. Somehow I manage to contain the scream that is threatening to burst from my head. I know if it gets out then I'm in – the men in white coats will come take me away. That's how close I am.

End up back on the floor pouring with sweat and sobbing. Don't know what it was, maybe stress, maybe my inner voice telling me I must stop trying to live a lie. I must stop trying to be what I'm not. For downstairs in the bar I had arranged for certain people to be meeting with me. They were going to put me to a test to see if I was deserving of their company. Their criminal company.

I go to that meeting in a state of automation. I'm handed several bank cards, a Parker pen, a piece of paper, and asked if I can match the signatures on those cards. I take a deep breath. That stress disappears in an instant, and I watch these signatures flow off my writing hand as if I am born to do this. I look up and see the biggest smile of admiration and hear the words, 'I think we can find a lot of work for you' from one of those glamorous figures I'd admired from afar.

'Work?' I asked. 'I thought this was all about not having to work.'

'It's what we call it. You'll see why.'

I saw why all right. Next day, in a dizzy trip from one bank to another with a series of cheque books and bank cards drawing out £30 at a time, starting at 9.30 a.m. opening and finishing that evening at a Bureau de Change somewhere in the city at eight o'clock, I had cashed a total of £2000. One third of that was mine, close to £700.

How excited I was to have proved myself to 'the firm' as the cockneys usually referred to an organised group, usually criminals. The term covered a wide range of activities, starting with the gangsters at the top of the chain. Looking back, of course they would welcome me. I had the signature-forging talent that most of them didn't have. They only knew how to procure the cheque books. But I don't want to turn on them now as some reformed do-gooder. They saw me coming. I had a neon sign on my forehead that said in bright red letters: Stupid. Trusting. Naïve. And they were low-energy types, like most criminals, using others to their best advantage. I was the one who'd rushed into their welcoming arms, I wasn't forced at gunpoint.

Forget any bullshit about morality. I didn't have it then. Of course I have since acquired a moral code which looks back on this in some horror, but I'm damned if I'm going to apply the judgement whip now. I only knew that this ill-fitting personality of mine seemed at long last to have found its own company. For these guys were tough, which I probably was too. They were proud and unpredictable, and most of all free spirits. Welcome to your own, Alan. At long last you've found your own kind.

I believed I would rapidly become like one of these people: self-confident, sure of myself and my position in the world, that I would soon carve a name for myself with my own efforts. I was contracting, but this time with an illegally applied pen, and not on building sites but in banks. I was a bank robber, with a pen as my gun. I was a bank robber who was soon wearing a Saville Road pinstriped suit and living in a nice apartment. As far from a novelist as you are likely to get. How odd that I should read William Faulkner throughout this period, and discover his epic novel, *Light in August*, the study of a complex character of mixed blood who was even more lost than I. Whilst I was at reading Faulkner, his rhythms, his Biblical writing style was implanting itself in me.

Life felt far from likely to slip up as I revelled in this new lifestyle. Life in the fast lane, I thought. Made it, finally, and not going to let it go. Money, but more important a sense of status, and with it this newly-found confidence. The lie was being lived with complete blindness now.

During the day – not every day, but two or three days a week, and not every week – I hit the bank circuit armed with my pen. A Parker, of course. All over London, Greater London, the smaller tourist towns within an hour or two's drive away. Once we happened by the Yehudi Menuhin School of Music, and I pointed at the sign outside this property and started to tell my two cockney companions who Menuhin was. They looked at me and one said, 'Is tha' right, Al? Well I'll be blowed.' Then he looked at me funny. We were supposed to be the bad guys.

We were a team, yet operated as individuals. We worked in pairs, with one 'minding' and the other signing. Sometimes a signature could go wrong, or the serial numbers on the cheques might be listed on the bank's hot list. A minder's job was to follow every movement of the signer's transacting teller to make sure no secret alarm was given. He had a signal called 'coating', another cockney expression which was a tug of a jacket lapel meaning go.

Had several incidents of running out of a bank whilst a teller was summoning the police or security and being driven by my minder at breakneck speed through the city streets or down some back country lane miles from London. You were on your toes all day and at night when you wound down it was a major winding down.

Go to seedy places all over south London, the East End, North London – pubs, gambling dives, illegal drinking clubs, council houses in huge, ugly apartment buildings – to meet people, strange people, weirdos and dangerous bastards, desperate gamblers getting money for their addiction, lifetime criminals, ex-pugilists, ex-cons, incredible charmers, men who looked like film stars, all to get connected, let them see the colour of our eyes and of course our money in exchange for their purloined cheques, including travellers cheques.

A couple of places they try you on, test your nerve, accuse you of something you're not, tell you you're a 'grass', an informer. I'm not a shy person in a situation like this and I make it quite clear I'll fight any man who says untruths about me. The funny thing about it is, your testing antagonist laughs and says, 'Oi, leave it out. Jus' seein' what yer made of, son. Come on, 'ave a nice drink wiv me.'

Everywhere I go in this new world is a new experience. A lot of the people I like; that cockney charm and humour, fast wit, and a certain dangerous side just letting you know it ain't all roast beef and Yorkshire pudding. The most gregarious person can turn ugly if the wrong button is pushed. But I understand fighters and rough men's pride; it's a simple enough thing: just respect them and let them know in turn that you have to be respected too. The biggest villains of them all you only see from a distance, can't get near them. But you're close enough to see they're of quite another world altogether.

People here live by thievery and criminal wheeling and dealing alone. You find there are families of different kinds of criminals, each usually specialising, some generalising. They talk a different language, cockney rhyming slang, and then there's another again amongst the criminal classes. The law-abiding workers and their criminal brothers and cousins and childhood friends fuse, they merge into one social force, of being with one another, needing each other, but each to his own in making a living. Villainy has been passed down for generations and it's a proud tradition, not something to be ashamed of. Sometimes I feel the spy secretly observing these people. Though of course I mean no harm. Just can't help my nature. I see everything, except myself.

I am a criminal. No ifs and buts. I'm in a new club, and quite literally too now that I'm a regular at a posh, private membership nightclub in Berkeley Square, where door attendants park your flash cars, call you by your first name, make you feel good, important, gangsterish without having to be the real thing. Gangster is well what I may become, though I didn't know at the time just how well off the mark my personality type is. A gangster is the most violent, ruthless man on his block – on the next door's block too, if he thinks he can get away with it. He's shrewd, trusts only a handful of people, sees conspiracies against him behind every door, and desires power, power, power. Whilst this poor would-be imitator desired only personal power, over my internal psychological enemy, namely myself.

At these clubs and fancy hotel bars we attracted the women and the envy of many men. Every night was party night; my mates drank Chivas Regal whisky and showed off with Dom Perignon champagne – by the brace, case if they'd had a good day. My tastes remained basic, being a beer or red wine man. Being in 'the club' meant you ran into and socialised with other professional criminals. They were virtually all Londoners and if they weren't Londoners they were Australians. The Aussies saw this as a kind of poetic justice that their great-great-grandparents had been transported from this country and Ireland as convicts and that they had come back preying on their ancestors' English masters.

The cheques came from the pickpockets. I met a few of these characters and found a tradition of handing their thieving legacy from father to son. It was considered perfectly normal and honourable. Time and time again we saw in the newspapers how those who fell foul of the law got lenient sentences, usually a term of suspended imprisonment, if they were from the upper crust and hefty sentences if they were from the working class. The son of a Viscount could have depraved, regular sex sessions with children as young as ten and get a fine and a telling off from the bench. A cockney from the East End could cash a book of cheques not his own and get two, three years in prison. Without question, demonstrably so, the working classes, and the criminal class amongst them, knew only too well that it was an uneven fight between the establishment and them, but they'd give it the best run for the money that wasn't their own that they could.

The other source of travellers cheques was, I was told, the hotel 'creeps' – men who specialised in robbing hotel rooms, a most un-savoury activity and presumably called 'creeps' for social reasons too, for I never saw a one. They always used intermediaries. Nearly all the pickpockets, everyone knew, had an extraordinary weakness in common: gambling. Every penny they made went on horses, dogs, cards, the Pools, whatever moved and could be wagered on.

No-one of us knew the other's business. Obviously we knew we were in the same game. But loose tongues could be dangerous. Socially we were often one, and we frequented the 'drinkers' in south London and north London, the illegal clubs owned by the gangsters and patronised by the Who's Who of the London underworld. I soaked it up, the sights, the voices, everything, like a sponge. I truly believed I was part of it and that this had turned out to be my destiny. Allow no other kind of thinking in. This is what I am, there is no more analysing, no more worrying myself sick about who and what I am – I've found it. And I was prepared to go down with the ship if that's how it turned out. And it eventually did.

Have beers with two of the Great Train Robbers, Jimmy Hussey and Buster Edwards. Associate for a few weeks with the man who sprang Ronnie Biggs, another one of the Great Train Robbers, from Wandsworth prison. Now this is really making it, so I thought. The glamour of it all. I did get a niggle of doubt looking at Buster Edwards, of such world infamy, wondering if any amount of money or notoriety is worth serving twelve years behind bars for, as he did. Such a warm character he was, and I remember vividly the conversation we had, how he bemoaned the decline of morality amongst his criminal fraternity. Buster was appalled at this new phenomenon of 'grassing', meaning ratting by criminals on their own mates. I remember being equally aghast at the thought of selling out your own pals and we sipped our beers and nodded in mutual lament over this! He ended up being a flower seller outside Coventry underground station. Some infamy.

Meet them all, or so it feels. Our activity has glamour, requires nerve and skill, makes plenty of money. We're playing our unlawful roles of various kinds of 'tourist' or 'overseas visitor'. The more respectable we look, the easier our job. These guys just love to dress up, they love acting out a role, say of a Spaniard, if that's what the name is on the travellers cheques, adopting accents and throwing in their own humorous variations whilst they're at it.

One guy hired Arabic clothes, including the head-dress, from a movie outfit hire shop to pass himself off as an Arab prince. One winter evening after a long day a mate and I drove past the famous Harrods store. A woman standing by the entrance doors waiting for someone in a beautiful fur coat was suddenly splattered with raw egg and I turned and saw my mate's hand pulling back in the car window and he was beside himself with laughter, with empty spaces in his half dozen tray of eggs. The poor woman was wiping frantically and incredulously at her expensive coat and staring up at the sky and at the street, in disbelief.

Eventually I meet the gangsters, just to say hello to. Our activities don't bother them. They have clubs and hundreds of poker machines in clubs all over the country, they own nightclubs, pubs; we're a source of mild curiosity, and we make sure they know we respect them.

I get to know the sons of two of the most notorious gangsters, one of whom was educated at a posh public school had and boarded there whilst his father served a long prison sentence! Not a bad chap either. And the father, once you got past that terrifying exterior, was a surprisingly softly spoken chap. Just as long as you didn't represent a threat to him or his interests, or appear a threat in his somewhat paranoid mind.

A gangster has to have something paranoid about him because everyone *is* out to get him, because of the lucrative position he has carved and hacked and doubtless murdered his way to. Yet amongst the gangsters I saw men who had a strong sense of 'family' within their cockney community, whether it was an affinity with a straight man selling vegetables, or an armed robber, or the little old lady from down the road.

Men who had done long prison sentences for armed robbery or any other major 'job' like that, wore their deeds and past sentence as badges of honour. They had fidelity to 'the Code' that required no explaining, nor justifying: you simply honoured certain behavioural codes and you got your respect from that. Or lack of it. They were the kind who never 'grassed' anyone, or did the wrong thing.

I get in deeper and see that so much of it is socially ordinary, like having regular Sunday lunches at a south London terrace house in a street stretched out like Coronation Street and peopled by a similar,

down-to-earth working-class types. "Ello, Al. Or right then?' The
women kiss you like their own. So do some of the men, if they really
like you. It's a strange feeling having a man kiss you, some big tough
nut from the Elephant and Castle, hard as nails, when your own father
has never kissed you. And yet it feels natural.

I help set the table with someone who might have killed men in his
younger bad old days, peel spuds with an ex-armed robber, a safe-
cracker. It's just another Sunday. Play cards with an array of current or
former crims, who get up and make a 'nice cuppa tea' for an elderly
visitor who's just popped in and call her 'darlin'' and make sure she has
a nice comfortable chair and 'Is there anyfink else you'd like, darlin'?'
before he sits back down and resumes his deadly intention to take as
much of your money from you as he can.

So it ain't all snarls and criminal plotting. And they've all got a
good sense of humour. Just that someone might call in the middle of
this extended and semi-adopted family Sunday lunch or card game
with cashmere sweaters for sale, stolen from Harrods, or silk dresses
hoisted from an exclusive fashion shop in Mayfair. And everyone
breaks off what they're doing to inspect the goods of these professional
shop-lifters. You hear their banter, their laughing recalls of how close
they came to getting 'pinched' and you know Harrods well enough
from your own purchases there, how elaborate the security measures
are, and you have to admire the cheek and verve of these thieves.
Unless you live in a monastery.

The same Sunday lunch there might be a telephone-call informing
us that someone they know has been 'pinched', meaning arrested for
some crime or other. Everyone duly laments, clicks their tongues, and
then starts making educated guesses on what the chances are of getting
a not guilty verdict, or if not, then how long the sentence will be. 'Oh,
that's an easy seven, maybe more wiv 'is form.' 'Form' meaning a long
criminal record.

There are aspects I hate. Like going to restaurants and our lot
behaving like mobsters. Not violent. Just crass. Order super-expensive
Dom Perignon champagne by the case. Dance on the tables. Be
uproarious, with not a hint of sensitivity to be seen, except for this
Kiwi sitting there squirming and dying a thousand deaths of

embarrassment. Though now that I've seen some advertising people and money-traders in action in trendy restaurants, I realise that this behaviour is common to anyone who isn't used to money, especially easy money.

While all this is going on, I still keep up with my old friends, the legit ones, from my days as Trianon Hotel barman. I love these guys. I still play rugby every Saturday for a respected, public school club. Know my team-mates as well as any, enjoy their company after the game, sometimes go to a middle-class party where the night ends up in games of Charade. Drive from there across the city to a pub in south London, get down dirty with the criminal class. Maybe it's my half-caste existence, of being able to go from one to the other. I can play rugby with the hound types and go and get drunk with the hares.

I don't realise that I'm seeing as much, if not more, of my straight friends as the ones I'm supposed to have thrown my total lot in with. I reckon I can choose my friends, but a few of the others are starting to reckon not. One night I'm confronted and asked to choose. I tell that person to go to hell, I'll be friends with who I like. Fortunately I have enough support within to withstand this attempt to claim me.

But a few of the company go wide of me and make it obvious. I hear someone sneeringly refer to me as 'the barman' when I'm the most prolific and skilled at signature-forging of them all. One of my closest allies tells me to understand these blokes. They're all lifetime criminals, as he is. They've known no other way of life, never held down a regular job, live by their own rules, have fathers and grandfathers and great-great-grandfathers who lived on the wrong side of the law. They're fanatically loyal to one another and resent anyone from the outside getting close. It's their way of looking out for themselves. 'Everyone does it,' my mate tells me. 'Cops and crims, lawyers and safe-crackers. They all look out for each other.'

I met men newly released from prison, which never failed to trouble me somewhat. It was as if I was being given a reminder of what my fate might be, or was certain to be. Except I ignored the warning.

Sometimes I'd go to Sunday afternoon sessions in a south London pub where the locals would take turns up on stage doing a number. Mostly old people, pensioners, men and women, singing war songs, and Vera Lynn was guaranteed to figure in the choice of singers to imitate. I saw hard men, tough nut criminals with tears in their eyes at some old biddy rendering 'Lilli Marlene' or 'When the Lights Go On Again.' The same men who could go out and shoot someone or bludgeon them with a baseball bat. I understood the contradiction and still do. Mankind is a contradiction. As this type would argue: the English Lord hands his title down to his next in line and so does the commoner criminal.

Good mates and close siblings and girlfriends were referred to as 'my' so-and-so. 'My Terry' would be someone's brother, or a best mate. An insult demanding retribution would go like this: 'He mugged off my Terry in front of everyone. We ain't standin' for that.' I loved their sing-song, rhyming slang style of speaking. I loved them, the cockneys. Let some of them be rogues and thieves and gangsters. There are plenty of equivalents in so-called normal society. They just call them by different names. I might not look up to any kind of gangster, but who am I to judge him if that's all he knows? He's thrown his hat into the ring and it could not be a more competitive, dangerous, deadly ring requiring not just physical might but mental power, and shrewdness and a certain kind of brain. Of course he's ruthless. I'm not saying love him. But he's an existence, another colour on this weird and wonderful earth. I don't ever want to prescribe who and what kind of man I shall like or pass judgement on. Your heart knows and that's all that matters.

Later when I was serving time in prison, I was saved by a man who was doing his second term for armed robbery. I got into a fix with some black guys over the simplest, most minor thing. They were getting together a delegation to sort me out, because one of them had wanted to fight me in front of an officer and I'd called his bluff. Come around the corner, I invited him, and then called him a coward when he didn't take up my offer. Maybe they thought my accent meant I was some kind of racist. Certainly I was a white man in their eyes. I went to my armed robber pal and asked what I should do. He said he'd fix it and I never had any more problems from that quarter. He did this for no reward. I had no standing being a foreigner, no support, and this mate did it at considerable risk to himself if my antagonists had lumped him in with me. I've known lawyers with fewer principles and less courage than this man. Experiences like these blur the lines for me of who and what is a good person. I never assume anything from a person's occupation or position alone, not when I've been ripped off by lawyers and treated honourably by thieves.

I have no regrets about any of my experiences, other than the question of morality. I was not born into a criminal class, so I have far less excuse than some on this count, if any. But I'm damned if I'll be Mr Reformed Morality now, pointing the finger of judgement at others. At myself, yes. And that is all a man should do: judge himself in his own context.

eighteen

We were sitting around in a city hotel foyer ready to get a flight to Paris that night when I looked out the glass entrance doors and saw a bus. It was spilling out with very large men. I said to my mate, 'Look. There's a rugby team, they're racing each other to the bar.'

Then I saw many of them were carrying batons. A few had guns. They burst in and some raced up the stairs and others filled the area we were sitting in. Everyone was told to be very still. I asked if this was a raid on IRA suspects, knowing quite well they were here for us. Moments later one of my mates is being walked out in handcuffs at gunpoint. Then it's over for me too.

Now, a year later, most of that out on bail and on a living gained from quite a few repeats of the same criminal activity, it's trial time for those who have pleaded not guilty and those who have not jumped their bail. I pleaded guilty to fraud charges against nominated clearing banks, namely of cashing cheques belonging to those issuing banks. The judge is far from happy that I am the only non-English defendant to answer my bail. He dishes out the prison sentence to me and me alone, and gives the other five guilty-pleaded defendants suspended prison sentences. Of course I bleated and said it wasn't fair, as it wasn't. But then nor were my crimes against the banks. For me, it's over. The party's come to an end. I am leaving behind a child and a de facto wife. I'm fated not to see freedom again for another nineteen months. Instant reform was my only thought as I left court in the van for prison.

That's me in that prison van, handcuffed to a burly Scotsman with dangerous eyes who's been given a hefty sentence of a minimum fifteen years for slashing a man with a knife so that he needed 830 stitches. I think about the others who fled. I doubt if the charges against them would have stuck. They'd been arrested by association. I wish them luck. They were born to be what they were. I wasn't. And I've had enough. Don't want to lose another child, though obviously there will be an absence of some couple of years from this next child of mine.

That's me looking out the van window as we go through the gates of this notorious prison. That's me going through the induction process – a foot wash in a chemical foot-bath; a shower and de-licing shampoo. These clothes, from Mayfair and Knightsbridge and Oxford Street and Church Road shops are irrelevant. Hand them over to be put in a plastic bag. And when you come to collect them you'll have changed.

You're another identity now. See there, the clothes a fellow inmate is handing you, that's what you are. A mirror of him, in denims and striped shirt and grey jersey and dark navy coarse wool jacket. That's you and everyone around you now getting into prison issue. Duff, you've lost, you're counted out.

You know what you're going to do about this situation. You've made sure to rekindle that dream. Write. Turn this into something, make it an opportunity. Though that doesn't for a moment stop your head ringing, your insides churning, and your heart feeling like it's been broken yet again. Hey, come on now, Al, you've been here before, as a thirteen-year-old, and then a fifteen-year-old. Didn't break you. You've graduated, boy. Even though no-one's saying congratulations. But this is what I say inside to keep myself together.

This is you, out in the mist swirling around these grim Victorian buildings. It is unbelievable, just unbelievable, but the mist curling at your feet is real enough. So are those security lights following your every step in this April dark. Of course I think I should have jumped bail. But there's my child. I couldn't desert another child again. Nor have a life on the run.

While I was out on bail, I made a phone-call to someone in the city and immediately got a crossed line. I listened for a moment and just as

I was about to hang up heard one of the callers mention a Maori word. I let them know they had a half-Maori on the third line. It turned out they were reporters relaying a story about Maori artefacts that were being auctioned at Christies by an Italian industrialist whose five-year-old son had been kidnapped and he needed to raise the ransom money fast. The New Zealand government had appointed someone to fly to London to bid on the country's behalf for the works. That New Zealander was none other than my uncle Roger Duff.

I told them who I was and naturally they thought it was a hoax. I had to answer all sorts of questions and one said he'd do some checking and ring me back. Half an hour later he called and in a most quiet voice loaded with expectation asked me what my uncle's middle name was. 'Shepherd,' I said. The reporter couldn't believe his ears. We calculated that it must be a billion to one chance of getting a crossed line with two people discussing my uncle who lived 13,000 miles away.

I immediately contacted Roger and Myrtle and had them to dinner at my rented Barnes semi-detached house in very middle-class suburban London where I was living with my then de facto wife Paula. We marvelled at the coincidence of the telephone-call. Being Kiwis we had one of those rulers at home with the different native timber insets and as Paula was pregnant, we wondered about calling the Kahikatea after the white pine tree or just Katea. My uncle, well-versed in matters Maori, advised that Katea was fine. A few months after returning to New Zealand my Uncle Roger had a stroke and died. I sometimes think it was his way of saying farewell to me.

Here in prison I've resolved I'm going to start writing on day one, which is tomorrow, as it's late now. Late, and mist hiding my feet. They're clumpy shoes manufactured in some prison, not Bally shoes. That's not a home, of semi-detached suburban London you've just left, with your Persian rugs and the oil paintings. It's a three-storey high brick building that has seen a million memories, each a human being, has housed a million stories over a century and more, and you're just one of them. You're going to be resident in a shared cell where one of those lights is glowing wanly against the mist.

'Just put your head down, Al, and do your bird.' These are the words of a friend. Bird is from bird lime, which rhymes with time, and

I have enough of that spread out before me to learn the disciplines of writing fiction. And think of the stimulus, the actual all-around presence of an array of interesting, bizarre, messed-up, dangerous, weird characters. Oh yeah, just think of that, and them. Just put your head down and do your bird.

●

The cacophony of everyday prison life is a scene from Dante's inferno. Doors clanging, inmates yelling, screws yelling, pipes banging, chairs clattering, grilles opening and closing, aggression so palpable you can touch it. How from this was I going to produce written works to be published around the world? Why hold on to an impossible dream, Duff? You're a loser and that's what you're going to stay. Yet that is not what I cling to in this madness of humans bereft of all sensibilities. I want to be someone. I *have* to be someone.

Mornings, three landings of cell doors get opened up and hundreds of men make with their full pisspots to empty them in the slosh sinks. Men sit shitting in toilet cubicles with no doors. Whilst others clean their teeth at nearby basins. The stench is gagging, your stomach heaves, your eyes stream. You're reeling in this onslaught of rank smells and low-life human beings. You're as miserable as you've ever been. What the hell has happened? Why didn't I run like everyone else?

At least one thing the borstal experience has given me – fear no-one. Even if you're trembling inside. Don't show it. I know the rules: anyone who so much as threatens you with a look, you whack. Don't ask questions, he's just trying to get the upper hand of making you think about him, worry about him – don't. Hit him. Or else he's got you and he'll hunt you down at his leisure and you become everyone's fair game. Maybe here they rape the weaklings too. How am I going to stand this? This cacophony of madness, of no sensibilities let alone sensitivity?

The place is vast. It's cavernous. I recreated scenes from this for my novel, *What Becomes of the Broken Hearted?* The prison scenes. I had already done my research – I lived it. I had the character, Mulla Rota, mopping a landing and making out to his fellow gang member leader that he was one of the boys, when inside his heart was broken. His will.

He couldn't do another day inside. He'd had enough. The reality I based that on is worse than described in the novel. For these inmates are this country's scum, its lowest forms of life, most of them. And I'm one. It sets up an air of unbelievable heaviness, as if every one of you is producing his bit to a crushing weight of truth, of harsh, ugly fact, that you're nothing. Just nothing. You're the ultimate chump, the big-time loser.

The paradox is that so many of these prisoners are here because they are nothing to start with. They got born to lives of abuse and neglect and stood no chance from the beginning. To be resident with such men is impossible to describe. I can only say that I know the true meaning of nightmare, the one where the landscape is peopled by these hideous inadequates of no morality, no self-respect, empty of dignity, foul of personal habits. Only a tiny percentage of men keep themselves separate from this seething of low-life masses. Which is what I did. From the very start. And woe betide any man who tried to drag me down to his level. This was as low as I was going to go: incarcerated but with a goal.

How ironic that I got a job in the library. The screw in charge was a wonderful man, sensitive, a reader, intelligent and took a shine to me immediately. He let me use the old typewriter in there with a broken comma key, and as long as I did my allocated work, I could spend the remainder of the time on writing.

One day I picked up a book called *Ragtime* by E.L. Doctorow. I started reading it that night, opting not to take my exercise period or recreation time with other prisoners. Instead I stayed in my cell and read this classic work and it switched on every literary light I had. It was as memorable a revelation as that book of Taylor Caldwell's in my solitary borstal cell, indeed more so because now I had a better understanding of literature.

This year, 1999, whilst in Los Angeles at the American Film Market, I needed a copy of my novel *One Night Out Stealing* as I'd met a distributor who was interested in it as a film project. Published by University of Hawaii Press in 1993 in the US, I expected it to be out of print, especially as it didn't sell that well over there. A friend took me to a book store he said stocks everything, and there was my novel sitting on the shelf under 'DU'. Right beside it was *Ragtime* by Doctorow. All those years later, from prison to this glittering store in Santa Monica, and now Doctorow and Duff are side by side. Not for a moment do I see us as creative equals, not even close. I know what my writing is and I'm no Doctorow, as much as I would like to be.

And who would have thought that I would have had my photograph taken with Robert Redford, one of the stars of 'the Sting', a film I had got to watch all those years ago in prison. Redford had come to the screening of *Once Were Warriors* at the Sundance Film Festival in Utah that he founded. Robert Redford coming to watch my movie, shake my hand, congratulate me after seeing it?

I was celled up with armed robbers and petty thieves and an ever-changing array of criminals. The armed robbers – usually meaning of armoured vans carrying large sums of cash – were the best. They had guts and principles and though they got the biggest sentences, took it with dignity. The worst types were anyone to do with drugs, as if a fundamental weakness attracts them to the drug trade.

In prison fights are as guaranteed as the sun coming up, no-one can avoid them. Violence rules on the inside. He who fights the best is considered the best. But me, I only used what physical abilities I had to defend myself and give out the signal I'd bow to no-one. I got attacked in another prison, where I finished my sentence, by a mad Irishman who bashed me across the face with a chair. I didn't give him a second chance. Violence is disgusting. But you live by the rules in there or you don't survive. Another man attacked me with a steel food tray and again my Maori warrior genes came to the rescue.

The vast majority of inmates are of pretty average intelligence and almost exclusively working class. A high percentage were professional thieves, but varied as to competency. I suspect all but a few were pretty average even as thieves.

I changed. Started to grow up at long last. I had a lot of growing to do but the process had started. And I never took my eye off that writing goal, writing every day until lights went out and every spare moment during the day. The friends I made tended to be the intelligent ones, though one Orthodox Jew I made friends with and nearly got my head torn off sticking up for against some blacks he'd ripped off, turned out to be the ugliest, most twisted betrayer of a friend you could ever wish to know.

But there was humour and many incidents that had you forgetting where you were for a time. Just as there were incidents that burned themselves on your brain. Like the man who got his eye knocked out by that same Scotsman I was brought in with. The man he attacked was an Arab terrorist who had shot up a coach-load of Air Israel hostesses in the city and who would later be released in a political move behind the scenes. Minus his eye.

'D' Wing was designated for those doing life sentences or twenty years and over. They came separately to the library and were as staunch a group as you could see, though few liked these crazy Irish political fighters. There were riots at the prison when I was there in 1979. We sat listening to this incredible din of men shouting, bellowing, roaring, and heating pipes under constant clatter of objects beating upon them. The noise alone is impossible to describe. We heard next day that the prison hospital had treated fifty-three prisoners for injuries, many of them serious. They'd brought over that they called the 'heavy squad' from the country's No. 1 punishment prison, where I'd spent three weeks on remand before sentencing. It was a hell-hole with bully, fascist guards to match. This specially trained squad tore the rioting prisoners apart, most of them IRA. I remember thinking at the time that this imprisonment experience was worth it, if only to be just in earshot of such extremists.

Nine months in this London prison; nine months of having to face up to myself, and not always succeeding. Time and again reverting to the immature child, the child wanting to lash out, to give up on the world, to be a permanent society reject. But then I had my new baby waiting out there, and two older children in New Zealand who had only a concept of me as a failure. And there was this voice deep inside that kept calling to me, too often only faintly, that it wanted to be heard, it must be heard, so I must keep going. Keep suffering, even when there seemed no good reason and it felt so unfair.

I survived this place through having a mental strength I didn't know I had, in resisting all criticism and doubts of my wanting to write my way out of this from my new peers. I had to tell them to go to hell and I used my physical qualities to keep them from trying to take away my dream, as they do with anyone inside who has a dream. They want to destroy it since it tells them they have nothing. If anyone wanted to fight about it, then so be it. I'd fight. And then keep right on with my writing, writing, learning this difficult craft, this impossible discipline with no guidelines, no set rules I could learn. Just hard graft. And every time I completed a few chapters, I would start again and then look back on what I'd written and throw it in the bin because each time I outgrew myself.

I was allocated to a prison in Northumberland. It was more of an open prison, with single cells that had plenty of light and a view of the countryside. I wrote every day and every night until lights out. My sister-in-law Pam kept me in touch with home with regular copies of *Rugby News*, which I read many times over. Paula, my daughter's mother, wrote nearly every day and her letters kept my spirits up, as did her visits every two weeks, involving a long train journey from London with our small daughter. My letters always promised that one day I'd make things up by being published.

For the first time I had the forced company of just myself for long periods. I turned that into longer periods by opting out of most communal activities. Dad wrote regularly and Mum wrote a few times in her neat, rather flourishy handwriting. I appealed against my sentence and set a legal precedent in the Appeal Court, which could not decide and so ordered another sitting. I'm ashamed that I bleated on so much against being the only one to receive a sentence, as if I had started to believe I was a complete innocent. But from your times of immaturity, hopefully you learn growth.

This period was a forced turning-point for me. I came to know myself a little better and learned to dig from myself the creative qualities that had so long been neglected and had begun to doubt that I had. Being released finally from prison is liberating in many senses. The experience of freedom is so marvellous that it feels almost worth going through a period of being locked up. I can remember being released like it was yesterday. I will always have it fresh in my mind. And that's probably why I so treasure and appreciate my freedom now – because I've lost it before.

nineteen

Even bad dreams end. And I've written near every day of it. Be some years yet, though, before I'm published. But even more significantly, years before I fully realise that self-esteem is a good part of the problem. It was when I was in a Christchurch pub having a beer with my older brother, and he said to me, 'You know what your problem is, Duff? You don't like yourself.'

I was shocked and confused. I thought liking yourself was the same as being vain and boastful and unacceptably over-confident. Memories started to trickle in. I heard voices, adult voices from my childhood, telling me I was a 'useless, freckle-faced shit' a 'fuckin' brain box', heard their disparaging nickname for me, 'jug-head' and the cruel sneering remarks on my other nickname, Chow, telling me that I had been found in the Korean War and adopted by my father out of pity. I saw my school reports being ignored or scowled at by adults meant to be my supportive relations. I recalled their scorn at my athletic achievements and academic achievements to boot, them saying, 'Oh yeah? Think you're clever and good at sport? You take my son on then, you little skite.'

Skite, show-off, blowhard, bookworm, all these standard terms resurfaced in my mind, as my brother's words echoed and echoed: 'You don't like yourself....' So, how do you get to like yourself?

My partner at the time, now my wife, was studying at university, and happened to have a book called *Transactional Analysis* which talked about this question of self-loathing and low self-esteem. It was not a light turned on for me but the very sun. I now had something to target. Though the book didn't promise miracles, just enlightenment to a fairly common ailment – of the heart, in my case. In lots of cases. I began to read the book and at last knew in more exact terms what my problem was. Though of course it wasn't a matter of reading the entire book and being cured. But at least it was light, blinding light.

Let me leap forward, into the unlikely future, to where I was told that my first novel, *Once Were Warriors*, had been accepted for publication in early 1990. I'm in the central Hawkes Bay rural town of Waipukurau, population about 4000. Here because my wife has a job running a home for the disabled, which itself is having a huge impact on me, a growing-up step after seeing people in wheelchairs, disabled, cerebral palsy sufferers, head injury victims, some of whom I became good friends with. I learned dignity from them and how to accept life's cruel fate with stoicism, even a kind of joy. We have a six-month-old daughter whom I've been taking care of during the day, writing during her sleep times, I had set up and then sold my Chinese takeaways shop from which I got the scenes in *Once Were Warriors* of Jake, drunk, purchasing his food from Chinese who were secretly in contempt of his drunken ways. For I had employed a Chinese cook who was exactly that, in total contempt of drunken regulars who spent the last of their money on our takeaways.

A couple of months previously I had finished the final draft of the novel at 5 a.m. after my literary agent gave me great advice on structure and a lesson on taking my voice out of the story (as much as Alan Duff is capable, that is) and writing with 'a sense of immediacy'. I had written to Chris Else of Total Fiction Services in response to an earlier critique of his on a draft of the book, asking whether I shouldn't just forget this stupid pipedream and do something else. I was thirty-nine after all and had been chasing this dream for about six years, writing almost full-time, getting money from contract insulation work provided by my dear friend Les Salter in Christchurch to keep me going. I'd done at least nine drafts, in different styles, trying to find my voice. First I lucked onto the American writer, Hubert Selby Junior's novel *Last Exit To Brooklyn* whose stream-of-consciousness style, devoid of conventional punctuation and spelling, gave the work a manic energy and immediacy. I knew it was a style I must learn to adapt my own literary voice to. Then Chris Else's advice slotted perfectly in with what I had gained from Selby's writing: a sense of immediacy. Chris's advice unquestionably helped launch my career.

It's 5.30 a.m. I go for a five-mile run and I'm running on air. Do my fastest time for the distance ever, the last part a fairly long and steep hill but it's as if it's flat. Wake my wife up and tell her I've written something that will make history. Don't know where this certainty comes from, I just hear myself saying it.

So now, after the agent has sent the last draft to the publisher, he has telephoned me to tell me himself: 'We'll be publishing your novel this year. Congratulations. We think it will do very well.'

I'm standing in the hallway of this Pukeora Hospital house that comes with Joanna's job and which I've painted up myself because it's a sad place, old and unloved over the years, and I've put the phone down and I lean against the wall and cry my eyes out. Have never felt such pure gladness, not before and not since. This was that dream at last realised – and not just the writing dream but the dream of turning my life around.

A book with my name on it was going to come out. It is not money, though I'm sure a money person's first $50,000, or million dollars, is a memory for life. This was different – not better, just different. A child had been born, and by being published, it was thus named and blessed. I don't know where the title *Once Were Warriors* came from. For a long while I spoke it in apology, till I started to realise that it stuck. I could not have thought of a better title.

Published. It means more than the word, for it is art. An act of creation that has no route, no map, no teachings or learnings to go by, nor a soul to help you. No teams to apply the collective effort to it, no-one but yourself and what feels like a stupidly impossible dream, which is what you start off with. A typewriter (back then), several reams of blank paper, and a lot of hope. And go over it and over it, still no clues, no place to go to check if your calculations are right or they're wrong – it is an act unto itself. And one where efficiency, which I admire, has no relevance. Even the sort of application and tenacity that is needed is quite different, say, from painting a house, or building one. There is a picture somewhere there in your mind that you have to coax on to the page, page after page, and keep it as a complete entity. A picture that stays with you until the very end, and then can flee on the last page. Finished. Failed. Project dead. Start again, start anew.

I phoned my father pretty soon afterwards. He was so pleased. I had never heard such a tone from him in all these tumultuous years of being the son wasting his talent. I was keenly aware, even in the giddiness of being published, that I had just sneaked in with salvaging this life. This is the same man whom I had been given special permission to telephone from a prison in England ten years ago to say that I had been granted parole. Now, I was to be published and would soon to able to call myself a novelist.

I told myself: I must never forget this, never forget this. The same words said to myself when gazing at my brother Kevin's body for the last time. Maybe that's what he was saying, that things would work out just as long as I remembered. That's remembering him and the waste his life was, and remembering that our father had done so much for us and yet we had failed him. Just as our mother had failed us. I knew with absolute certainty that if things went well for me I'd put it back into society. No doubt it accounts for a lot of my motivation for the Books in Homes programme and various other causes and young people I support. Because I know – I *know* – how close those who grow up with traumatic lives come to it collapsing into utter failure. The reason, if it isn't obvious, is that you don't have an emotional base, you lack self-esteem, self-love and therefore believe you must be worthless.

It is no different, I'd suggest, to the threat that constantly hovers over the dry alcoholic, of an abyss waiting for you if you slip up. Though I hasten to add I could never return to that criminal way of life, way of thinking, not the bad old days. But I remain grateful that the life I lived before that as a child and young adult, which is perhaps at least partly responsible for the wrong path I briefly took, is now far behind me. And now I can provide a voice, a conduit, an articulated means for others who have lived lives that have been negative.

●

I was nervous at meeting my agents, Chris Else and Barbara Else. I was ashamed of my past even if it was ten years behind me. I did not feel comfortable entering this new world. It was like entering someone's house, and I had an old psychological fear that I was disrupting their peace, their happy party. Though Chris and Barbara were most generous and sensitive in realising my uncertainties and could not have been more highly encouraging of my literary talent.

The next people to meet were my publishers, the Tandem Press husband and wife duo, Bob Ross and Helen Benton. We were meeting to discuss and maybe sign the contract. I was too happy to be nervous and also too broke not to ask for an advance considerably more than what was being offered. They agreed on the spot to the larger advance, which was just as well because I was building a new home and the floor concrete pour payment was due. We proceeded to start drinking Steinlager beers in this bar, and at one stage we called over a complete stranger – he was English as it turned out – to witness the signatures on the book contract. We said he could be a signatory to history being made, though I think only I believed it. Not out of vanity, but from this inner certainty that my funny old troubled life was destined to end up like this and with a lot more to come.

We had a discussion about how many copies *Warriors* would sell. The Arts Council had given it a maximum, first-time author publisher subsidy, though their advice, Bob told me, was that it would sell no more than 2500 copies. Well, Chris said 3-5000 copies, Bob said 5-8000 copies, which would make it a best-seller. And I said 25,000, which would be unprecedented.

On my return to Havelock North I wrote Bob and Helen a letter, stating that I'd better say this before publication that this book would make history. And to continue on this boastful line, I had also written to David Lange, former Prime Minister, asking him thus: 'How would the country's most eloquent man like to launch the career of one of New Zealand's greatest writers to come?' Lange wrote back and said yes, except he got involved in a hostage drama in Iraq and chose to go on the world stage rather than my tiny, new-born Kiwi one. It was with great delight that I told him at the Montana Book Awards ceremony in 1997 at which he, as one of the judges, awarded *What Becomes of the Broken Hearted?* Best Fiction Award, that had he launched my writing career he could have been famous too!

Before the launch I was highly nervous at the thought of making my speech, so I took myself to a Toastmasters group in the hope of learning the techniques of public speaking. I only wanted to get through this one occasion. Except at the class, in listening to the various club speakers and talking with them, I realised I had under-valued myself and my own strength of personality. So I never went back.

At the launch in Auckland I had a bus-load of relatives and whanau from Rotorua there to support me, and my Auckland-based brother Nick and his wife Pam were also specially there for me. My speech I cannot remember, though the day itself was one of the happiest of my life. I was not to know that from then onwards I would give hundreds of speeches to a huge diversity of groups and organisations, nor would I know what the book and the subsequent movie would go on to become. I met Maurice Shadbolt that night and Witi Ihimaera. I re-member inscribing in Witi's copy of *Warriors* a thanks to him for being the first, meaning the first Maori novelist. We partied at my brother's house that night and I knew then that my life had changed forever.

Despite the changes I am still a person of simple outlook who is more satisfied with gathering shellfish at some secluded beach than sitting in some trendy place in Auckland or wherever. And despite my growing involvement in the film world, I remain indifferent to Hollywood. I have learned to love my friends so much, and I still have my old mates, the Kiels, and Les Salter whom I insulated pipes with. I particularly enjoy my involvement with the children in the Books in Homes programme. I enjoy my own children of course most of all, especially knowing that they have grown up totally loved and encour-aged. It is children's potential I love most, and I like doing my tiny bit to help youngsters find that. My own potential was so close to being lost forever. I could have been another statistic, either back in gaol or killed in a bar brawl or a drunken road crash. I have found my voice at long last, as I promised my step-grandmother all those years ago in that letter from prison. I believe I have a lot to contribute, and desire to do so humbly and without reward. Most of all I have found love, and that is more than a man can ask.

Dea r Nga ere,

Tha nks for your le tter.   Well a t the moment I'm w a iting on a
pa role decisio͏ꞯ w hich if fa voura ble could see me home by Xma s - thiˢ
yea r!   It's a gony for Pa ula ha ving to w a it on the answ er as
it is for me.   I'm not doing this sentence a ny ea sier tha n whenI
s ta rted.   But I don't q uite a gree w ith you when you say tha t it's
a wa ste of a young life.   It might w ell be ha d I not been in need
of s uch a period in my a lwa ys dra ma tic (Yhe a hcing ha s been second
ra te how ever)life.   I've been plucked out of a river of my own making
a nd I8m gla d I w a s.   I'd ha ve been sure ly drow ned otherwise.   I
think it's bes͏t to w a it a nd s ee w hat I8ve ma de of this imprison-.
ment.   I'm confident more tha n a few people a re in for a surprise
but I ma ke no ꞉predictions from my pres ent prone s ta te.   Just look
out for me though for I ꬰa ve ha d s omething to s a y.   This time I8ve
sa id it.
Those poems of mine a mba ra ss me.   I don't know w hat Dad sees in them.
They w ere just burs ts of voice from a fle d͏gling a rtist who didn't
know w ho the hell he wa s.   He's not that that certain who he is
now but his voice has lea rned a refinement w hich is beginning to
a ppea l even to him.

There is one poem how ever w hich I q uite liked although I dont know
if da d got it publis hed .   He w a s going to tr y the Listener
a s fa r a s I know .   It's c a lled " Father. Fa ther?"   It
ha s a nice rolling rhythm w hich I ha͏ve s ince w orked pn.   I enjoy
w riting pros e rather tha n poe try.   I get the bes t of both w orlds
then.

Ro ger Paulin the Ca mbridge University tutor came to visit me a while back
Ha ve you met him?   He's q uite nic e and a t ypica l Duff- highly
intelligent a nd a t times unsettling.   He has re a l Duff eyebrows
da rk a nd pondering a s if he is forever wondering c ontempla ting great
a nd wis e thing s .   I do w ish I ha d known Oliver from a n adult view.
I'm in no doubt a t a ll that I miss ed out on something w ith his passing a t the time of my ver y troubled coming.   I wa s in Borstal at the
time and I s till remember his letter to me   "It doe sn't lat forever."
Well?...No of cours e it doesn't but it feels like it at times !
I got a nice letter from Alison yes terday.   At last she is w riting
to me a s a n a dult to a nother instead of a n a unt to her teenage
nephew .   I might a ppea r (my a ctions) childish to certa in narrow-
visioned people but I'm a man benea th it all.   Des pite my being
here I have always behaved- in the past 6 or 7 yea rs a nyway- w ith
loya lty a nd integrity to my friends and though I broke the law I would
not dream of stealing from a n individual a nd have never done so.   These
a re different times   and I ha ve grown up in a n a nyw ay tumultuous
childhood a s you well know .   But my head is hi gh.
Love to you a nd be a ssured, this Duff will ma ke his mark.
                                                 Alan.

The letter I wrote from prison to my step-grandmother, Ngaere, in 1980.

216